BEHAVING BADLY

The Life of Richard Harris 1930–2002

Cliff Goodwin

First published in Great Britain in 2003
by Virgin Books Ltd
Thames Wharf Studios
Rainville Road
London
W6 9HA

610003

A catalogue record for this book is available from the British Library.

ISBN 1 85227 957 5

Typeset by Phoenix Photosetting, Chatham, Kent
Printed and bound in Great Britain by CPD, Wales

From a nine-year-old girl who fell in love with Albus Dumbledore and her mother who fell in love with King Arthur.

– entry in Limerick Book of Condolence

BEHAVING BADLY

PROLOGUE

One forgets too easily the difference between a man and his image,
and that there is none between the sound of his voice on the screen
and in real life.

— Robert Bresson

It must have seemed to Richard Harris, as it did to Bull McCabe, the
irascible unforgiving landowner he played in *The Field*, that he had
reached a time in his life when compromises were no longer an option.
It was a time beyond the edge of shame when, facing the prospect of a
new oblivion, Harris declared, 'I want to make worthwhile movies again.'

In the final scene of the film, McCabe wades into the Atlantic Ocean
and vents his frustration and anger and fear by beating the waves with
his stick, challenging the tide and the consequences of his own actions
to sweep him off his feet just as, years earlier, Harris had bloodied his
fists in frustration on the bonnets and windscreens of cars whose drivers
were not brave enough to run him down.

But McCabe was not Harris. This was no alter ego. This was far more
complicated. McCabe, as the actor readily admitted, was a character
created from a life of weaknesses and defeats: from a remarkable
international debut in *This Sporting Life*; from the bitterness and rivalry
of Hollywood; from a million-selling record and a few outstanding, yet
unsold, books of poetry; from a couple of half-decent adventure films;
from the long history of drunken adventures; from the near-fatal
accidents and illnesses; from a string of dreadful B-movies; from the
abandoned wives and necessary lovers; from the careless friends; and
from the curious years of self-imposed retirement.

A recent generation of film fans has judged Bull McCabe as one of the
actor's principal masterpieces. Perhaps Harris had – unwittingly – put
more of himself into the part than he intended. If that is correct, only his
true friends can appreciate how close to the truth Harris got. The rest of
us, and that includes his fellow actors, can only admire his determination
and sense of craft and guess at the real measure of his talent.

Harris, it would seem, ranked among that rare breed of actors who
openly confess their dislike of the film industry. 'There are far too many

prima donnas in this business and not enough action,' he repeatedly claimed. This was one reason he rarely watched modern movies – and hardly ever his own.

His personal obsessions leaned heavily on his integrity as an artist: industry, independence and incorruptibility; an avoidance of imitation; a disgust of sloppy workmanship; a hatred of cant; and a compelling competitive spirit.

Once, in his youth, he aspired to do well at rugby, to play for Ireland and, when he was not leading his team to victory against the English, to write hard and thoughtful poetry. In later years he had another sport. Just as the rest of us enjoyed listening as he did it, he enjoyed deflating the egos of his fellow actors who, he claimed, talked like Oscar winners but delivered only polychrome trash. Harris detested the aura of celebrity and elitism. 'Actors are not important,' he insisted. 'Not like Beethoven or Van Gogh or Francis Bacon.'

It was all good headline-making stuff. But Harris's own shortcomings were just as real and almost never denied by the actor himself. His notoriously short temper could be ignited at any time by almost anything. Sometimes, what started as a drunken spat congealed into a rejection of someone he loved – and who loved him – which lasted for decades. Disloyalty, to Harris or his friends and family or his profession, provoked instant and public retribution. Ask Michael Caine. On the other hand, an act of kindness or loyalty produced a tender, equally public and lasting declaration of faith.

If the star of *This Sporting Life*, *Camelot* and *The Field* had been diminutive or sickly or contemptibly feeble, paid to live out a stronger man's fantasy, he would still have been one of the world's greatest actors.

But he was no weed. He was six foot two, broad-chested, manly, attractive and hungry. It was this fusion of ruggedness and sensitivity, machismo and originality, that came to be Richard Harris's unstoppable movie myth. It is a compulsive legend, made all the more compelling by his apparent disregard for his own life while showing endless concern for the welfare of others.

Perhaps he sometimes looked down the road from which he had come, wondering where it all began, where the false starts and wrong turns had been – 'I do my job and I do it well. Sometimes I succeed, sometimes I fail. Sometimes I'm brilliant, sometimes I'm not. It really doesn't matter.'

Perhaps, also, he sometimes looked back to a clearer scene, to a country and a town to which he remained true; to the early mornings of his childhood and of playing in the neatly kept garden of his home on the outskirts of Limerick; to the clamour and chatter and laughter of a large warm family; to the smell of his father's work clothes stiff with flour dust; to his mother's busy love; to the summer upheaval of moving to Kilkee, where he would paddle in the cold Atlantic waters; and then, each night, to the silence that came when the family and the house finally went to sleep and he was left to fashion his dreams in what, to a young boy, must have seemed the still point of his world.

CHAPTER ONE

By his late teens Harris was already fourteen stone and an athletic six foot one. Much of his school rugby career was spent packing down as a rebellious and wandering lock, though 'I was too busy and knackered scoring tries to bother too much with scrummaging.' It was, he claims, his first case of miscasting.

Harris's dedication to rugby – and to *winning* at rugby – received some unusual benefaction. In 1947 Crescent College met PBC Cork in the final of the Munster Schools Senior Cup. Harris was forced to watch the impressive but indecisive match from the sidelines. Before the replay, one of Crescent's forwards left the college to start work and Harris, still only sixteen, was called into the team alongside his older brother Ivan. The danger player in the Cork side was a full-back named Mick Brosnahan, who Harris had a hunch would turn out in the fly-half position. For three hours each day Harris and his Crescent teammates practised 'nobbling' a fly-half. When their coach, Father Guiunane, finally arrived he called Harris to the sideline. 'I'm utterly appalled,' said the priest puffing hard on his cigarette. 'We'll win this match by fair means or not at all.'

When, on match day, the dreaded Brosnahan trotted out on to the pitch wearing a Number 10 fly-half shirt, 'Harris, a quiet word,' whispered Father Guiunane through a cloud of blue smoke. 'You may continue with your plan.'

CHAPTER ONE

If a farmer fills his barn with grain, he gets mice. If he leaves it empty, he gets actors.

– Bill Vaughan

There is no question that Mildred Harty had a haunting beauty about her. In that first full decade after World War One, her Celtic ancestry brought a shine to her red hair and a perfection to her pale skin, which turned more than her share of Limerick heads. Below her high forehead her soft eyes possessed a quiet confidence. And her tight distinctly Scottish lips and mouth complemented the delicacy of her jawline.

Of course the years had passed down more than a genetic code and a certain, if rather pleasing, physical appearance. Roughly translated from the Gaelic, her family name meant 'descendent of Faghartach', a byname for a noisy and vociferous person. It was a reputation she was quite capable of living up to. But there was also an inherited fire within Mildred's soul, an unshakable family loyalty and religious certainty that would ultimately prove capable of withstanding everything fate and the English could throw at it.

The shy but determined Mildred knew little of the young Ivan Harris when they were first introduced, and then only what Limerick gossip and her own mother had told her. Despite the fact that the Harris family money had helped to found the town's Crescent College, Ivan was sent to England to be educated. After six years at Downside, a Benedictine boarding school attached to Downside Abbey near Bath, Ivan returned to Limerick tall and wiry and ruggedly handsome. What Mr and Mrs Harty wanted for their daughter was a strong, socially reputable marriage. For Ivan's parents the priority was a good, clean, childbearing Catholic girl to safeguard the future of the Harris dynasty. Love was a secondary consideration.

Years later Mildred's most famous son would ask his mother if she and his father were in love when they married. 'No,' she said. 'We were matchmade.' It was true. Bound by tradition and family responsibility, Mildred Harty and Ivan Harris were brought together by a matchmaker and told to get on with it.

Somewhere in the distant past, Harris's paternal ancestors travelled from England to Ireland. Lieutenants Edward and William Harris were both officers under Cromwell, but there were other Harrises already living in Ireland before the arrival of the Lord Protector's Model Army. Seventeenth-century records show that the penalty for one Harris family's 'treachery' of going over to the Irish was a forfeiture of its lands. In various issues of the *Cork Historical and Architectural Society Journal* there are accounts of the 1722 will of Joseph Harris of Cork. Also of the Harris Affair, 'an account of the death of William Harris as a result of being tossed in a blanket'.

It is not known whether these Harris's – Harris is itself a corruption of the French first name Henri – were related to the Harris family, which, by the early nineteenth century, had settled in Limerick and already begun to amass a business fortune. The first patriarch of public note was James Harris, the actor's great-grandfather. By 1864 James Harris's empire had grown to include not only Limerick's largest flour mill but a company dock and warehouse at Steamboat Quay and a bakery in Henry Street. The family home, Hartstonge House, was rambling and comfortable and richly furnished, with its own private chapel.

An astute businessman, James Harris also appreciated the value of publicity. In the spring of 1868 he came to the rescue of a French balloonist whose disastrous attempts to depart from the town had caught the public's attention. Monsieur A Chevalier arrived in Limerick during the first week in May. While the aeronaut and showman unpacked his equipment on Steamboat Quay, his assistants toured the city drumming up interest in flights aboard his 'magnificent and novel sailing balloon' *L'Esperance*. 'This remarkable Aerial Machine,' proclaimed his poster, 'is the first of the kind ever constructed; it can be elevated and depressed without discharging gas or ballast, and is especially constructed by Mons. Chevalier (late of Paris) for scientific Aeronautic Observations and the study of the Atmospheric Currents.' Among Chevalier's other claims to fame were that he had remained aloft for two days and nights and travelled more than seven hundred miles with the fellow French balloonist Nadar, and that he had received the Légion d'Honneur 'for the invention of an iron Aerial Machine, which is driven by Steam Power, and ascends in the air without the use of any gas'.

To witness the uncrating and assembly of his balloon, Chevalier charged onlookers a shilling (5 pence) for outer-circle seats and two shillings to watch from a closer enclosure. Those who wished to make 'partial and other ascents' could do so by private arrangement. James Harris, while happy to allow the Frenchman the use of his quayside yard, preferred to keep his feet firmly on the ground. During one test flight, *L'Esperance* was damaged and needed extensive repairs. The delay prompted a flurry of street-corner bets on which Limerick citizen would be brave enough to make an ascent – and whether they would survive.

On 16 May the *Limerick Chronicle* published a letter from Chevalier addressed from the Harris's riverside yard:

Dear Sir,

Allow me to inform the gentry and public of Limerick that the injury sustained during the last inflation is completely repaired, and I intend to perform my promise, weather permitting, by ascending in my balloon on Thursday next, 21st of May, at three o'clock, from Mr Harris' premises, Steamboat Quay, who was kind enough to give me the use of it, free of any charge. The scientific manager, Mr Baker, will give me every facility in his power to secure a successful ascent, and supply the required quantity of gas at high pressure. In this voyage, I will be accompanied by a lady and a gentleman. Hoping to be still favoured with the patronage of the gentry and public of Limerick, who have expressed so much sympathy for my unavoidable accident, and returning them my sincere thanks.

I remain, dear sir,

Your obedient servant,

A. Chevalier.

The *Munster News* reported that Monsieur Chevalier 'ascended at 3.30 p.m. from Mr Harris' yard and was last seen heading for Castleconnell'.

Fiercely loyal, James Harris remained lifelong friends with the colourful Scots-born textile magnate, ship owner and three-times Limerick mayor Sir Peter Tait, who, in less than thirty years, went from rags to riches and back again.

James Harris was a political liberal but also a staunch and devoted Catholic who lost no opportunity in forestalling the ambitions of his Protestant rivals. During the final quarter of the nineteenth century, he was elected secretary of the harbour board and became a markets trustee and a shareholder of the Limerick Race Company. Harris was also a stakeholder in the Catholic-funded citizens' tugboat *Commodore*, which engaged in more than one riverboat war with its *Privateer* rival, owned by the Protestant families of Bannatyne, Spaight and Russell.

James Harris died in 1895. In his obituary the *Limerick Chronicle* described him as a 'kindly and genial' man who had 'gained himself a host of friends' during his seventy-year life.

There was little chance that the Catholic–Protestant rivalry would be laid to rest with James Harris. When the family firms of Bannatyne and Spaight each announced they were branching out to offer the city's wealthier inhabitants the chance to lease telephones and connect to the expanding national network, the Harris board announced a Catholic competitor. Calls were not cheap: a three-minute connection between Limerick and Dublin cost an exorbitant 1s. 6d. (7½ pence).

By the time Ivan Harris inherited control of the family business in the late 1920s, he and his wife had moved into Overdale, one of Limerick's finest houses. The lifestyle was easy and enjoyable, with maids to keep the huge rooms clean and aired, nannies to look after the ever increasing Harris offspring, and gardeners to look after the large garden. The Harris empire extended to a pan-Ireland chain of flour mills and baking-powder mills and more than two dozen town bakeries. It was an empire that made them jealously rich and powerfully influential. By the time Ivan Harris's third son, Richard, was born on 1 October 1930, it was also a kingdom under fatal attack.

Three-hundred and fifty miles away in London the board of Rank, Britain's biggest flour merchant, voted on a move to corner the Irish market and instructed its managers to destroy the competition at any cost. It was a campaign that would eventually take more than fifteen years to win. One of its first targets was the Harris flour and seed mill in Limerick. Whatever Harris charged Rank undercut. Farmers who stayed loyal were eventually enticed away with still lower prices and under-the-table incentives. 'I saw it all dwindle,' recalled Richard Harris. 'We went from being rich to being poor.' One by one the servants were let go until Mildred Harris was forced to scrub her own floors and wash the sheets and shirts for her husband and eight children.

Richard Harris's earliest memory is of the 'good and the rich' times. His brother Noel had just been born. When he was little more than a toddler Harris recalls pushing his baby brother's pram down Limerick's Post Office Lane when he asked his mother if he would ever be that age again. 'No, Richard, you won't,' said Mildred Harris.

At one time, Ivan Harris wanted to send all his sons to England to be educated, like him, at Downside. Ireland's independence and the war with Germany made that impossible. World War Two was just a few months old when the Harrises enrolled their son 'Dickie' at Limerick's Crescent College.

Around this time, or very soon afterwards, Harris began to write poetry. At first they were naïve innocent verses scribbled in a spidery child's hand on scraps of paper or 'illegally' into his school notebooks. As he moved into adolescence – which he always claimed came exceptionally early – he experimented with various styles of handwriting. The subject matter never changed. The poems were a personal and private literature that the young Harris never read aloud or shared with his parents or seven brothers and sisters. By the time he was twelve he was recording his days and experiences in a kind of sing-song shorthand.

Like his mother Harris was an instinctive and intuitive hoarder: he later claimed he had squirrelled away every poem just in case, one day, he could make money from them. Ivan Harris's advice was more down to earth. 'Invest in property,' he advised his children in turn. 'That way when take you a piss at least you're pissing on your own land.'

'In Our Greenhouse' – later published in his first collection of poems called *I, In the Membership of My Days* – was written sometime in late 1942. It describes the magic of fantasy every child sprinkles on its surroundings, in the young Harris's case the garden at Overdale: of playing Tarzan in the apple tree with Sally, a neighbour's daughter who would later become his first teenage girlfriend; of escaping man-eating crocodiles by climbing the branches of an overhanging plum tree; of hoisting his sister's knickers on the washing pole as a white surrender flag; of playing James Cagney, with whom he would later act, and being executed for his crimes on the makeshift electric chair of the outside toilet. In 'our lane' behind the house the boys would collect old rags to scrunch and tie into a rugby ball and Harris would dream of leading a victorious Ireland against England. And then there was his father's car, which successively became a bomber to blitz the Germans, a destroyer he captained on his hunt for submarines, and an armoured car to chase the enemy. 'My brother died five times. He said I was lousy shot, but the truth was he was a bad loser.'

Tall for his age and with a crop of hair that already shared a stubborn individuality with the nine-year-old head beneath, young Dickie Harris plunged into the Crescent College regime with notable indifference. The school was owned and staffed by Jesuit fathers, an educated and severe order that interpreted any fleeting lack of concentration as a lapse in devotion – and an outright refusal to learn as a mortal sin. Salvation, as the Crescent's latest pupil soon found, could be achieved only through suffering. The spiritual weapon the fathers found most redeeming was a vicious leather strap.

'A grammatical mistake in homework, or a moment of foolishness in class, and the good father would write out a little chit from his docket book,' recalls the television and radio presenter Terry Wogan in his autobiography *Is It Me?*. 'Depending on the seriousness of the error or transgression, that chit would be good for three or six heavy welts across the hand from a reinforced leather strap.' Each lunchtime and afternoon a queue of boys would assemble to receive their 'biffs' from the college prefect of studies. Only the brightest and the most diligent escaped.

Others found the Crescent regime less brutal. Bill Whelan, creator of the *Riverdance* spectacular, who would later owe his breakthrough as a composer to Richard Harris, attended the college between 1957 and 1968. 'Of course we got the odd slap at school but there was nothing extreme in my opinion,' claims Whelan. 'I am always amazed at how former pupils exaggerate their memories of the Crescent punishment.'

In the classroom, Harris found little to interest him. Most subjects were barely tolerable; the rest he gave up on. He was not alone. Much against the Jesuit tradition of learning and academic excellence, Crescent College created a special class for its 'eleven hopeless cases', of which Harris was one. Expelling or arranging for the pupils to be transferred to another academy would have been seen as an admission of failure. To hide its collective shame, the school denied the class's existence – to the other pupils and their parents – even ordering that no written record be kept of its presence. On paper, the boys took their places each day alongside the other pupils in their year. In reality, they shuffled into a classroom at the far end of a long corridor, where their rebellious minds could be contained in a form of academic quarantine.

For the 'forgotten few' examinations were as boring and worthless as the learning they were designed to test. During one end-of-term examination, Harris waited until the papers had been distributed before folding his into a neat row of paper houses; when that was done, he put his head on the desk and fell asleep.

At the end of one Christmas term Harris returned home with his school report. Ivan opened the buff envelope with accustomed resignation. Opposite the list of printed subjects each teacher had written his son's end-of-term mark: mathematics – 2; French – 1; geography – 2;

algebra – 0. The accumulated total failed to reach the 40 per cent pass mark for a single subject.

At the bottom of the report was a tear-off slip on which parents were expected to add their own comments. Ivan unscrewed the cap of his prized Parker pen and wrote, 'Dear Father McClaughlin, I am very pleased with my son Dickie's progress at your school.'

One apocryphal story still doing the Limerick rounds involves an American journalist collecting material for a magazine feature on the now-famous Richard Harris. Having spoken to his family and friends, the journalist made an appointment with the Crescent College head. The head was polite but insistent: 'I would prefer it if you did not mention him in connection with this school.'

There were two subjects in which Harris excelled. Both took place outside the confines of regular classroom routine and both remained his absorbing passions for the rest of his life.

'As a family we were great singers,' Harris once said. 'Not in the professional sense, but music and singing were always in their hearts.' At school – in the great wood-lined hall – Harris's gregarious nature thrived amid the chaos of school plays. His performance in the William Vincent Wallace opera *Maritana* won him a standing ovation. And in his early twenties he earned equal praise at the Victoria Hotel's impromptu concerts for his delivery of a long sequence from *On the Waterfront*, complete with American accent and Marlon Brando's threatening whisper.

Since he was a child, as soon as he could walk and almost certainly as soon as he could pick up and run with a ball, Harris also became fanatical about rugby – 'My dream was always that I would play for Ireland.' It was an ambition that slotted in well with the ethos of Crescent College, which honoured its rugby team members with special treatment and extra privileges – not that he saw much of those. What it did give Richard Harris was sex appeal and hero status.

For some, Limerick would remain the 'last bollard on the dark edge of Europe'. It was the furthest place from which to travel. Only the desperate and the bravest travelled west to America. The rebellious and the ambitious turned their backs on the Atlantic and headed east to Dublin, and then, if you really had nothing to lose, to London.

'Limerick gained a reputation for piety, but we knew it was only the rain,' recalled Frank McCourt in his memoir *Angela's Ashes*. Fifty years on, Harris would have a violent and highly publicised dispute with the

Pulitzer Prize-winning author over their differing memories of childhood Limerick, but the one thing they would never fight over was the weather. 'Out in the Atlantic Ocean great sheets of rain gathered to drift slowly up the River Shannon and settle forever in Limerick. The rain dampened the city from the Feast of the Circumcision to New Year's Eve. It created a cacophony of hacking coughs, bronchial rattles, asthmatic wheezes, consumptive croaks ... The rain drove us into the church – our refuge, our strength, our only dry place.'

Harris was growing up in what was then Ireland's third-largest town. Limerick did not qualify as a city because it did not have a cathedral. What it did have were dozens of churches, all Roman Catholic and all providing that strange complexity of fear and faith that only Catholicism engenders. 'Limerick was more Roman Catholic than the Vatican,' recalls Terry Wogan. 'Not a lot of Christianity, if by that you mean love and tolerance of your fellow man, but plenty of religion.'

Whether you were poor and hungry and sharing a two-room slum behind St John's Castle or, like Wogan, born into a comfortable lower-middle-class family from Elm Park, the Church permeated your house, your clothes, even the air you breathed. And, unlike the smell of warm sugar from Cleeves Toffee Factory on the Ennis Road, it could not be blown away by the sharp Atlantic storms or washed clean by what seemed like Limerick's ceaseless rain.

For the town's few wealthy families, such as the Harrises and those with ambition enough to claw their way up the financial and social ladder, the Church was eager to help. 'They had something called the "Arch-Confraternity", a sort of Catholic Freemasonry, except that there was secrecy,' explains Wogan in his autobiography, *Is It Me?* 'If you got into the Arch-Confraternity, you let the whole of Limerick know about it. You had arrived: a pillar of the Church, a pillar of the community; people bought you drinks and paid your fare on the bus.'

There was little, if any, contact between the Harris and the Wogan families. Unlike Ivan Harris, Michael Wogan was not a member of the Arch-Confraternity, a situation the presenter attributes to his father's impish sense of humour. Terry Wogan was born in August 1938 and for six years, while his father managed Leverette & Frye, one of the town's more upmarket food emporiums, he remained an only child.

Limerick's divisions, recalled one of Harris's friends, Desmond O'Grady, ran deep and through almost every aspect of the city's business and social life. 'It was a caste-divided city of Catholics and Protestants, urbanites and suburbanites, Laurel Hill and Presentation girls, Jesuit and

Christian Brother boys. The rugby, rowing and church clubs were equally divided,' explained O'Grady.

Only one thing could be guaranteed to unite this deeply divided society, either on the blood-spattered grass of Thomond Park or against a wider enemy. Limerick, as Harris explained many years later in an American documentary, is the home of rugby. 'Not only in Ireland, but throughout the world. Rugby is sacred on these streets. To say anything against rugby on these streets will get you into very serious trouble.'

Rugby was not only almost a religion in itself – whereby you were baptised by being taken to a match and held aloft to celebrate a try before your first birthday – but was also organised into traditional religious areas. Limerick's junior teams were based and recruited from parish boundaries, allowing players to defend not only their championship ranking but also their neighbourhood honour. Junior matches, like interschool clashes, were bloody and hard and desperately serious.

By his late teens Harris was already fourteen stone and an athletic six foot one. Much of his school rugby career was spent packing down as a rebellious and wandering lock, though 'I was too busy and knackered scoring tries to bother too much with scrummaging.' It was, he claims, his first case of miscasting.

Harris's dedication to rugby – and to *winning* at rugby – received some unusual benefaction. In 1947 Crescent College met PBC Cork in the final of the Munster Schools Senior Cup. Harris was forced to watch the impressive but indecisive match from the sidelines. Before the replay, one of Crescent's forwards left the college to start work and Harris, still only sixteen, was called into the team alongside his older brother Ivan. The danger player in the Cork side was a full-back named Mick Brosnahan, who Harris had a hunch would turn out in the fly-half position. For three hours each day Harris and his Crescent teammates practised 'nobbling' a fly-half. When their coach, Father Guiunane, finally arrived he called Harris to the sideline. 'I'm utterly appalled,' said the priest puffing hard on his cigarette. 'We'll win this match by fair means or not at all.'

When, on match day, the dreaded Brosnahan trotted out on to the pitch wearing a Number 10 fly-half shirt, 'Harris, a quiet word,' whispered Father Guiunane through a cloud of blue smoke. 'You may continue with your plan.'

After leaving Crescent College, Harris played for the old boys' team, Old Crescent, before joining Garryowen Rugby Club, which trained and played on the Thomond Park Rugby grounds. With Harris in the Garryowen squad, the team went on to win the Munster Senior Cup. Harris wore his injuries like badges of honour and revelled in his invincible fitness. He was, he boasted, a gladiator on the battlefield of Thomond Park – where he scored eleven tries in various junior and schools games.

Feared for his unforgiving tackles, Harris did not, however, always get things his own way. One member of St Mary's Rugby Club squad was a no-nonsense player called Ducky Hayes. Taking the field for his school's old boys' side, Harris made the mistake of clashing with Hayes head-on. Semiconscious and with his face covered in blood, Harris was stretchered off the Thomond Park pitch and treated in the casualty department of the nearby City Home Hospital.

'A few minutes later he was back,' recalled Hayes. 'All you could see were the slits of his eyes, his face was bandaged so much.' The crowd greeted the reappearance of Old Crescent's star player with shouts of: ''Tis the return of the Phantom – no, 'tis the Mummy.'

In 1945, a new culture swept the streets and bars and back alleys of Limerick. With World War Two over, Ireland was released from its declaration of neutrality, and Shannon Airport, fifteen miles up the Ennis Road from Limerick, became a major staging post for American troops on their way to and from occupied Germany. For the seven-year-old Terry Wogan 'it brought new sounds, new flavours, the almighty dollar, and a sinful touch of forbidden fruit to Holy Catholic Limerick'. To Harris the drawling, gum-chewing, back-slapping B-movie cowboys and gangsters he had so carefully watched at Saturday afternoon cinema came alive – and he was desperate to be one of them.

By his early teens Harris and his cohorts Paddy Lloyd and Gerry Murphy were doing a weekly round of the town's five cinemas. Each visit to the Carlton or the Lyric or the Savoy – which still offered an intermission speciality act and fifteen minutes of Wurlitzer singalong – was governed less by that day's feature film that by a recent misdemeanour and the length of a subsequent manager's ban. With money short, the trio would pool their resources to buy a single ticket. As the lights dimmed for the start of the programme the ticket holder, usually Harris, would slip out of his seat and help his friends in through the fire exit or toilet window. His departures were equally ingenious and considerably more public. After watching a screen cowboy tumble to his death at the Savoy, Harris emulated the dead villain by hurling himself head first down the cinema's sweeping staircase. At the Lyric, Marlon Brando's Oscar-nomination performance in *Julius Caesar* so impressed him he began to echo the star's lines out loud – 'Friends, Romans, Countrymen, lend me your ears ...' When Harris started to get more laughs than Shakespeare's tragedy the manager decided it was time to call the Garda and Harris was frogmarched, still reciting, from the premises.

Limerick's newest cinema opened on 17 November 1947, and within a few weeks would present the teenage Harris with one of his first entrepreneurial opportunities. Converted from the city's old Athenaeum Hall, the six-hundred-seat Royal opened with Cole Porter's hit musical *Night and Day*, starring Cary Grant and Jane Wyman. Its new owner, Mary Collins, intended her cinema to be the grandest and plushest of Limerick's nine such establishments and staffed by 'knowledgeable and caring' assistants. As commissionaire, she hired a six-foot-six ex-army boxing champion called Denis Hayes, who had appeared as an equestrian stuntman in Lawrence Olivier's epic *Henry V* and cherished a personal note of thanks from the actor–director.

Dressed in his elegant maroon and gold uniform, Hayes soon earned a reputation as the city's leading authority on cinema matters and show-business gossip. During performances, it was part of his duty to patrol the balcony and attempt to halt the cascade of Cleeves toffee wrappers and other more dangerous missiles aimed at the patrons in the more expensive seats below. His job was not helped by gangs of rampaging youngsters abandoned by their older siblings while they 'shifted' their latest date in the darkened back rows. At the start of one matinée performance, Hayes wanted some help, and approached a youth who appeared to share his interest in films.

'You can guard the balcony for half an hour, young man,' said Hayes, 'while I slip out for cigarettes.'

'For half-price next Sunday?' offered the teenager.

Hayes agreed and slipped out through the fire exit and across the road into Collin's pub. When he returned, everyone in the balcony was sitting bolt upright: 'The only thing I could hear was the hum of the projector and the occasional sob from a red-eared kid,' he recalled. His partnership with the 'young pup' continued until Richard Harris left for London.

On his own, Harris took films far more seriously. 'I often went to the cinema and stayed all day,' he later confessed. 'I would go in for the matinée, stay for the middle show and leave after the evening performance.'

For the town's motorists, the longer Harris stayed indoors and off the roads the better. Not long after passing his driving test he made spectacular contact with a corporation bus. When he somehow managed to repeat the incident he was summonsed and fined and banned from driving for life. He never drove a car again.

At seventeen, and like his older brothers before him, Harris left school and joined the family firm. The flour mill at Mount Kenneth was barely making a profit, certainly not enough to support a third and hungrier generation of Harrises. It was an opportunity, the company's latest recruit explained to his new employer, for him to break with family tradition. He wanted to do something else. Anything else. He certainly didn't want to learn the benefits and failings of various strains of wheat or to master the intricacies of double-entry bookkeeping. At home there were rows and hurtful accusations. In the end, Harris agreed to follow his siblings into the firm – but pushing a broom instead of a pen.

There was barely enough work in the Mount Kenneth flour lofts to keep Harris occupied. What there *were* plenty of were mice and rats. At first Harris used a stick to shoo away the vermin. When he acquired an air rifle he hid among the sacks and sniped at the foraging rodents.

Sean Leonard was a Limerick teenager who remembers his contemporary's mischievous sense of humour. Leonard was employed in his uncle's butcher's shop about seventy yards up the road from the Harrises' flour mill. 'Always full of talk and craic', Harris would first admonish the butcher for allowing a queue to form, and then push his way behind the counter, pick up a knife or cleaver and announce, 'Right you are, who's for two pound of round?'

Mary O'Meara's family owned and ran a small grocery shop in Bellinaccurra, about a mile and a half outside the city. She remembers Harris as 'tall and carefree and gay' and always with a pretty young woman on his arm. 'Everyone knew Dickie Harris,' adds O'Meara. 'Even at that age he was a rugby hero to a lot of people. If Dickie wasn't playing that week some of my friends wouldn't bother going to the match. We all expected him to one day play for Ireland, he was that good.' Once a week she would drive the family's Commer van into Limerick to collect sacks of flour and rolled oats from Ivan Harris's store in Henry Street. 'An eight-stone sack of flour was nothing to Dickie,' recalls Mary O'Meara. 'He would toss the sack over his shoulder and skip his way to the van before hurling it in the back.'

By early 1948, though, the Rank stranglehold on the flour business was proving ruinous. The Harris business, which at one time had been one of area's largest employers, was haemorrhaging money daily. Ivan Harris informed his wife, but not his family, that he was thinking of closing the remaining mill and taking a lease on a small Limerick shop. From there he could at least earn a living selling flour direct to the public and other retailers. The end, when it came, was triggered by mischievous disloyalty from Ivan's own troublesome son.

Weary of sweeping floors and shooting rats, Harris persuaded his fellow mill workers they were being poorly paid and that the only solution was to strike for higher wages. Surprised by the militancy of his workforce, many of whom he had grown up with and knew as friends, Ivan arrived at his riverside premises one morning to be confronted by a wall of strikers brandishing banners that announced, 'Your son says we should have more money!'

Years later Harris would use the story as a piece of interview self-mockery. It was, claims one of his near relatives, 'the biggest single act of treachery Dickie performed on his family. It may not have killed off the business, but it was certainly one of the final nails in the coffin. Ivan was bitterly hurt.' It took almost a decade for Harris, by then an Oscar-nominated actor, to redress the balance.

Beneath the window of Harris's Overdale bedroom was a galvanised tin roof. It was his escape route for the nights when Ivan Harris forbade his troublesome son to go out. And, shimmying up an overhanging tree, he would remove his shoes before clambering barefooted back into his room from an all-night date.

During the summer before his 22nd birthday, Harris noticed that the climb left him unusually breathless. He dismissed it as the start of another summer cold. The infection dragged on for days, leaving him tired and chesty and soaked by nightly sweats. When he began coughing up blood his mother called the doctor.

Tuberculosis was a legacy of the crowded and unsanitary living conditions that still existed in many Irish cities in the early 1950s. Not only was it considered a fatal disease, but recovery for those who did survive could take as long as three years and patients were invariably admitted to an isolation hospital. For those left at home the stigma of having a family member in a sanatorium was almost as embarrassing as the disease itself. It was a burden Mildred Harris was not prepared to bear. Her son would be confined to his bedroom and treated at home.

The trickle of friends brave enough to visit the invalid eventually dried up and Harris, frustrated by his physical condition and uneasy about the curb on his rugby ambitions, was left to find his own distractions. His imagination roamed and rebounded about the room. The light bulb became his captive and the door and dresser knobs his servants. 'I would have conversations with inanimate objects,' he recalled, 'and invent hundreds of people who trooped through my room and spoke to me as they went.' He was a castaway; a highwayman; a red Indian; the king of England; the Pope. In his mind – from within his mind – came instant sin and instant absolution.

He read and reread a copy of *Hamlet*. It filled him first with excitement and possibility and then, as he paced his bedroom reciting the lines, it swelled the room itself with a special kind of magic. 'Hamlet is a part which can be compared to a man given a pistol, blindfolded and told to fire it off in a room completely papered with targets,' the veteran classical actor Ralph Richardson once said. 'If he goes bang, bang, bang, he'll hit three targets.' Harris fired off stray shots – 'O shame! where is thy blush?' – at whoever came into his room.

Harris also began searching inwards in a self-search that he once mentioned had never stopped, and as his guide he chose the tortured genius of Vincent van Gogh. Since the Dutch painter's suicide in 1890 almost eight hundred books and articles and theses had appeared around the world. In van Gogh's letters the 23-year-old Harris found endless inspiration:

> To act well in this world one must sacrifice all personal desires. Man is not on this earth merely to be happy, nor even simply to be honest. He is there to realise great things for humanity, to attain nobility and to surmount the vulgarity of nearly every individual.

And advice: 'Don't take things that don't really concern you very closely too much to heart, and don't let them hit you too hard.'

And, possibly for the first time in his life, he also found a shared suffering. In 1879 van Gogh wrote to his brother Theo:

> If I had to believe that I were troublesome to you or to the people at home, or were in your way, of no good to anyone, and if I should be obliged to feel an intruder or an outcast, so that I were better off dead, and if I should have to try to keep out of your way more and more – if I thought this were really the case, a feeling of

anguish would overwhelm me, and I should have to struggle against despair . . .

Unlike van Gogh, Harris never felt the need to take his own life. Harris's 'suicide' was escape – from the same feeling of entrapment he sensed closing in when his father demanded he should work in the flour mill office. 'There were six boys and two girls in the family,' Harris explained years later. 'I was lost in the middle and when the tuberculosis eased off I was left with an identity crisis. I was free to become something, but what? I chose acting partly because I knew I would have to create an identity for them to recognise; I wasn't just child number five. I wanted them to realise who I am. For my mother and father to say, "Hey, we've got a friend called Richard Harris in the family. That's him up there on the stage." '

Mentally, Harris was now fitter and sharper than at any time in his life. Physically he was a wreck. The TB left him physically weak and it was two years before he was allowed out of his Overdale bedroom to sit, wrapped and coddled, in the sunshine of the garden. By the winter of 1953, desperately thin but even more determined, he was back striding the streets of Limerick. One former classmate, Tom Stack, was surprised to see him carrying a copy of John Steinbeck's *East of Eden*. 'It was a revelation,' he recalled. 'At school Dickie had shown little interest in literature.' The trainee priest was glad to see the illness had failed to dampen his friend's sense of humour and energy and listened as Harris explained his plans to earn a living on the stage. 'It was eating him up and I could see he would never be satisfied until he was an actor.'

To convalesce, his parents packed Harris off to Kilkee, where they hoped the crisp Atlantic breezes would clear his lungs. Since the turn of the century the women and children from the better-off Limerick families moved the sixty-odd miles up the County Clare coast to Kilkee, to be joined each weekend by the town's husbands and unattached young men.

Kilkee possessed the safest bathing beaches on the west coast and had attracted bathers since the end of the eighteenth century. Its regular celebrity visitors included the *King Solomon's Mines* author H Rider Haggard, Charlotte Brontë and the poet Lord Alfred Tennyson. By the 1930s it was one of the few resorts anywhere in Europe still enforcing a strict bathing code. The beach was divided into three. Council-employed inspectors toured the sand to ensure men were confined to the middle section – where they frequently swam naked – and women remained unmolested in the two outer areas. To protect their modesty still further, female swimmers changed in Victorian bathing boxes, which were then winched into the sea up to their axles to allow the occupants a dip away from preying eyes. As a child, and under his mother's protective eye, Harris would build sandcastles and play on Kilkee's crescent-shaped beach. As a teenager he, with friends, roamed 'Limerick-on-Sea' looking for mischief.

In the late 1940s Harris made sure he was always in Kilkee for the last two weeks of July and the annual squash racket 'world' championships. The mixed pairs of players use a racket and a tennis ball stripped of its fur. The game is played on the beach against a wall built during the relief scheme that followed the Great Famine of the mid-nineteenth century, which forms the base of the squash alleys. A loosely strung racket was essential. 'A highly strung racket would not control the ball,' said Harris. 'I knew where the holes in the wall were and where the bounce was.' Between 1948 and 1951 Harris was unbeatable. For four consecutive years his name appears as a world champion on the original Tivoli Cup.

His body still painfully stiff and his muscles too weak for strenuous physical exercise, Harris in his early twenties preferred to roam the Kilkee streets away from the sea where there was a sullen mix of curates and daffodils and the raffish scent of Mooney's pub, of Boland's bakery, of McCabe's the licensed victualler and of Ryan's, the black-painted and unforgiving funeral parlour. During the Easter holidays a university drama group touring the west coast arrived in the resort. Harris introduced himself and volunteered to help the backstage crew set up scenery and arrange the props. It was his first involvement with a theatre company and Harris took any job that needed doing, even cooking the students' meals.

Back in Limerick he sought out and joined the College Players, an amateur theatrical group, which ran weekly acting workshops. One member recalls Harris's arrival. 'He was basically very shy,' she says, 'but when he started to act you could see the show-off in him coming out. He was a born actor, the problem was he was unwilling to learn.'

His chance came when he was offered the part of Ellis in a production of August Strindberg's play, *Easter*. 'Working with Dickie was a delightful experience,' remembers a fellow College Players actor and future producer, Kevin Dinneen. 'From that one role we could see his future was on the stage.'

By now Harris had earned himself a new reputation: he was still a mischievous rebel, but he was now a reader and a thinker and for most of Limerick that branded him a Bohemian. He had also taken up with two friends who shared his ambition, if not his direction.

Desmond O'Grady was a would-be poet whose literary guru was James Joyce and who insisted on wearing a woollen sweater and a long, black coat. A 'modern school' artist dressed in crumpled and paint-stained country clothes, Jack O'Donovan refused to remove his battered tweed hat. Harris, as the thespian of the group, had taken to wearing a duffel coat. His inspiration was Marlon Brando and the recently fashionable New York school of acting.

The Left Bank cafés and London's newly emerging coffee bars were still a long way off, and the trio of eccentrics had to make do with a corner of the Savoy tearooms, where a sympathetic waitress kept their teapot refilled with free hot water. The nineteen-year-old O'Grady was already saving hard to finance a move to Paris. And it was here that Harris first announced – at least to his friends – that he had abandoned his plan to join the Dublin-based Abbey Theatre Company in favour of a London drama school. The equally ambitious Jack O'Donovan was a less enthusiastic traveller and remained in Limerick to become head of painting at the town's College of Art and Design.

Late in 1954 the Anew McMaster repertory company returned to Limerick. A classical actor-manager of the old school, McMaster had toured Ireland in 1952 with a selection of Shakespearean productions. It was after one performance that Harris was inspired to buy his copy of *Hamlet*. Now McMaster was back with a lighter selection of plays, including a stage adaptation of Stanley Weyman's 1894 novel, *Under the Red Robe*.

At each venue, McMaster recruited extras from local amateur drama societies. Harris and a fellow College Players member, Michael English, auditioned and were accepted. His brief, downstage appearance in *Under the Red Robe* would mark his professional stage debut. McMaster also confirmed what Harris had known and decided on for months. 'If you want to be an actor, my boy, you must go to London.'

The advice was constructive but not yet compelling. And anyway, before he left for England Harris had a date in Dublin to watch a rugby final between Ireland and Scotland. He and three friends planned to hitchhike to the capital on the Friday before the match. After a succession of lorries and vans had passed, they finally arrived in style in the back of a new car, which still smelled of leather and wood polish. His first impression of Dublin – 'tatty and deliciously disgraceful and full of churches' – would never leave him. The women, shockingly pretty against the grubby shop fronts and pub windows, somehow lacked any form of taste with their emerald and electric-blue cardigans and dresses. There was also a carelessness about the gutters and rubbish-strewn streets populated by fleets of dented and paint-worn buses, all looking like much-played-with Dinky toys.

That night the quartet planned to visit a dance hall to 'show Dublin girls what sexual monsters we Limerick boys were'. Shuffling through the streets, Harris spotted a poster for Luigi Pirandello's *Henry IV*, starring Michael MacLiammóir. 'You go to the dance,' announced Harris. 'I'm going to see this play. This is what I'm going to do with my life – I am going to be a professional actor.'

The following Monday, Harris called his father and mother together to announce he was off to England to train as an actor. Mildred begged him to stay. And when that failed she begged her husband to order him to stay. 'Go, go,' said Ivan shaking his head. 'For God's sake, go.'

Within days Harris had pocketed his £21 savings, bought himself a steerage ticket to Liverpool and followed his dream across the Irish Sea to England.

CHAPTER TWO

The LAMDA audition was at four o'clock on a Thursday afternoon. At 3.45 p.m. Harris was still rehearsing his lines more than four miles away on the far side of Hyde Park.

It was gone five o'clock by the time Harris reached the Cromwell Road. He was out of breath and desperate. A bespectacled little man was turning the key in the main door of the LAMDA building.

'Quick. Quick,' panted Harris. 'Take me to Michael MacOwen.'

'I am Michael MacOwen,' replied the academy's principal.

'Good,' said Harris. 'You've discovered me.'

When he attempted to apologise and explain why he was late, MacOwen, who was still resolutely barring the entrance, informed Harris the drama school was full.

'But you must take me,' demanded Harris. 'I've checked out the record of your academy and you haven't had one success. Not one. Now I am going to be your first success.'

Impressed by his would-be student's youthful confidence and Irish cheek, MacOwen – who before taking over at LAMDA had been drama director with the Arts Council – unlocked the door and dutifully led him into the academy theatre. Alone and illuminated by a single spotlight, Harris went through his Shakespearean set pieces. It was enough. All Harris had to do now was live up to his doorstep promise.

Two decades after he left the London Academy of Music and Dramatic Art, Harris met his former principal in a television studio's green room. They chatted politely until Harris asked MacOwen what he had thought of that first performance. 'Truthfully?' Harris nodded. 'It was the worst audition I have ever sat through. It was truly awful,' he said.

CHAPTER TWO

I was planning to go into architecture. But when I arrived, architecture was filled up. Acting was right next door to it, so I signed up for acting instead.

– Tom Selleck

Externally, Richard Harris was formed on the playing fields of Crescent College and the rugby pitches of Thomond Park. Despite his illness, he still walked and held himself like a sportsman, and his lean Irish face and broken nose gave him the look – at least to himself – of being slightly ugly. He loved to win. But at 24 he still had that gentle, boyish sort of cheerfulness that had never been trained out of him.

Internally, he had been shaped by his mother and his two sisters and every woman he had ever fallen in love with. But he had not yet been moulded. That would be left to a succession of women he would meet in London. The first of whom sat opposite him now.

'What are you going to do for us, young man?' said the middle-aged woman whose aristocratic voice and perfect vowels betrayed her attempts to dress like her would-be students.

'Something from Shakespeare.'

Harris delivered the piece he had rehearsed. The audition panel looked sideways at each other. No one spoke. Finally the woman asked, 'And what right do you think you have to enter our profession?'

'The same right you have to judge me,' replied Harris.

The woman reached for a miniature brass bell. Behind him the door opened and a small man waved Harris out of the room and out of the building. The man was little bigger than a dwarf. He showed no fear, especially not to a disrespectful Irishman twice his height.

As he stepped out of the Royal Albert Hall the August sunlight hit Harris full in the face. So, too, did his first rejection. The Central School of Speech and Drama did not want him. He decided to walk off his disappointment. He blamed his failure on the snobbery of the selection panel, his choice of material, his physical appearance, his age (he was five or six years older than most applicants), his too-sharp tongue. Years later, Harris finally conceded the truth: 'Perhaps it was because I just wasn't good enough.'

Someone suggested he should apply to the London Academy of Music and Dramatic Art. It was a relatively small drama school, which, as Harris soon discovered, had several things to recommend it. Situated on the Cromwell Road, the northern boundary of the expatriate Irish enclave of Earl's Court, it was just a minute or two's walk from his temporary lodgings – a distinct advantage after a heavy night's drinking. LAMDA was also the only establishment in London offering classes in the acting technique known as 'the Method', a discipline famously employed by Marlon Brando, one of Harris's cinema heroes.

The LAMDA audition was at four o'clock on a Thursday afternoon. At 3.45 p.m. Harris was still rehearsing his lines more than four miles away on the far side of Hyde Park.

'Now is ... Now is the winter of our discontent made glorious summer by this son of York ... Now is the summer of our ...'

An old man on a park bench squinted over the top of his newspaper at the young man walking in a figure-of-eight around the trees and apparently talking to some invisible being.

'... and are our yesterdays as righteous fools ...'

Harris's nose suddenly made contact with something cold and shiny. 'You all right, lad?' His eyes focused on a silver-crested button. 'This is no way to behave in one of Her Majesty's Royal Parks.'

The Irishman straightened to his full height to find himself eye to eye with a policeman. 'I'm rehearsing,' said Harris. 'I'm an actor.'

'That explains it,' said the officer, shaking his head. 'One of those.' It took Harris more than half an hour to talk himself out of night in the cells.

It was gone five o'clock by the time Harris reached the Cromwell Road. He was out of breath and desperate. A bespectacled little man was turning the key in the main door of the LAMDA building.

'Quick. Quick,' panted Harris. 'Take me to Michael MacOwen.'

'I am Michael MacOwen,' replied the academy's principal.

'Good,' said Harris. 'You've discovered me.'

When he attempted to apologise and explain why he was late, MacOwen, who was still resolutely barring the entrance, informed Harris the drama school was full.

'But you must take me,' demanded Harris. 'I've checked out the record of your academy and you haven't had one success. Not one. Now I am going to be your first success.'

Impressed by his would-be student's youthful confidence and Irish cheek, MacOwen – who before taking over at LAMDA had been drama director with the Arts Council – unlocked the door and dutifully led him into the academy theatre. Alone and illuminated by a single spotlight, Harris went through his Shakespearean set pieces. It was enough. All Harris had to do now was live up to his doorstep promise.

Two decades after he left the London Academy of Music and Dramatic Art, Harris met his former principal in a television studio's green room. They chatted politely until Harris asked MacOwen what he had thought of that first performance. 'Truthfully?' Harris nodded. 'It was the worst audition I have ever sat through. It was truly awful,' he said.

'There was no doubt Richard had charm,' MacOwen explained. 'A born actor he wasn't. As I watched him my heart sank, but I thought that any young man with the gall and the cheek to stand up and give a performance like that has got to have the confidence to make it.'

For the first time Harris found himself eager to learn. Being accepted by his fellow students – most of whom had grown up in postwar Britain, with its rationing and deprivation and two lost years of National Service – was a luxury he had long since learned to live without. Limerick or London, he continued to carry the sense of isolation he had grown up with and brought with him to England. 'I was an outsider in my own family and at LAMDA,' he said. 'It was like, "Oh Jesus, here he is again. He doesn't conform. He doesn't do what we tell him." '

In his home town, Harris had professed a devotion to acting among his café aesthetes. His pose was that of a sweaty and untutored philistine. In London, and particularly at LAMDA, his aim was not to stand out but to appear to be a mysterious and dangerous man from Ireland. He was a good four or five years older than the majority of students. Thin but muscular, as if he were recovering from some potentially fatal disease – which, of course, he was – and with a broken nose and the disconcerting habit of using a profanity at the most inappropriate moment, he was delighted to be taken for anything but an actor. But Harris is philosophical about his early life in London. 'It was probably the best time and the most fun,' he admitted. 'When things become too easy and challenges are diminished by success, one is inclined to become very complacent.'

There were three drama schools of note in London in the mid-1950s. One was the Central School of Speech and Drama, about to move from its original home within the Royal Albert Hall to its new purpose-built campus at Swiss Cottage, and Harris's first unsuccessful choice. The second was the London Academy of Music and Dramatic Art, where he was now a student. The third, and most prestigious, was the Royal Academy of Dramatic Art, or RADA, founded in 1904 by Sir Herbert Beerbohm Tree, one of the great Victorian actor–managers. Among its students at the time was a dedicated young actor called Peter O'Toole. Another was an eighteen-year-old would-be actress and part-time debutante by the name of Elizabeth Rees-Williams.

The only daughter of David and Constance Rees-Williams, Elizabeth had grown up a privileged yet stubbornly resolute teenager. Her childhood was divided among various preparatory and boarding schools, her paternal grandparents' home in South Wales and long summer holidays on the Brittany coast. In 1945, when his daughter was eight, Rees-Williams abandoned his family-breed Liberalism and was elected as Labour Member of Parliament for Croydon. A sure-footed and talented politician, he was soon promoted to Parliamentary Undersecretary of State for Commonwealth Relations and eventually Minister of Civil Aviation. After losing his seat in the 1950 general election, he was elevated to the peerage by Clement Attlee and opted for the title Baron Ogmore of Bridgend.

At seventeen, Elizabeth was sent to a finishing school in Switzerland. By the summer of 1954 she was back in London for 'the Season' and with her mind set on an acting career. As an attractive, lively teenager she was, by her own admission, 'lumbered with *joie de vivre*'. Between 10 a.m. and 6 p.m. she attended classes and rehearsals at RADA. By 6.30 p.m. she was back at her parents' Queen's Gate home, preparing for a night on the town.

'The Season may have been frivolous, irrelevant and crumbling tradition but it was fun and a necessary antidote to the exigent routine of RADA,' she recalls in her autobiography, *Love, Honour and Dismay*. 'So many parties to go to and so many people to meet.'

The inevitable end came late one Friday afternoon in January 1955. It was the start of her fifth term at the academy and her tutors had universally failed to detect any improvement in her potential as an actress. Outside the academy's Gower Street premises, London was shivering under the worst winter since 1947. Through the window of the principal's office, Elizabeth watched the start of yet another snowstorm. Principal John Fernald coughed to regain her attention and with 'faultless rhythm and exemplary economy' informed the teenager her days at RADA were over.

There were no tears. Her expulsion was a setback, nothing more. Trudging north through the snow along Gloucester Road, Elizabeth was concentrating on how to continue her stage career when she heard a voice. 'It's no night to be out for a stroll,' said the young man holding open the door of a Daimler car. 'I thought you might like a lift.'

'I'm going to Queen's Gate,' said Elizabeth, brushing the snow from her coat and slipping in beside the driver.

Progress through the worsening blizzard was slow. 'I'm an actor,' Elizabeth's rescuer informed her as they turned right into Kensington Gore. His name, he added, was Peter Prowse.

'That's funny,' said Elizabeth, 'I'm an actress. At least I was until an hour ago.'

Elizabeth turned to thank Prowse for the lift. 'Look, I'm up for the lead in *Winter Journey*,' he said. 'The auditions are tonight. If you're interested, I could take you along and introduce you to the director. I know he's still looking for someone to play the ingénue.'

Prowse was a colourful and idiosyncratic actor who did his best to conceal his South African birth behind a rough Cockney accent. The son of an Indian Army officer, he had come to Britain in the late 1920s and, as the family fortunes dwindled, grew up in poverty in London's East End. Prowse turned to acting when World War Two and his career as a Royal Navy lieutenant-commander came to an end.

Two hours later the thirty-year-old actor was back at Queen's Gate. 'The director's a very young man,' he said on the five-minute drive to Earl's Court. 'He's putting up his own money for the production.' As they pulled up outside a busy coffee bar the light from the windows reflected the doubts in Elizabeth's face. 'Oh, don't worry,' added Prowse, brushing aside a flop of blonde hair from his forehead. 'He's only using this place for casting and rehearsals.'

The Troubadour was owned and run by Michael and Sheila van Bloeman. Steamy and crowded, the snack bar was a long way from the glittering nightclubs and bubbly parties where the teenager was accustomed to spending her evenings. On each pine table flickered a candle, throwing a dim but warm light on to the plain whitewashed walls. To Elizabeth it seemed that every customer was wearing either a beard or at least the makings of a beard, and the obligatory ex-navy duffel coat. Born in Canada to Dutch parents, Michael van Bloeman was operating the establishment, with his wife, on a unique but still profitable 'cash and reputation' basis: those who could afford it paid cash for their food and drinks; those who couldn't were fed anyway, promising to repay the debt from their next performance fee or when their reputations as actors or artists had been recognised.

Prowse took Elizabeth by the hand and led her through the maze of tables to where a young man was reading an outsized book. She was suddenly very nervous. The man's face was pale and waxen in the candlelight and his tired eyes rubbed sore and bloodshot. He seemed to be concentrating overly hard on the contents of the book and it wasn't until he raised his head that Elizabeth realised the man's shoulder-length red hair gave him the look of a van Gogh or Rembrandt figure.

'This is Richard Harris,' said Prowse. There was no flicker of interest. 'Richard, this is Elizabeth Rees-Williams.'

Harris slammed the book shut and leaped to his feet. He nodded twice, once for Elizabeth to sit and once for Prowse to follow him, before padding barefoot across the café floor to where some steps disappeared into the darkness of an apparently unlit cellar.

As she sat alone, Elizabeth's confidence was draining almost as fast as her realisation that her mother's fur coat was drawing some unusually antagonistic glares. In a few years' time she would be able to put names to the faces: Mort Sahl, the sardonic American comedian and actor, tried out most of his early material on the Troubadour's customers; the French mime artist Marcel Marceau was another regular; and Ken Russell, the *enfant terrible* of 1970s cinema, cast one his first films from among the coffee bar's patrons. But at that particular moment Elizabeth was trying to concentrate on a man in the far corner playing a guitar and repeating the same tune over and over again. Just as she was about to leave, Prowse's head appeared in the cellar doorway. 'Come on, he wants to meet you.'

A single unshaded bulb cast a sinister light over what, to Elizabeth, looked more like a Gestapo interrogation scene from a war-themed B-movie. Harris sat behind the small wooded table. Prowse stood in the half-shadow by his side. And from the floor rose the unmistakable smell of damp crumbling stone.

'Here,' ordered Harris, waving a sheet of script toward Elizabeth's face. 'Read this. The Girl.' The part was for an abused young woman. The unkempt would-be director gave nothing away. After fifteen minutes, and even fewer words, he waved Elizabeth away. She returned to the outside world and fashionable society unaware Harris had already made up his mind to change her life for ever.

Elizabeth's debut as a professional actress would be a shocking and revealing experience. The first revelation came a week later, when Harris telephoned to say she had got the *Winter Journey* part. That evening, at her first Troubadour rehearsal, she discovered her director and impresario was still attending the London Academy of Music and Dramatic Art and had less formal training than she had.

Harris would make *his* own discoveries too. Arriving for rehearsals late one evening, he saw Elizabeth getting out of her boyfriend's MG sports car. The cast's best-kept secret was out: not only was he employing the daughter of a peer of the realm but someone whose dedication to completing the 'canapé circuit' had cost her a place at RADA. Elizabeth's fate was sealed: 'The first time she is late for rehearsals she is out on her social arse.'

Elizabeth kept her place, but lost her innocence. For the next two weeks the coffee bar's cellar would become a battleground of ideas and egos, where the company members thought nothing of hurling foul language or furniture to get their own way. The most bitter and violent skirmishes were fought between Harris and his leading man. Prowse was a dedicated and strong-willed individual who attempted to give his own authoritative performance and rarely accepted his director's demands without a challenge. Harris, as Elizabeth would later recall, displayed 'all the fanaticism of his rashness. He never lacked the courage to follow through his chosen course, no matter how daunting the odds.'

The odds against success were considerable. Harris's inexperience as a director not only allowed him to be bullied by his cast, but he was also cornered by the lack of rehearsal time and a fast-approaching opening night – he had already booked the Irving Theatre, situated down a Leicester Square side street, for a two-week run.

The Irving Theatre was a tiny venue with a single aisle down the centre of the auditorium. During the final rehearsals Harris paced up and down the aisle, stopping in mid-stride and sometimes with his back to the stage, to listen to a particular speech or troublesome piece of dialogue. Each fluffed line or late entrance would be followed by a vicious hiss or sharp intake of breath depending on the severity of the transgression. For the actual performance he would add a colourful collection of four-letter words. Elizabeth's father, Lord Ogmore, had his own vivid memory of the play's director. 'Richard had his shirt hanging out of his trousers. Out of the *seat* of his trousers. The only time I have ever seen that.'

Winter Journey was a moderate success, attracting enough critical attention – 'a brave effort' – to fill most of the seats and allow it to complete its run, but Harris reluctantly admitted he had 'backed a loser'.

The day after the play closed, Elizabeth returned to the theatre to collect her clothes. Harris was already there. The pair chatted. Released from the pressures of the production, he spoke gently and passionately about his plans with a magnetic energy that seemed to fill the entire dressing room. When Harris unexpectedly invited Elizabeth to visit his cousins in Essex, she felt compelled to ask him to share a pair of tickets for a Leicester Square film premiere. 'And I'll take you to dinner afterwards,' announced Harris.

Since his arrival in London Harris had still not found a permanent home. Mostly it was money. More often it was prejudice. Landladies, in all but the poorest areas of the capital, still protected their grubby bedsits and overcrowded bedrooms with scribbled No IRISH signs. What lodgings were available were quickly snapped up. In the summer, Harris tucked his belongings under his head and curled up on an Embankment bench. If it rained he would pay 2s. 6d. (12½ pence) for a dosshouse dormitory bed, where he would sleep fully clothed and with his arms clamped around his cardboard suitcase – 'If you removed as much as a dirty handkerchief from your pocket somebody would steal it by the morning.' When the weather turned colder he bummed a sofa in a friend's flat. By early 1955 he was spending most nights on the floor of a bedsit in Nevern Place, off the Earl's Court Road. The room was being rented by Robert Young and Len Taylor, another hopeful actor who exchanged free meals at the Troubadour for his dish-washing services.

The thought of reserving a table for after the premiere had not occurred to Harris. When Elizabeth suggested a nearby nightclub restaurant he readily agreed. 'You'd think in a posh place like this they'd be able to afford real flowers,' Harris said nodding to the brightly decorated swizzle sticks in the centre of each table. He was deadly serious. Confronted by the French menu, he followed Elizabeth's lead by confidently announcing, 'Yes, that looks good. I'll have some of that too.' Several months later Harris admitted he had no idea what he had eaten – and had paid for with an entire two weeks' rent and food money.

By their second date Richard and Elizabeth had plunged into an 'unnerving and all-consuming' affair. They made love whenever and wherever the opportunity arose. Unsure of where they wanted the relationship to go, the pair agreed to see each other only on alternate days. It was a frustrating ordeal: Harris lost concentration on his LAMDA classes and Elizabeth, by now an absent debutante, ignored several invitations to exclusive country-house parties.

'I simply wanted to be near him,' said Elizabeth. 'I felt other men were shallow by comparison. When I'd been taken out in the past, I had enjoyed the anticipation; deciding what to wear, how to fix my hair. I enjoyed the fun of flirtation. I relished the teasing. Now suddenly that had gone; the intensity of my feelings for Richard transcended sensual pleasures and conceits. I didn't care what I wore or how I looked.'

With at least one professional appearance on her résumé, Elizabeth set about launching her own acting career. A walk-on part in a theatre-club production of Arthur Miller's *All My Sons* was followed by an equally nerve-racking appearance strapped into a skidding car for an industrial film extolling the virtues of the seatbelt. In the spring she was offered a £7-a-week job as an assistant stage manager and juvenile lead with Warrington Repertory Company.

Money remained tight, although never as desperate as Harris or his appearance would suggest. He may have arrived with little more than £20 in his pocket but his income was secure. Among his inheritances were a house in Ireland, rented out for £6 a week, and a portfolio of Guinness shares, which he sold off in slices to pay his LAMDA term fees.

The fatal flaws in Harris's character were his joy of social drinking – not yet a problem – and his almost pathological aversion to landladies. One kept him habitually poor. The other perpetually homeless. When the two collided, the result was explosive. By the summer of 1955 Harris had replaced Len Taylor as Robert Young's Nevern Place flatmate. One night in a nearby pub the actor was delivering an accurate and colourful impersonation of their landlady when the glass partition between the snug and the public bar slammed back. 'And you, Mr Harris,' announced the framed face of his subject, 'you can piss off out of my house right now and never come back.'

By now there was no doubt in Elizabeth's mind that this was the man she was going to marry. She missed him terribly. When she could stand it no longer she caught the Saturday midnight train from Warrington to be with Harris in London and in whatever bed he had been able to scrounge for the day. That night he would deliver her to Euston Station for the overnight train back to Cheshire. When Warrington Rep disbanded for its summer break, she returned to London and Harris and his apparently endless need for new lodgings. Even with the deposits paid from her annual dress allowance, the bedsits were getting depressingly worse. 'This has got to be the bottom of the fucking barrel,' Harris declared one afternoon in a room that seemed as damp and joyless as the weather.

'We can't go on like this,' said Elizabeth. 'We have to do something.'

'Yes,' admitted Harris, picking at the remnants of some mouldy net curtain.

'Perhaps we could stay somewhere together,' she said. 'Get something more permanent.'

'Get married you mean? Is that what you're saying?'

'Yes.'

All Elizabeth had to do now was persuade her parents of the benefits of an out-of-work Irish actor for a son-in-law.

The following Friday, the doorbell rang at Lord and Lady Ogmore's North Kensington home. Hughsie, the family's elderly maid, shuffled along the corridor and opened the door. 'There you are, boy,' she said, depositing a bag of laundry in Harris's hurriedly outstretched arms. 'And don't forget the starch.'

To prepare her for his parental encounter Harris had posted a message on the LAMDA student notice board seeking etiquette advice for someone dining with a peer of the realm. Do you shake hands or bow? Is it 'your lordship' or simply 'sir'? What Harris forgot to ask was how to pick up the conversation when you cross your legs to discover you've forgotten to put on your socks. Or when the baron in question asks you if you wish to marry his daughter, you say yes, and his wife throws her arms in the air and runs screaming from the room, her wounded animal howl disappearing with her footsteps down a long and distant corridor.

Lord Ogmore had a certain sympathy for his future son-in-law. His favourite literary character was Dickens's roguish and out-of-work actor Alfred Jingle, who plagues the Pickwickians and with whom they have a series of embarrassing encounters. And, as a young man in Cardiff, the peer had performed in several amateur productions and even written the words and musical accompaniment to his own play. At least it was something in common with the tall, awkward, over-deferential Irishman his daughter claimed to have fallen in love with.

Ogmore considered his daughter's prospects – and the prospect of a head-on clash with his strong-willed but still underage offspring – and consented to the marriage.

Desmond O'Grady, one of Harris's former Savoy tearoom confidants, saw the public announcement of the impending marriage in a borrowed newspaper on his way back from Paris. It was 1956 and he wanted to be back in Limerick by late spring. The would-be poet decided to stop over in London and call on his old friend. He found Harris in a 'depressingly bare' bedsit just off the Earl's Court Road. The pair talked about poems and plays and argued over *Finnegan's Wake*. O'Grady slept on the floor and they pooled their money to buy drinks and share a single plate of fish and chips in a nearby restaurant. 'Two penniless paddies in London cut a pitiful picture,' O'Grady later recalled.

At about the same time, a tatty, beer-stained script was landing on Joan Littlewood's Theatre Royal desk. Some pages were folded in half with handwritten notes scribbled on the back. Sometimes the typing went careering off the sheet. By page 5, the controversial and fiery director knew she was reading something special. Littlewood turned back to the title page: *The Quare Fellow* by Brendan Behan.

Littlewood's acceptance letter included an invitation for the author to work on the play during rehearsals in London and enough money to get there. A few days later, Behan's reply arrived: 'Drinking with some Toronto Irish. Send us an injection.' When Behan had finished guzzling the replacement fare he announced he was ready to leave. This time – for the third time – Littlewood sent a prepaid ticket and an AA map of the capital.

Behan was the son of a Dublin house painter and was a fierce Republican. In 1939 he was arrested for his involvement with the Irish Republican Army and sentenced to a period of Borstal training, an experience he had already used in his first play, *Borstal Boy*. The title of his latest script, *The Quare Fellow*, was the nickname given to a prisoner about to be hanged for murder. By the time Behan arrived in London in 1956, he was 36 years old, with 'a coxcomb of black wavy hair, a Roman nose, a few teeth missing and a pronounced stutter'.

The Theatre Workshop, whose home was the Theatre Royal, had already started work on the play, but there was, Behan pointed out, one problem: not one of the cast was Irish. Brian Murphy was from Portsmouth, Max Shaw was a Polish Jew, Glynn Edwards was from the West Country, Gerard Dynevor was Welsh and the rest of the cast were Cypriots. And there was still one small part to fill.

On the next corner from Harris's latest lodgings was a pub. As he drank half-pints of stout one evening, a conversation at the next table caught his attention. Harris leaned back to listen. Brendan Behan's new play *The Quare Fellow* was being produced at the Theatre Workshop and they were still looking for cast members. 'Jesus Christ,' whispered Harris, 'I'll have a try for that.'

It was gone eight. Harris wondered if anyone would still be in the theatre office. He borrowed a telephone directory from the landlord and four pennies from O'Grady and dialled the number.

Gerry Raffles was still at his desk when the telephone rang. 'There's only one part we haven't cast yet,' the theatre manager told him. 'How old are you?'

'Twenty-five.'

'No good,' said of Raffles. 'This part is for a fifty-year-old man.'

'I look fifty,' replied Harris. 'I haven't had a good meal for four months. And I haven't slept for days. Just take a look at me.'

'Be here at ten tomorrow morning.'

To get there, Harris needed to borrow more money from O'Grady. The journey seemed to take forever and he counted down the sixteen Underground stops to Stratford with growing apprehension.

Once he was there, Raffles handed him a copy of the script. Never a good reader, Harris stumbled his way through a few lines. He could see from the man's face he was not impressed.

'Perhaps,' snapped Raffles with the edge of a man who had just wasted several minutes from a busy morning, 'if the script is too difficult you would like to try an improvisation.'

Irritated by Raffles's smugness, and convinced he had blown his chances, Harris imagined himself back at his Earl's Court local describing the audition to O'Grady: 'He was a cold insensitive bastard. A man with no imagination, a fellow with no compassion, and no understanding. Wouldn't you know such a man would turn me down?'

As the tirade reached its bitter climax Harris caught the sound of a single hand clap. The applause approached the stage through the darkness of the auditorium. Just visible behind the glare of the footlights was a small round woman wearing what looked like a bargee's cap.

'I think we found our Mickser,' announced Joan Littlewood. 'The part is yours. Start Monday. Six weeks.'

CHAPTER THREE

The marriage of a baron's daughter to a handsome and promising actor attracted most elements of the press. The following Monday's *Times* and *Daily Telegraph* carried serious reports of the service and near-complete lists of the peerage present. The *Daily Express* fashion editor, however, was far more interested in Elizabeth's 73-year-old cream satin and lace dress and train, which once belonged to her Great-Aunt Rhoda. All carried pictures of Mr and Mrs Richard Harris descending the church steps on their way to the reception.

From Leicester Place, the wedding party was transported to the House of Lords, where they were joined at the reception by three hundred guests. It was a volatile mix: devout Irish Catholics mingled with teetotal Welsh Methodists; austere great-aunts dressed in high necks and bonnets looked down their noses at brothers-in-law and cousins in Gaelic kilts; and lords and countesses attempted to mingle and exchange small talk with shopkeepers and publicans. During the reception, Elizabeth was congratulated by the campaigning Lord Longford. The Catholic peer asked if she was considering converting to Rome. Before she could answer, her father butted in: 'My daughter's spiritual immortality concerns me rather less at this moment than the question of the daily bread.'

CHAPTER THREE

A man who strains himself on the stage is bound, if he is any good, to strain all the people sitting in the stalls.

– Bertolt Brecht

'Right,' said Joan Littlewood, slowly running her eyes over the 26-year-old Irishman. 'Get 'em off.'

'What?'

'Take your clothes off,' demanded Littlewood. 'Take them all off.'

Richard Harris made sure the stage and wings were empty before slipping off his shoes. 'And your shirt.' The actor removed his shirt. 'And your trousers.' Once again Harris reluctantly complied. 'And your underwear.'

'What?'

Across the footlights the only sign of Littlewood's presence was the constant wisp of blue cigarette smoke.

'Take your pants off. There's no one here but me.' Harris removed the last item and stood naked and shivering in front of his new employer. 'Now make me believe you are fully dressed,' ordered Littlewood. 'That's what actors do. Until you're prepared to expose yourself and vomit up your secrets on stage you'll never be any good as an actor.'

An outspoken, rebellious, indefatigable tyrant, Joan Littlewood was a self-confessed bastard: both literally and figuratively. World War One was still less than three months old when Littlewood was born into a working-class family in London's East End. Before the war was over the precocious toddler would shock her parents by announcing she wanted to be 'famous'.

Littlewood's acute mind and artistic talent earned her a scholarship to a Catholic school and a place at the Royal Academy of Dramatic Art. When she realised that RADA was neither socially nor politically congenial she left to study art. In 1934, and still a few months short of her twentieth birthday, she began working for the British Broadcasting Corporation in Manchester, where she soon became a founder member of Theatre in Action, a left-wing drama group.

For five years the company toured the industrial North, performing in factory canteens and church halls until the outbreak of World War Two forced the group to disband and Littlewood to earn a living from her writing. In the weeks after VE Day Littlewood teamed up with Gerry Raffles (whom she later married) and the playwright Jimmie Miller – pen name Ewan MacColl – to launch the Theatre Workshop. Despite winning considerable praise for its late-1940s tours of Germany, Czechoslovakia and Sweden, at home the company led a vagabond existence, playing one-night stands all over Britain. It was during this period the Theatre Workshop was booked to perform *Alice in Wonderland* at the Theatre Royal in the heart of London's East End, where, in 1953, it returned to set up its first permanent home.

In the traditionalist corridors of the London Academy of Music and Dramatic Art Joan Littlewood's name was whispered with awe and equal resentment. For many she was the most exciting producer–director to emerge in Britain since the war. But it was her methods and her conviction that a theatre should be something more than a place of mere entertainment that magnetised scores of young actors and actresses.

For Theatre Workshop rehearsals, Littlewood insisted the stage be always flooded with pink light. 'The creativity she managed to collect in the centre of that pink floodlit stage was unbelievable,' recalls Victor Spinetti. 'It was somehow magical and electric and everyone knew it was something very special.'

As *The Quare Fellow* progressed Harris attempted to concentrate on his role despite the thunderous interruptions from the stalls. Sitting one or two rows back, Behan would chain-smoke as he listened to the dialogue of his play, occasionally erupting in a splutter of laughter. 'Did I write that?' he bellowed across the footlights. 'I'm a fucking genius.'

As the theatre's two resident Irishmen, Harris and Behan became immediate and lasting friends. But there was more to it than a countryman's shared poverty and love of alcohol (Behan had once lugged a cello halfway across Dublin to a pawnshop he knew would give him the price of a round of drinks): there was something in the playwright's rebellious spirit, in his social values, that could well have been Harris's own. 'I respect kindness in human beings, first of all,' explained Behan. 'Then kindness to animals. I don't respect the law. I have a total irreverence for anything connected with society except that which makes the road safer, the beer stronger, the food cheaper and old men and women warmer in winter and happier in summer.'

The riotous Behan did much to turn *The Quare Fellow* into a cult play.

On the first night – 24 May 1956 – the playwright leaped on to the stage and joined in with the opening song, 'The Old Triangle':

A hungry feeling came o'er me stealing
And the mice were squealing in my prison cell.
And that older triangle
Went jingle jangle
Along the banks of the Royal Canal.

For most of the evenings that followed he would arrive drunk and equally enthusiastic. After he had been repeatedly dragged from the stage one evening, the management had no option but to call the police. Behan was hauled away to spend the rest of the night in the cells, only to return the next afternoon apologetic but unrepentant.

Meanwhile, Littlewood was putting in extra time with the company's latest recruit. 'Don't practise how to say a line,' she tutored Harris. 'You say the lines which are not written. Take them on a journey. If your attitude is right then whatever comes out of your mouth will be right.' Four decades later, Harris summed up his time under Littlewood's directorship: 'You could get a PhD in the theatre after two years with her, she was so extraordinary.'

Once a run was under way, Littlewood had a unique way of keeping the cast on its toes. Somehow she had perfected the knack of scribbling in a notebook while never taking her eyes off the stage. 'You never knew where she was sitting,' recalled Harris. For each performance she would take a different seat in the house: sometimes way up in the Gods, sometimes in the front row just visible through the glare of the footlights. The next day Littlewood rounded on any cast member she felt was getting stale. 'Change that, you're getting too used to it,' she would hiss at her latest victim. 'It's dead, dead. It's getting stale. Change it.'

The wedding was set for Saturday, 9 February 1957. All that remained was for Elizabeth to be officially introduced to her Irish in-laws. Harris and his fiancée would spend the Christmas holiday at Overdale.

Limerick had changed, of course, but not as much as Harris. With her arm in his, he guided Elizabeth around the streets of Limerick and through what seemed to her an endless clutch of family and relatives. They met up with friends in a dozen or so pubs and hotels before Elizabeth returned each night, her head swimming from alcohol and affection, to stretch out on her lover's old bed and try to make sense of it all. 'That holiday taught me a great deal about Richard,' she would later write. 'About the problem of being the middle son in a large family, about what made him the kind of man he was – and the kind of man he was still to become.'

One night towards the end of the run of *The Quare Fellow*, there had been a knock on Harris's dressing room door. The caller was a tall, thin man wearing heavy spectacles, who introduced himself as Arthur Miller. The American playwright was so impressed with Harris's performance as Mickser that he wondered whether he would like to try his hand at a longshoreman in his new play, *A View From the Bridge*, which would be staged at the Comedy Theatre. Back in London from Limerick, Harris started rehearsals for Arthur Miller's play. Attempting to find the character within his role as an American longshoreman was not easy.

Elizabeth, meanwhile, began a search of her own: finding them somewhere to live. A few nights later she took Harris to Paddington to look at a one-bedroom flat. It was smaller than she had hoped, with an alcove kitchen hidden by a curtain and its own bathroom down the hall. The rent was £6 a week. With her future husband earning £10 a week during the play's run, they would have precious little cash for food.

At the Comedy Theatre, the author and producers were facing a cash crisis of their own. All production companies were legally obliged to submit scripts to the Lord Chamberlain's office. Most were passed for performance with few, if any, amendments. But the censor was refusing to grant a licence for Arthur Miller's play unless a scene, in which the leading man, Anthony Quayle, kisses another actor on the lips, was changed. Miller claimed the homosexual encounter was a vital part of the plot and refused to cut or rewrite it. The stand-off meant either abandoning the production or attempting to stage the play and face almost certain prosecution. In the end the theatre management turned the Comedy Theatre into a club for the duration of the play's run, charging the 'members' a small fee and effectively putting it beyond the Lord Chamberlain's jurisdiction.

On the second Saturday in February 1957, a Rolls-Royce collected Elizabeth and her father from 34 Alexandra Court in Queen's Gate and delivered them to a Leicester Place church in the northeast corner of Leicester Square.

The Church of Notre Dame de France had been carefully chosen as an architectural compromise: it needed to look like a Catholic church for Harris's Roman Catholic relatives – most of whom expressed a deep concern for the couple's salvation – while possessing an Anglican feel for Elizabeth's extended family, the majority of whom arrived clutching Methodist bibles and hymn books. Both sets of guests were not disappointed. Destroyed during the 1940 Blitz, Notre Dame – originally purchased for the Victorian French community living around Leicester Square – was rebuilt and completed less than eighteen months earlier. Its angular design and tall brick walls are more reminiscent of an office block than a church.

The marriage of a baron's daughter to a handsome and promising actor attracted most elements of the press. The following Monday's *Times* and *Daily Telegraph* carried serious reports of the service and near-complete lists of the peerage present. The *Daily Express* fashion editor, however, was far more interested in Elizabeth's 73-year-old cream satin and lace dress and train, which once belonged to her Great-Aunt Rhoda. All carried pictures of Mr and Mrs Richard Harris descending the church steps on their way to the reception.

To one of Elizabeth's society friends who watched Harris await the arrival of his bride, it was a match doomed to failure. 'They were so different it was farcical to imagine how they came to know each other,' she recalls. 'Here was this elegant twenty-year-old girl – sometimes awkward but always charming – marrying a loud uncouth Irishman who looked so out of place in his morning suit and haircut that you wonder if there was any future in it.'

From Leicester Place, the wedding party was transported to the House of Lords, where they were joined at the reception by three hundred guests. It was a volatile mix: devout Irish Catholics mingled with teetotal Welsh Methodists; austere great-aunts dressed in high necks and bonnets looked down their noses at brothers-in-law and cousins in Gaelic kilts; and lords and countesses attempted to mingle and exchange small talk with shopkeepers and publicans. During the reception, Elizabeth was congratulated by the campaigning Lord Longford. The Catholic peer asked if she was considering converting to Rome. Before she could answer, her father butted in: 'My daughter's spiritual immortality concerns me rather less at this moment than the question of the daily bread.'

Ivan Harris was not at his son's wedding. Instead he sent £25 with instructions to spend the money on a honeymoon. The couple duly obliged by blowing the cash on a champagne supper and a single night at the select Stafford Hotel within sight of Buckingham Palace, but not before Harris had delivered his matinée and evening performances at the

Comedy Theatre. The next morning, with just enough change for a taxi, Mr and Mrs Richard Harris departed for Paddington and married life.

Donal Donnelly was a small, companionable actor who possessed the disconcerting habit of pointing his chin when he spoke like an aggressive leprechaun. Unlike Harris, whose single-mindedness refused to allow him to do anything but act, Donnelly supported himself by working as a waiter or Christmas postman and sleeping in any warm corner he could find. Right now he was sleeping in the hallway of the Harrises' Paddington bedsit. It was not the ideal start to married life, but Elizabeth did not seem to mind her 'uncomplaining' lodger even if her mother found the arrangement 'somewhat distasteful'.

The Theatre Workshop's reputation, like those of most of its actors and actresses, was growing with each production. With Joan Littlewood's direction it was a company which attracted a daily delivery of new and unproduced scripts.

Littlewood rested her feet on her desk and began reading the two plays that had arrived in the morning post. She gave up on the first after two pages. The second, *You Won't Always Be On Top*, was a little better. It had no plot, no drama and no women, and the entire play was based on a single rainy day on a building site . . . it was the kind of challenge Littlewood loved.

First the research. 'There were building sites all round us,' recalled Littlewood in her autobiography, *Joan's Book*. 'A pint with a ganger over at the Lion and we were in. Of course the actors wanted to try their hand at everything.' To produce the Henry Chapman play the Theatre Royal stage was stripped bare. Each evening during its run, Dudley Foster, as the foreman brickie, added to his wall of real bricks; Brian Murphy sawed and hammered his way through yards of wood; Dudley Sutton sloshed out real tea; and Harris trundled his wheelbarrow back and forth loaded with whatever he thought his fellow actors might need. The trapdoor, centre stage, was suitably disguised for two weeks as a building-site hole.

In the reviews, the plaudits were plentiful:

> The play is performed against and upon the most spectacular and elaborate setting I have ever seen in the legitimate British theatre. Using every horizontal square yard of the wings and every vertical square yard of the back wall, John Bury [the designer] has reproduced a three-storey building in course of construction, complete with scaffolding, cement-mixer, workmen's hut and

no-man's-land of plank-traversed mire. It is an astonishing achievement.

— Kenneth Tynan, *Observer*

The language and the people are vividly alive, often wonderfully funny, occasionally touching, and Mr Chapman has replaced the grip of a story-line with something just as effective: accurately drawn and absorbingly interesting characters.

— *Liverpool Daily Post*

It is not a profound comment on our times, but who cares about that? The profound comment is that such a play – an entertaining chunk of life about the way nine-tenths of the British people live – should be such an unusual event … It superbly catches the rhythm and feel of a day's manual work: the cold, the greyness, the long stretches when people are only half speaking their thoughts: my boots leak, women are beautiful, it's taken mankind thousands of generations to get here.

— Wayland Young, *Tribune*

Infinitely the best London play of the month is at the Theatre Royal, Stratford-atte-Bowe. Henry Chapman's play is kicking with humour, richly observant, Chekhovian in its cartography.

— Penelope Gilliatt, *Vogue*

The Arts Council, keeping up its side of Littlewood's lifelong feud about money and support, delivered its own preproduction verdict. Asked to provide a guarantee against losses a member of its drama panel replied:

I am sorry but I am unable to make head or tail of this play. It seems to consist of a series of disjointed and more-or-less meaningless conversations between a set of peculiarly uninteresting workmen on a building site. It also has the disadvantage of being so abominably typed that it is almost unreadable.

Almost a month later the company returned from its New Year break to start rehearsals for *The Celestina*. One by one the cast dried up. Bemused by the silence, Littlewood turned to find two men standing on the stage behind her.

'Joan Littlewood?'

'At your service,' replied the diminutive director.

'Gerry Raffles, John Bury and Richard Harris?' The three men nodded. 'We're here to serve a summons on you all.'

'What for?' asked Harris.

One of the plain-clothes police officers read from the sheet of paper he was holding. 'That unlawfully, for hire, you did present parts of a new stage play entitled *You Won't Always Be On Top* before such parts had been allowed by the Lord Chamberlain, contrary to Section Fifteen, Theatres Act, 1843.'

'And the author?' someone asked.

'A similar summons has been issued to Henry Chapman, aged 47, builder's labourer, at Hastings.'

The date for the hearing was set for 16 April 1957. In the intervening three months Littlewood and her co-defendants discovered some unusual and heavyweight allies, among them Harold Lever, the Labour MP for the Manchester constituency of Cheetham, who would become Paymaster General in a future Harold Wilson government. A barrister by profession and a financial wheeler-dealer by inclination, Lever had represented Littlewood and Jimmie Miller in 1940, when the pair had faced censorship charges. This time Lever had enlisted the help of a fellow barrister and future Lord High Chancellor, Gerald Gardiner. After talking over the case, the pair agreed to defend all five for free.

The night before the court case, Harris shared his first stage lead with an assorted but appreciative Theatre Royal audience. In a George Bernard Shaw double bill, the Workshop presented *Man of Destiny*, with Robin Chapman playing Napoleon, and a dramatisation of Shaw's correspondence with Ellen Terry. 'Richard's G.B.S. was a little wild,' recorded Littlewood, 'but good value.'

Next morning, before the hearing started, the tall, grey-haired Gardiner nudged Littlewood aside. 'They tell me the magistrate's been in the building trade all his life,' he said with a heavy wink. 'We'll see.' When Harris and his four co-defendants entered the court they looked around to see the press bench elbow to elbow with reporters and the public gallery packed with fellow actors.

The prosecution outlined its case. Among its more serious claims were that Harris had urinated, in full view of the audience, into the stage's open trapdoor while impersonating Winston Churchill, and that Dudley Sutton had allegedly raised his fingers in a V-sign. As witnesses, the Crown called two policemen who had apparently made extensive notes while sitting through a performance of *You Won't Always Be On Top*. Their technique was not up to Littlewood's. 'Brickies were given carpenters' lines, and carpenters the brickies',' she remembered. Periodically an outbreak of coughing and spluttering would ripple through the public gallery and the magistrate found it necessary to blow his nose. 'It was all good comedy stuff.' Two and a half hours later, Harris and his co-defendants emerged from the court guilty but unpunished – and warned not to commit the offence a second time.

By the late spring, *A View From the Bridge* had ended its West End run and Harris joined his wife and unofficial lodger on the audition circuit.

Elizabeth was the first to find work. As she prepared to spend the next few months with a summer repertory company in Blackpool, her husband faced the prospect of being both homeless and unemployed. To save money he accepted a room at Queen's Gate with his parents-in-law and almost immediately got a call from Joan Littlewood. She was staging a modern-dress version of *Macbeth* and there was a small part for Harris. The pay wasn't much – £4 a week for the month-long rehearsal period and £6 during the performance – but neither were his four lines.

To mark his arrival as a classical actor Harris invited his family to attend the first night. Dressed in a soldier's uniform and brandishing a sword, he waited in the wings for his cue. His mind was suddenly and inexplicably blank. As he marched on, his mouth opened, but it wasn't his own voice he heard booming across the stage. From the front row Mildred Harris announced, 'That's my son. Isn't he marvellous?'

Alone and the focus of everyone's attention Harris needed to extricate himself with at least a sliver of dignity. He raised his sword and bellowed the first thing that came into his mind – 'Grrrr!' – before stamping off, stage right.

'As a Shakespearean debut it was a bloody shambles,' confessed Littlewood. 'But it was bloody marvellous theatre.' Backstage Harris waited for his inevitable dressing down. When the director finally arrived she announced something far more terrifying.

The Theatre Workshop had arranged to swap directors for a future production. Littlewood was off into East Berlin to stage *Unternehmen Olzweig*, a translation of *Operation Olive Branch*, at the Maxim Gorki Theatre, while France Jamnik would be directing Pirandello's *Man, Beast and Virtue* at Stratford East. 'Oh, and by the way,' added Littlewood over her shoulder. 'In the meantime I want you to come on tour with us.'

By 1957 the future of the Theatre Royal was looking bleak. The building needed extensive repairs and, no matter how good the productions, its grubby and threadbare interior was affecting attendances. An appeal to the Arts Council met with a predictable refusal. An undaunted Littlewood announced that the company was going on tour to raise the badly needed cash. The backbone production would be *Macbeth*, and the first stop Switzerland. On the way to Zürich, the train stopped at some unannounced station and Harris and Brian Murphy stepped down to stretch their legs. A few minutes later Littlewood looked up from writing the *Macbeth* programme notes to see the rest of the cast dragging the pair aboard the rapidly accelerating train.

Just as the company was concluding its three-day Swiss run, Littlewood received an invitation to perform the Shakespeare tragedy at the Moscow Art Theatre. The company packed its bags and caught the first through train to the Russian capital. While the others slept on the overnight express, Littlewood had insisted on giving Harris extra lessons. 'Richard had fire in his belly,' she recalled, 'but his accent and his speech rhythms were pure Irish. I stayed up all night showing him how to use the iambics.'

No matter how poor they were or how precarious their careers, Elizabeth was determined they would never again be homeless or rely on her parents' charity. Not long after her return from Blackpool she celebrated her 21st birthday. Elizabeth decided to invest her £150 inheritance in a more permanent home.

The frontage between Hogarth Road and Earl's Court Gardens was barely long enough for three or four shops. Beside the post office was a window filled with unusually large items of female underwear and a crude banner announcing, OUTSIZED GARMENTS FOR THE FULLER FIGURE. Between the two was a brown-painted door whose colour was a gloomy portent of what visitors could expect at the top of two flights of stairs.

It was up this narrow uncarpeted stairway that the Harrises dragged their few possessions in the late autumn of 1957. Elizabeth had spent the best part of £100 on a five-year lease and the rest on the bare essentials of furniture. The kitchen was filled mainly by wedding gifts and the second-floor bedroom with a large four-poster bed donated by her grandparents. Her mother and father had bought them a green antique tin trunk, which doubled as a wardrobe and dining table.

After nine months of marriage they were barely surviving. Harris, it seemed, was in perpetual rehearsals at the Royal Court and doomed never to earn more than £6 a week, exactly what they paid out each week in rent. To keep the men in dark-blue mackintoshes from the door – Harris was convinced only meter readers and bailiffs wore mackintoshes – Elizabeth decided to replace her attendances at auditions with a weekly visit to the local pawnbroker. One by one her rings and brooches and the garnet earrings she once loved to wear disappeared from her jewellery box. It was a humiliating and ego-bruising experience, but at least this way she was returning with money in her purse.

Another money-making scheme proved less successful. Harris's generosity, which had tolerated Donal Donnelly's hallway encampment, now extended to a 'bedraggled line of bleary-eyed' strangers who sneaked in after the pubs closed and whom Elizabeth first met queuing for the bathroom early the next morning. If there were going to be strangers in the maisonette at least they could pay for the privilege: £2 a week for the single bedroom and £4 for the top floor, a double. The venture ended when one cherubic-faced lodger attempted to leave with most of their wedding presents.

Man, Beast and Virtue ended its Royal Court run and transferred to the Lyric Theatre in Hammersmith. Harris was getting changed and preparing for the end of production celebrations when a well-built but rather shy man knocked at his dressing room door and introduced himself as Cliff Owen. Posted on a board beside the front entrance of the Lyric were copies of newspaper reviews and features on various members of the cast. The television director explained that he had noticed Harris's name in most of the stories and, with the play already into its final half-hour, decided to slip in and put a face to the name. Owen was still looking for someone to play a blind Irishman in a Joseph O'Connor drama called *The Iron Harp*, and wondered if Harris would be interested.

For most of the next day Owen's secretary attempted to make contact with Harris. Minutes after arriving home the telephone rang. Could he make an audition by four o'clock? Harris said he could. The only chance of getting to Owen's Soho office on time was by taxi, and the only money for the fare was inside the gas meter. After prising off the padlock, he grabbed a handful of coins and raced out into the Earl's Court Road. Harris made the audition with seconds to spare. An hour later he was still waiting to go in when the secretary informed him the part had already been filled and he might as well go home.

Harris's simmering temper finally boiled over. He pushed aside the secretary, slammed back the office door and skidded to a halt inches from Owen's startled face. 'I broke my bloody neck getting here,' he bellowed at the director. 'I've robbed my gas meter for a ten-shilling taxi fare when I could have got here for sixpence on the tube. That's a criminal offence. It's also two days' food for me and my wife. Like it or not you're going to hear me read for that fucking part.'

'OK,' said Owen, handing Harris a script. 'Let's hear you read.'

There was no time for his fear of reading to kick in. Harris rattled through the lines the best he could. When he'd finished, the blood and the self-doubt flooded back in to his face.

Owen let him stew. The silence extended into minutes. Jesus! thought Harris. How do I get out of this? Suddenly a broad grin spread across the director's face.

'Congratulations,' he said. 'You've got the part.'

Harris's hand-to-mouth poverty was about to end. His single television appearance in *The Iron Harp* would earn him £50 – more than an entire eight-week run at the Royal Court – and land him his first studio contract.

CHAPTER FOUR

Two weeks later, close enough to their third anniversary to be sentimental, Elizabeth received a telegram: 'How about a honeymoon in Paris?'

When she walked into Le Bar au Ritz her estranged husband was sitting relaxed and smiling beside a bucket of chilled champagne. 'Honeymoons, however late, should always be memorable,' Harris announced as he poured two glasses of the vintage wine.

They made love and slept in one of the most expensive and stylish suites at the Ritz. Over dinner at Maxim's, they held hands and attempted to rekindle their marriage. They also made each other a promise: that, no matter how bitter the fights and how desolate their time apart, their reconciliations would always start in an elegant hotel bedroom. 'We shall have a series of beautiful affairs,' added Harris.

It was a pact that would see them through the next spectacularly volatile decade.

CHAPTER FOUR

For an actress to be a success, she must have the face of Venus, the
brains of a Minerva, the grace of Terpsichore, the memory of a
Macaulay, the figure of Juno, and the hide of a rhinoceros.
                                                    – *Ethel Barrymore*

'Come on. Come on. You've got to see this young man.'

Robert Lennard knew there was no point in arguing with his wife. He
hauled himself out of the bath and reached for a towel. By the time he
padded his way, half naked and shivering, into the lounge *The Iron Harp*
was almost over. His wife was right, though. What little he saw of Richard
Harris's television debut convinced him here was an actor with a big future.

Over the years Lennard had felt that same back-of-the-neck tingle
when he first saw a handful of other actors, among them Richard Todd
and Robert Shaw. His latest discovery was a suave, self-confident young
man called Laurence Harvey. 'Bob was a man who truly cared for those
actors whose careers he was able to influence,' said Todd.

At his office the next morning the casting director for the Associated
British Film Company scribbled a list of theatrical agents. The first one
he tried was Jimmy Fraser.

A mile or so across London the telephone rang in Fraser's office. For
the last quarter of an hour a 27-year-old Irish actor had been attempting
to persuade one of the few agents with a reputation for nurturing new
talent to take him on. Fraser looked unimpressed and excused himself to
answer the phone. 'Did you see a young actor called Richard Harris on
the television last night, Jimmy?' asked Bob Lennard.

'I did.'

'Do you know who represents him?'

Fraser smiled at Harris. 'I do,' he said.

'Let's meet.'

'What do you have in mind?'

'A seven-year contract,' suggested Lennard.

'I'm not sure we would be interested in anything like that.' The agent
shrugged his shoulders apologetically for the interruption. 'We could
certainly talk.'

Fraser replaced the telephone. 'So that's settled,' he said, offering his hand to his latest client.

The seven-year deal, signed a few days later, put Harris on a guaranteed salary while the Elstree-based film company offered him scripts in line with his growing reputation. For the first year Harris would receive £30 a week – less his agent's commission – rising by £10 each year until his hoped-for star status gave him enough clout to renegotiate the contract. It would be almost six months before Associated British Films found a role it considered suitable. In the meantime its publicity machine was ordered to start promoting its 'newest star in the making'.

Within weeks the staff at ABF's press office found themselves in a unique position. 'From the beginning it was a matter of trying to keep up with Harris,' explains one of the press officers who found himself charged with moulding the actor's early screen image. 'Until Harris came along the actors and actresses on our books were all well groomed and well behaved. We would ring the newspapers or magazines and attempt to persuade them to do an interview or cover a publicity appearance. With Harris you would come in on a Monday morning to find all the telephones ringing and think, "God, what's he done now?" '

During a celebrity evening at the Royal Festival Hall, someone on Harris's table broke a glass. It was a genuine accident, but when the bill arrived the management had charged for ten replacements. The waiter seemed unconcerned by the mistake and unwilling to reduce the charge. 'All right,' announced Elizabeth, rising unsteadily to her feet, 'if you're going to charge us for ten glasses we still have nine to go.' One by one she hurled the remaining goblets to the floor.

Worse was to come. As they emerged from the hall, Harris spotted a group of uniformed policemen and, assuming they had been called to deal with his overzealous wife, decided to take pre-emptive action. Spreading his arms and dropping his head he rugby charged the unsuspecting constables – shunting them through a plate-glass shop window. No one was seriously injured and Harris escaped with a police caution and several stitches to a gash in his hand.

The next morning Elizabeth awoke to find her husband silent and moody. He felt guilty about his own violent behaviour, but ashamed by what he saw as his wife's deliberate display of indignation. She had made an exhibition of herself. She had let him down in public. They had been married for less than a year, but to Elizabeth her husband's parochial double standards appeared as an unwelcome crack in their relationship.

For the first time 'Richard's overbearing personality became suffocatingly apparent,' she recalls.

Harris's daydream – their joint daydream – of fame and money and freedom was already tainted by his newfound cachet. Even Elizabeth's announcement that she was pregnant with their first child failed to calm him. Harris was intent on surrounding himself with an ever-expanding group of colourful hangers-on, most of whom ended up drunk and crowded into their Earl's Court flat. 'I had become an outsider in my own home,' Elizabeth confessed in her autobiography, *Love, Honour and Dismay*. 'I was feeling sick, fat and very lonely. The London I once knew seemed a million miles away from the life I was now leading. I could take the poverty but this lack of privacy was beginning to destroy me.'

Harris's insensitivity blinded him to his wife's deepening depression. There was no one she could turn to: her parents were in Africa and both her brothers abroad. In her darkest moments she hated herself and she hated Richard. One evening when Elizabeth could take it no more she hid herself in the bathroom and unwrapped a new razor blade. As the blood began to seep from the cut in her left wrist she started to feel faint. Before she could complete the job she hit the floor. She was still unconscious when she arrived at a nearby hospital. While the medical staff closed the wound, Harris explained away his wife's attempted suicide, still a criminal offence in the 1950s, as an accident that had happened while she was trimming linoleum.

Three months after signing his film contract, Harris had still not been offered a picture. He regretted the deal, but not the £30-a-week retainer, and began to wonder if Robert Lennard's promise of 'big screen roles' hadn't landed him in a contractual straitjacket. 'We just didn't feel he was right for any of the films we were making at that time,' explained a former Associated British executive. 'You have got to remember that Richard was one of an emerging new breed of actor. The public were used to gentlemen screen idols with ties and white cuffs and impeccable manners, not wild young men like Peter O'Toole and Albert Finney and Alan Bates – and Richard Harris.'

Lennard's vision began to take shape – appropriately through a swirling Scottish mist – in the early summer of 1958. Harris departed for Oban and his first small part in a gentle comedy about three old ladies who swap their life in an unpleasant old folk's home for a remote Irish island. At its best the film would never be more than a studio vehicle for its three elderly but still energetic stars, Sybil Thorndike, Kathleen Harrison and Estelle Winwood.

While her husband was away, Elizabeth moved to her parents' Kensington home. Overdue and slightly anxious, she finally went into labour on the 2 August. Harris, a day or so back from Scotland, was given permission to be present at the birth and held his wife's hand as she was wheeled into the labour ward of Queen Charlotte's Hospital.

Surrounded by midwives and what seemed an endless flock of white-coated student doctors, Elizabeth tried to relax with the occasional whiff of gas and air. Dull moans and high-pitched screams drifted over the top of the curtained cubicles. The delivery was easy and uncomplicated – at least for the mother. When Elizabeth looked up, her husband was gone. Harris had fainted at the very moment his son Damian was born.

Dispatched on medical advice to recover in the Rose and Crown opposite the hospital on Goldhawk Road, Harris returned for a more dignified look at his first child. 'He just sat and stared and stared at his son,' recalls Elizabeth. 'When he was finally persuaded to pick him up they both looked so vulnerable: one so tiny and helpless, the other so large and tender.'

In the middle of September Harris and his wife and their six-week-old son flew to Ireland. For ten weeks the family lived in a small rented house on the outskirts of Dublin. Each morning Harris was collected by car and driven the twelve miles south to Bray and the nearby Ardmore Studios. United Artists had hired the studios' single sound stage and backlot to make an action melodrama about the Irish Republican struggle called *Shake Hands with the Devil*.

The film's director, Michael Anderson, had just finished making *The Dam Busters* and persuaded Michael Redgrave to sign up a second time. It was Anderson's work on the wartime epic that also won over the film's star, the 59-year-old veteran American actor James Cagney. For more than a decade Cagney had dominated Hollywood with his tough-guy characters. In *Shake Hands with the Devil*, he played a downbeat but no less ruthless IRA terrorist living and working in 1920s Dublin as a surgeon.

Back in London and with Christmas fast approaching, Harris reflected on his year. In less than twelve months he had secured himself not only an agent but a studio contract, made two feature films and become a father. It was about to get even better.

Michael Anderson was 'instantly impressed' by Harris's enthusiasm and determined professionalism. Even before the Ardmore shoot was completed the director earmarked the Irishman for his next picture. 'It was quite obvious Richard had a lot to learn,' said Anderson. 'But it was equally obvious his acting possessed that special quality.'

This new film would have an impressive pedigree. With an Eric Ambler script, adapted from the bestselling Hammond Innes novel, Harris would be working alongside Charlton Heston, Gary Cooper and, for the second time, Michael Redgrave. Better still, *The Wreck of the Mary Deare* was to be shot in Hollywood. With the contract signed, it was clearly time for a celebration – and a second assault on the Royal Festival Hall.

With Lord Ogmore as president of the London Welsh Society, there was never any question of banning his daughter and son-in-law from the South Bank venue. Placated by promises of good behaviour, the management agreed to allow the Harrises to attend the society's annual ball. Among the official guests was the Welsh-born actress Siân Phillips, escorted by her fiancé, Peter O'Toole. With so many Welshmen under one roof it was inevitable the gathering would degenerate into an impromptu glee club. Harris and O'Toole responded with an uninvited and uncensored Irish cabaret. The hushed silence was rapidly overtaken by a wave of noisy protests as dozens of indignant Welshman besieged Ogmore's table threatening to resign and demanding the pair's immediate expulsion. The vindicated management duly obliged.

The next morning's flight to Los Angeles proved equally stimulating and came very close to ending Harris's career. Shortly after their Super Constellation airliner had passed into American airspace from Canada, one of its four engines burst into flames. After extinguishing the blaze, the crew circled the wastes of North Dakota, dumping fuel before landing. A replacement plane eventually arrived and took off for California. This time they were looking down on the Rocky Mountains when one of *its* engines exploded in flames, and they were forced to make an emergency landing at Salt Lake City. What should have been a nonstop flight over the Pole took almost 48 hours. The Harrises arrived in Los Angeles fraught and exhausted and determined, for the sake of their son, never to travel together on the same plane again.

Hollywood was not a good experience. *The Wreck of the Mary Deare* was being filmed at MGM's Culver City studio and was a strange amalgam of seafaring action and courtroom melodrama. To shoot the shipwreck scenes, the crew built half the ship so that it could be plunged into the huge backlot water tank. Harris spent several uncomfortable days drenched and clinging to the prop as it was hit by machine-generated waves and lashing rain. Gary Cooper, who endured the same on-set battering, had recently been diagnosed with cancer but insisted on continuing with the film despite the pain and discomfort. Each evening

Harris returned to Elizabeth and their motel suite invigorated by his day's work but sore and scratchy that, despite working with two of Hollywood's top stars, he had not been accepted into its social circle. There was no hearty backslapping, no after-hours drinks, no party invitations.

The Harrises had arrived at the 'fantastic end of America' but did not yet belong. Instead they were left to wander the grey and dirty stucco streets of Jack Kerouac's 'ragged promised land' and waste their days off in downtown cinemas. Four years earlier the Beat writer had walked the same streets. Things hadn't changed much. 'Great families off jalopies from the hinterland stood around the sidewalk gapping for the sight of some movie star,' Kerouac wrote in his autobiographical novel, *On the Road* (1957). 'When a limousine passed they rushed eagerly to the curb and ducked to look: some character in dark glasses sat inside with a bejewelled blonde ... Handsome queer boys who had come to Hollywood to be cowboys walked around, wetting their eyebrows with hincty fingertips. The most beautiful little gone gals in the world cut by in slacks; they came to be starlets; they ended up in drive-ins.'

Frustrated and disappointed, Harris struck out at the only person within reach. His cheerless moods would suddenly erupt into a sour and spiteful verbal lashing. Things would be said and flung until Elizabeth was reduced to tears and her husband, exhausted and ashamed, would slink off to spend the next few hours in silent but determined self-examination. 'I no longer felt at ease with Richard,' Elizabeth remembers of those days. 'I didn't like to think of it as fear, more a certain weariness.' Whatever it was, she was more than happy to leave Hollywood before him. Elizabeth decided to make the five-day Atlantic crossing from New York to Southampton on the *Queen Elizabeth*, while Harris would fly home alone.

'During that crossing I realized that my life had not only changed it had practically stopped,' said Elizabeth. 'I'd stopped reading books, stopped listening to other people's views, stopped developing as a person. There seemed to have been so little time for introspection, for ideas, for curiosity. I got used to listening to the comments and criticisms made by Richard; it was so much easier to repeat his views than to form and express my own.'

For an actor making only his fourth film, Harris was clocking up an impressive list of leading men. James Cagney, Gary Cooper and Charlton Heston would now be joined by Robert Mitchum and a return to Ireland. Once again, the plot would involve Republican terrorism. For *A Terrible Beauty*, Harris had graduated to the role of a 'fanatical IRA man'.

Despite his surly reputation, Mitchum got on well with Harris and, when Elizabeth arrived at Bray, the couple were invited to Robert and Dorothy Mitchum's nearby rented home for a meal. Some nights the quartet drove up to Dublin for dinner. As they ate in a cosy restaurant favoured by visiting show-business personalities, a man suddenly appeared at their table and asked Mitchum to autograph a piece of paper. The actor obliged, only to be interrupted a second time by the same man with a different piece of paper. The pestering continued until Mitchum took the latest scrap of paper and scribbled, 'Up your arse – Kirk Douglas'. The sound of the man stamping and muttering his way across the dining room and back to the star's table was nothing compared with the slap he laid on Mitchum's face. In total silence the American finished what he was saying to Harris before inviting his attacker to lean a little closer. 'Next time you do that,' whispered Mitchum, 'make sure you drop me good or I'll break your mother-fucking neck.'

Three years with Joan Littlewood may well have taught Richard Harris how to act, but it was being in the company of international stars that taught him a vital lesson in dealing with studio executives and directors. He made it a point never to demand special treatment or private jets. For *Shake Hands With the Devil*, James Cagney arrived in Dublin with no bodyguards, secretaries or hairstylists – just himself and his suitcases. Despite his ill health while making *The Wreck of the Mary Deare*, Gary Cooper asked only that his wife be allowed to accompany him on set. Again, on *A Terrible Beauty*, Robert Mitchum's only companion was his wife. Four decades later Harris's abhorrence of all things pretentious still held good. 'I saw John Travolta in Cannes once,' he slammed. 'He was on his private jet. The doors opened and he gets off with eight bodyguards. Eight bodyguards!'

It was about this time that Harris heard that JP Donleavy had adapted his novel *The Ginger Man* for the stage and was hoping for a London production during the summer of 1959. The novel was based on the American-born Donleavy's experiences as a Dublin Trinity College student after the war, and it takes as its hero the roguish Sebastian Balfe Dangerfield, who is in Dublin to read law. It appears that all Dangerfield's studies have given him are a quick tongue for wheedling loans to buy more drink and a verbal charm that comes in handy for bedding women. Dangerfield is married and has a young baby – an inconvenience for him, but a tragedy for his wife. When Harris heard that Jason Robards, eight years his senior, was about to be offered the part, he telephoned his agent. 'I should play the Ginger Man,' he announced. 'It's me. It's my life.'

The producers agreed. Rehearsals for *The Ginger Man* were delayed to allow Harris to finish filming *A Terrible Beauty* in Ireland and the director, Philip Wiseman, to find someone to play Dangerfield's smelly, sex-obsessed but deprived friend Kenneth O'Keefe. He settled on a newcomer called Ronald Fraser. The play opened in the tiny Fortune Theatre in London's Covent Garden in September to a standing ovation. Bernard Levin added to the euphoria by claiming that the members of the cast, which included Wendy Craig and Isabel Dean, 'wore their parts as if it were their skin'. The next morning the management announced it was expecting the play to run well into the New Year.

It was time, Elizabeth decided, for them to move up in the world. Despite her husband's habit of 'assimilating into his own life the characters he enjoyed playing' – and at the moment he was more than happy emulating Dangerfield's rumbustious lifestyle – they were at least financially secure. Their rows, on the other hand, were becoming more frequent and less forgiving. When Elizabeth threatened to leave him, Harris was usually too drunk to take the threat seriously. Perhaps a new home in keeping with his status would provide his ego with the bedrock it needed.

By early October Elizabeth had taken a lease on a partly furnished apartment in Allan House, an impressive red-brick and white-stone block just round the corner from Kensington High Street. At £15 a week, it was an extravagant but necessary move upward to an address that seemed to attract a growing band of actors and actresses on the verge of celebrity. The most famous was Sid James, who lived there before *Hancock's Half Hour* made him a star and whose ex-wife and daughter were still Allan House residents.

The day they moved in, Harris departed for his evening performance at the Fortune, leaving Elizabeth surrounded by a jumble of furniture and half-empty tea chests. He returned with JP Donleavy and casually announced that the writer would be staying the night. It was not the first 24 hours in their new home Elizabeth had planned. 'Donleavy disturbed me,' she later confessed. 'Not only did I dislike him, he made me apprehensive. I had the feeling that he enjoyed creating tricky situations just to see how one would cope and what sort of dialogue we would inflict on each other.'

The next three weeks would have delighted Donleavy's sense of domestic mischief. Harris was taking full advantage of the Covent Garden pubs near the theatre, which kept their own irregular hours to serve the fruit and vegetable market porters. Each performance seemed an excuse for a celebration. And each drunken and rowdy return to Allan House prompted the inevitable argument. When Elizabeth could take no more she scooped up her year-old son and departed for her parents' Alexandra Court apartment.

Attempts at reconciliation failed. So, too, did *The Ginger Man*. Instead of the bullish six months predicted, the production closed after just six weeks. For Harris, by now in a flat of his own and struggling to come to terms with what looked like the end of his marriage, the blow was softened only by the prospect of an Irish premiere for the play.

The Ginger Man ended its London run on Friday, 23 October. During the weekend Harris flew to Dublin. After a brief Sunday night rehearsal, the play opened at the Gaiety Theatre on Monday, this time with the Irish actor Godfrey Quigley taking the part of O'Keefe. By the time the curtain fell there were already demands from the management to trim a seduction scene and cut references to the Catholic Church.

The *Irish Times* claimed Harris's performance swung from magnificent to boring and declared the sex scene the 'most offensive ever performed on a Dublin stage'. The city's two evening newspapers were equally damning. Sitting through *The Ginger Man* was, according to the *Evening Herald* critic, 'murderously like watching a film in slow motion'. While the *Evening Mail* branded it 'tasteless, trivial and empty'. The personal secretary to the archbishop of Dublin pleaded for the script to be edited and rewritten. Donleavy refused without some kind of 'official' order.

Harris was also under pressure to withdraw from the production. He later admitted, 'I received messages, unofficially and indirectly, that as a Catholic I should not appear in plays of this nature.' When he telephoned the archbishop's secretary and asked him specifically what it was that was wrong with the play and what were the references that were offensive to the Catholic Church, the priest advised him to consult his spiritual adviser – before slamming down the phone.

The play went on for a second night. The next morning the *Irish Independent*, the country's biggest and most influential daily, delivered the fatal broadside: '*The Ginger Man* is one of the most nauseating plays ever to appear on a Dublin stage and it is a matter of some concern that its presentation should ever have been considered. It is an insult to religion and an outrage to normal feelings of decency.' With the cast and writer determined to complete the advertised run, it was now up to the theatre's owners to take action. On Thursday morning they announced the Gaiety Theatre had closed.

Harris's dedication to the play and his career cost him dearly. Carousing with the cast had left him thin and drained and more dependent on alcohol than he cared to admit. And after just 31 months of marriage, Elizabeth filed for divorce. 'This play has ruined my life,' Harris admitted to Donleavy, 'but I think it's a classic.' To 'rid his system of *The Ginger Man*', as Elizabeth phrased it, Harris checked himself into a Cornish nursing home for two weeks.

Harris was back in London barely a day when his father telephoned from Limerick. His mother was dying of cancer.

For months Mildred Harris had kept her terrible secret, first from herself, and then her husband. Now, when there was no hope, she finally shared it with her family. The illness was destroying her body but not her faith in God or her pride in her favourite son's achievements. 'Dickie's arrival at Overdale seemed to give her a deeper strength,' recalled a member of the Harris family. 'Whenever she opened her eyes Dickie was there holding her hand. That was something none of us had the courage to do. He stayed with her every waking hour until the very end.'

Haunted by his mother's death – and morbidity in general – Harris desperately needed to submerge himself in a new project. The opportunity to escape came while he was still in Ireland. His agent called to say he had been offered a small part in an American television play. The drama, starring the 57-year-old British stage actor Eric Portman, was being filmed in New York. Harris caught the next flight from Shannon.

It was the break he needed. Two weeks later, close enough to their third anniversary to be sentimental, Elizabeth received a telegram: 'How about a honeymoon in Paris?'

When she walked into Le Bar au Ritz her estranged husband was sitting relaxed and smiling beside a bucket of chilled champagne. 'Honeymoons, however late, should always be memorable,' Harris announced as he poured two glasses of the vintage wine.

They made love and slept in one of the most expensive and stylish suites at the Ritz. Over dinner at Maxim's, they held hands and attempted to rekindle their marriage. They also made each other a promise: that, no matter how bitter the fights and how desolate their time apart, their reconciliations would always start in an elegant hotel bedroom. 'We shall have a series of beautiful affairs,' added Harris.

It was a pact that would see them through the next spectacularly volatile decade. 'I found hotel rooms erotic,' Elizabeth candidly admitted in her autobiography. 'I welcomed the anonymity and transitory feeling hotel rooms gave us. We became different characters, new personalities, for those few days of reconciliation. It gave a new excitement to our marriage.'

Few actors enjoyed working at Elstree studios. Associated British Pictures kept a tight rein on its production staff and, more seriously, on its performers. The studio managers were instructed to keep a 'black book' and record details of set arrival times and the number of takes each actor or actress required to complete a scene. Staff on the gate contributed to this Big Brother intrusion by noting exactly who went across the road to the Red Lion public house for a lunchtime drink and what time they returned. It was hardly the best place to team up two rebellious young actors intent on enjoying themselves.

Richard Harris and Laurence Harvey had been recruited with David McCallum, Ronald Fraser and the veteran actor Richard Todd to make up the doomed World War Two patrol fighting the Japanese and itself in the film version of Willis Hall's play The Long and the Short and the Tall. For Richard Todd it would turn out to be the most unpleasant film he ever worked on.

Shooting started in mid-June 1959 on an Elstree set dressed with lush palms and steamy streams to resemble the Malayan jungle. By the end of the first week it was clear things were not going to plan. Harris and Harvey had formed an out-of-hours drinking alliance and were attracting the attention of the studio boss, Vaughan Dean.

According to Richard Todd the 'real irritant' was Laurence Harvey. The Lithuanian-born actor was playing the irrepressible and vicious Cockney wide boy Bamforth, a role originally offered Peter O'Toole. 'With his consuming desire always to be the centre of attention, he became a mischievous and disruptive influence on our working days,' recalled Todd in his autobiography, In Camera. 'A lot of time was wasted while he clowned around, and his influence started to affect some of the other actors.'

Harvey – real name Larushka Mischa Skikne – arrived in England in the late-1940s from South Africa, where he had served as the youngest member of an army entertainment unit commanded by Sid James. It was in 1949, on the top deck of a London bus, that James gave the inexperienced Skikne his stage name. Scouring the Oxford Street shop fronts, James rattled off the names without success until they arrived opposite Harvey Nichols. 'OK,' announced the future *Carry On* star, 'it's either Laurence Harvey or Laurence Nichols.'

By coincidence Harris and Harvey shared the same birthday, although Harvey was two years older. The pair spent each lunchtime across the road in the Red Lion. To the frustration of the director Leslie Norman, they returned for the afternoon session on time but considerably overindulged. In desperation, Dean cornered Richard Todd, as the film's senior actor, and asked if he could do something to curb the pair's boisterousness.

That evening Todd invited Harris into his dressing room for a chat. 'I told him what an ass he was making of himself and how he was letting himself be led into being a nuisance.' Todd, who fully expected a less gentlemanly response, watched in amazement as tears began to well in the Irishman's eyes. Harris apologised and promised to keep his midday drinking under control; the film finished on time in mid-August.

During the final weeks of production another set of actors and technicians moved on to the Elstree lot. *The Rebel* would be Tony Hancock's first feature film since his elevation to Britain's best loved radio and television comic actor. Hired as a one-line extra for a Paris café scene was another young actor still to deliver his breakthrough performance – Oliver Reed.

Late one afternoon when shooting on both films had finished Oliver Reed went in search of his old friend Ronald Fraser, who was starring in *The Long and the Short and the Tall*. Knocking on the door to Fraser's dressing room, Reed physically jumped as the door was wrenched open. 'What do you want?' spat an obviously irritated Richard Harris.

'Is Ronnie Fraser at home?' asked Reed.

'Yes, he is,' said Harris.

Reed leaped backwards once again – this time to avoid the slamming door making contact with the end of his nose. 'I didn't hold a grudge against him for that,' Reed admitted. 'After all, I was a nobody and he was a big star.'

From the Elstree jungle, Harris moved to the flight deck of a Shepperton bomber. For the $6 million World War Two epic *The Guns of Navarone*, he had a small part as Squadron Leader Howard Barnsby, who pilots a commando raiding party on its mission to destroy a German gun cave hidden in cliffs on a Greek island. Unfortunately for Harris, his character remained grounded at the studio southwest of London while the film's stars – including Gregory Peck, David Niven, Anthony Quinn, Stanley Baker and Anthony Quayle – jetted off to Rhodes for the location filming.

Sometime between shooting and the release of *The Long and the Short and the Tall*, several of the film's stars gathered for dinner in a King's Road restaurant. Sitting each side of the Harrises were Laurence Harvey and his actress wife Margaret Leighton. Suddenly, a tall, well-dressed man appeared at the table. '[Rex Harrison] was exactly as I imagined him,' says Elizabeth. 'Handsome, elegant, worldly and so very English.' He was, she also recalls, rather frightening. He had an aloof quality about him that was inhibiting. I had the feeling it was better not to speak at all than to say something less than brilliant.'

Harrison was 52 years old and had been married three times: to Collette Thomas, Lilli Palmer and Kay Kendall, who had died the year before. He was, admitted one of the many women in his life, incapable of spending an evening by himself. Although Elizabeth Harris did not know it at the time, she had just been introduced to her second husband.

CHAPTER FIVE

On the first day of the northern shoot for *This Sporting Life*, Anderson arranged his cameras around the Wakefield pitch, and the club's professional players, hired as extras but looking more like gorillas in striped jerseys, trotted on to the field and began to warm up. 'Is this what you do all day?' Harris called to the nearest Neanderthal. 'Kick this little ball over that little bar?'

'Ay, bloody 'ell you've got to, lad,' the gathering team mumbled in unison.

'That's a simple kick,' taunted Harris. 'Give us a kick, then.'

The ball was scooped up and placed about forty yards from the goal line.

By now Harris was enjoying himself. He picked up the ball and repositioned it. The Wakefield players winked at each other. Harris took a couple of steps back before returning to the ball. This time he wanted a smudge of mud removed. Smirks and wide toothless grins.

As he paced backwards to take the kick, Harris closed his eyes and said a little prayer inside his head. 'If there's a God in heaven,' he pleaded, 'put wings on that ball and carry it over.' The entire ground fell silent, rising to collective cheer as the ball flew over and through the goalposts.

CHAPTER FIVE

Acting is the expression of a neurotic impulse. It's a bum's life. The principal benefit acting has afforded me is the money to pay for my psychoanalysis.

– Marlon Brando

The 1960s came as a culture shock at the end of what had been a static and backward-looking decade. With the Beatles and the pop revolution came the surprising revelation for the British that they could be beautiful. But this Technicolor decade began in black and white and predominantly in the stark and unfamiliar landscape of the North.

'England,' recalls playwright John Osborne, 'was more like a sleepy village after the war. It was very difficult to get anyone's attention.' Within a decade England would become a hothouse of writers and directors and, more importantly, stars. By 1967 there would be 76 pictures in production in Britain, but the seeds of this success were sown more than fifteen years earlier and, satisfyingly for Richard Harris, in the mud and blood of a rugby pitch.

At nineteen, David Storey unwittingly found himself living one of the great literary and dramatic themes of the 1950s – he was 'an artist isolated in an alien society'. Born and brought up in Wakefield, Yorkshire, Storey was a natural and talented writer. He was also a gifted rugby player. His final weeks at school brought two offers; a scholarship to study at the Slade School of Art in London, and a chance to play rugby league as a professional. Storey accepted them both. Each Friday night he would catch the train north to join his team. On Sunday evening he returned to the capital physically bruised and mentally broken by the taunts of his father and former schoolfriends, all duty-drawn to a life down a Yorkshire coalmine.

Storey's only hope of survival was as 'an armoured protagonist', and in 1954 he started to write down his experiences. His rambling notes suddenly came into focus one Saturday afternoon during a rugby match at Leeds. The ball landed at Storey's feet and he hesitated. 'I knew that if I picked it up I would lose my teeth,' he recalls. Another player scooped up the ball and was smashed in the mouth by a flying boot. 'He looked at me and swore and I suddenly had the vision of my hero.'

Two years later Storey had collected enough material for a novel. It took another four years of rejections and rewrites before *This Sporting Life* was published. Its hero, Arthur Machin, was 'a self-absorbed, intuitive kind of creature and a hard, physical, extroverted character' existing, as Elizabeth Harris would later describe it, 'somewhere between the time old family snobbery went into decline and working-class chic began to flourish'.

A haze of intrigue and film-industry politics separates the publication of David Storey's bleak first-person novel and its screen release. At the heart of the double-dealing was the Yorkshire-born film executive, Tony Richardson.

In 1958, deciding it was time to direct films instead of plays, Richardson joined forces with John Osborne to launch Woodfall Productions. When no British individual or institution would back them, the pair sought finance in America and eventually made contact with Harry Saltzman, the future producer of the James Bond films. Woodfall's first film was of Osborne's play, *Look Back in Anger*, on which it turned a small but respectable profit. When an adaptation of *The Entertainer* – also a play by Osborne – failed disastrously, Saltzman became fractious about his lost percentage and was elbowed from the company. Richardson urgently needed finance for his next film, *Saturday Night and Sunday Morning*, and persuaded Karel Reisz, the Czech-born director and film critic, to sign up as producer. What Reisz didn't know was that 'the abominable Richardson' had rigged their contract so that his new producer didn't see any profits from the highly successful *Saturday Night* until all *The Entertainer*'s debts were cleared.

While all this was going on, Richardson was also shuffling the pack on the director Lindsay Anderson. 'Lindsay had read and been impressed by David Storey's novel,' explains Reisz. 'He took it to Tony at Woodfall as a project for himself.' After reading the novel, Richardson informed Anderson that he wasn't interested. What he didn't tell him was that he had already made an offer for the film rights. Richardson was eventually outbid by Julian Wintle and Leslie Parkyn, who already had a distribution deal with the Rank Organisation, but when that partnership foundered Wintle asked Karel Reisz if he would like to direct *This Sporting Life*. 'But it was Lindsay's project,' continues Reisz, 'and I didn't want to direct it anyway, as the material seemed too close in some ways to *Saturday Night*. So I offered to produce it with Lindsay directing, and Wintle agreed.'

Anderson was a homosexual, and was also given to pre-emptive and irrational outbursts of rage. The trigger was invariably creative anxiety or sexual frustration and, when the two elements combined, the effect could be devastating.

Both Anderson and Reisz felt no one but the author should write the screenplay. Storey was hesitant but agreed. The artistic squabbles with Anderson began almost immediately. 'We had three terrible rows,' recalls the writer, 'and I could never quite make out why they erupted.' Part of the problem was that both men were on new and high-pressure ground: it was Anderson's first feature film as director and Storey's first attempt at a film script. The climax came one night when the pair were in the North of England scouting locations. After an apparently amiable dinner, Storey rose to go to bed. Without warning, Anderson's face drained white with rage and he bellowed: 'Come back here, you cunt!'

On 23 January 1961, and back in London, Anderson confided his ambitions for *This Sporting Life* to his diary. He hoped it would be

a film about all of us and our lives right now – of Karel, Albie [Finney] and Zoe [Caldwell] – and Jill [Bennett] and Willis [Hall], and our aspirations and egoism and unhappiness. This was obviously the way *L'Avventura* affected Karel – a film *d'auteur*, a firsthand work, not a dramatic construction well directed by somebody – which is what *Sporting Life* will be unless I can get inside it and make it a personal allegory. But it is here that my intuitions and aspirations have been all too swift and all-at-sea.

One hurdle still faced Anderson, Reisz and Storey: who should play Arthur Machin? From the outset Anderson, supported by Storey, visualised Albert Finney as the complex and troubled rugby professional. The producer was not so sure: whispers of Finney's 'awkward' behaviour during the filming of *The Long and the Short and the Tall* were still circulating. Next they considered Sean Connery, but the trio agreed he was not right for the part. Finally, the director suggested Richard Harris, whom he had seen on stage as *The Ginger Man*.

When Anderson contacted Harris's agent he was informed the Irishman had already departed for Hollywood to start work on *Mutiny on the Bounty*. The script for *This Sporting Life* was not yet complete, so the director posted off a copy of David Storey's novel and an outline of the film. Within days, Harris replied with 'a marvellous letter full of enthusiasm'.

Richard Harris's first instinct was to reject the invitation to appear in *Mutiny on the Bounty*. Although convinced of the film's potential, he was worried that his own part, as one of the mutineers, John Mills, was too small and out of step with his rapidly rising reputation. A month or so later a new screenplay arrived giving him more lines and a higher profile. Once again, Harris refused to consider the part. Even the offer of more money was not enough. When the casting director finally asked the actor what it would take to get him to sign up, Harris cheekily demanded equal billing with Marlon Brando.

There was a choking gasp from the other end of the telephone. 'Impossible,' the man said. 'Brando is the star.'

'OK,' conceded Harris. 'Equal billing with Trevor Howard.'

Another pause. 'But Howard is better known than you.'

'Not at my age.'

Two days before the rest of the cast were scheduled to fly out to Tahiti, the production company rang back. Harris had won his first round of contractual brinkmanship.

The 9,500-mile journey to the French Polynesian island would be long and tiring. After they had jetted to San Francisco, a second airliner would ferry them across the endless miles of the world's biggest ocean to Honolulu. With a little luck an ageing and noisy South Pacific Airways plane would be waiting to take them on to Tahiti. Harris habitually travelled light. He arrived at London Airport with one small suitcase and clutching a bottle of bourbon.

'Good morning, Mr Harris,' said the airline check-in clerk.

'How do you know me?' enquired a puzzled but flattered Harris.

'I recognised you from your hand luggage,' she said.

Marlon Brando was originally approached by David Lean to play TE Lawrence in *Lawrence of Arabia*. After a Paris meeting with the director and producer Sam Spiegel, the trio were only days from publicly announcing Brando's portrayal of the World War One hero when the actor was offered the part of another British military legend, this time the mutineer Fletcher Christian. MGM had hired Carol Reed to direct a $5 million remake of the 1935 epic *Mutiny on the Bounty*. Much of the casting was complete, including, at Reed's insistence, Trevor Howard as the authoritarian Captain Bligh. Faced with the choice of six months in the desert or half that time on the Polynesian island of Tahiti, Brando opted for the *Bounty* – 'I would have dried up in the desert like a puddle of water.'

Shooting was scheduled to start on 15 October 1961. When the 37-year-old actor flew into the former French colony he found the 110-strong location team of Hollywood technicians in chaos. A replica of HMS *Bounty*, powered by diesel engines and a third larger than the original to accommodate the cameras, had arrived from Canada but still needed attention. As did the Eric Ambler script. Ambler was on a $3,000-a-week contract and on his fourteenth rewrite. Without a completed and Brando-approved screenplay it was possible to film only background shots. And few, if any, of the seven thousand native extras had been recruited or trained. Things had not improved when Harris arrived a few days later.

Six weeks after her husband, Elizabeth completed the same journey. It was Christmas Eve. She arrived in Tahiti holding her exhausted son in one arm and dragging an artificial Christmas tree with the other. Shuffling a yard or so behind was their young Welsh nanny.

There was no husband to greet them. Harris was at sea, filming aboard the *Bounty*. And, anyway, the date on the telegram announcing his wife and son's arrival had somehow changed during transmission from the 24th to the 27th. The luxury house Harris had rented outside the capital Papeete would not be ready for another three days; until then the family would have to share the actor's small beech hut. Elizabeth waited until the next day to deliver her 'special Christmas present' – she was expecting their second child.

Delays clocked up, dragging the film behind schedule and into the red. But not all the problems were of Reed's making. No one had accounted for the vagaries of the Pacific weather: unforecast and instant squalls appeared from nowhere and the light, which changed almost by the minute, forced several scenes to be reshot from scratch. The $750,000 replica *Bounty* was also giving problems. Built in Nova Scotia to eighteenth-century Admiralty plans, the ship proved troublesome to sail, with its decks cluttered with lights, cameras, cables, generators and more than twice its original complement. It was dangerously top-heavy and bounced and bobbed and felt as if it were about to turn turtle. Harris, never a good sailor, frequently joined other members of the cast and crew depositing their last meal over the side.

Another problem was Brando's apparent inability to learn the script. Long after the film's release Harris maintained that the American star would stick his lines on Harris's forehead. 'He doesn't play a scene with you,' explained Harris. 'Everything's secret. He doesn't pour on the coal in the first take, but lets it go on to the eleventh and suddenly it clicks for him. 'That's it,' he says and walks off. Meanwhile your best take may have been three. It's a self-centred sort of art.' At other times Brando took great pains – what Harris called Marlon's Method – to found his acting on authenticity. For Bligh's death scene Brando insisted on a layer of ice between himself and the bedclothes so that his shivering fit seemed more real.

Spying a crack, Harris nagged and worried at these imperfections until he lost all respect for his acting hero. Brando was already trapped on a road that, by tradition, allowed and encouraged an actor to think he was larger than the production itself. What Harris inadvertently – at least at first – found himself bringing down was not only Brando, but his own belief in the Method, on which they had both so diligently built their careers. During the 1940s and 1950s the Stanislavski Method was hailed as something very close to authorship, allowing the continued regeneration of an actor's spiritual integrity. In reality and within the hair-trigger atmosphere of a film set, it encouraged only chaos and delays. Harris's admiration for Brando disintegrated.

In an interview shortly after shooting ended Harris claimed the rift between the two actors started one day when Brando failed to hit the Irishman hard enough. After the third feeble blow and as many retakes, Harris taunted Brando by asking: 'Shall we dance?' From then on, alleged Harris, the American star refused to act with him, forcing Harris, in the final scene, to talk to an out-of-shot packing case. Perhaps the footage ended on the cutting room floor. Nowhere in *Mutiny* does Brando strike Harris. And, during the portrayal of Fletcher Christian's death, the film's final scene and the last sequence to be shot, Harris is clearly in shot.

Not surprisingly, Brando remembers the film differently. To him it was all an MGM plot. With rumours of Carol Reed's imminent sacking, Brando later claimed he was the obvious patsy for the studio bosses – 'just as Twentieth Century-Fox had used Elizabeth Taylor as a scapegoat for its miscalculations and production excesses on Cleopatra'.

In Brando's mind at least, MGM would go to any lengths to feed the rumour machine, even planting a studio spy on his personal staff. 'Reporters in the entertainment press, who didn't like me for refusing to give interviews, and who seldom did any independent digging on their own unless it involved titillation, accepted what MGM's press agents said,' he claimed in *Songs My Mother Taught Me*. 'It fit their preconceived notion of an eccentric, cantankerous Brando, and quickly the distortions were carved in granite.'

What had started as a handful of prerelease gossip stories to a few select journalists quickly turned into a feeding frenzy. News from Tahiti was being 'leaked' daily to the world's press. Most top American and British papers had their own reporters on the island. One veteran show-business writer recalls, 'It was like something out of a spy novel. You would receive the official press release and then, if you were one of the favoured few, on the back would be a telephone number or the name of a local bar. That's where the real story could be found.'

For the first time in his career Brando hired a press agent to short-circuit and correct the 'anonymous' tip-offs. However, 'though he was supposedly working for me,' says Brando, 'he was on the MGM payroll and had been instructed secretly to keep placing the blame on me.' This was a fact confirmed by a former studio insider, which the actor himself did not hear of until the late 1960s. 'At the time, I was still of a mind to ignore what people wrote or thought about me, so I hadn't paid much attention to what was going on until the stories of my alleged profligacy had been woven into the tapestry containing all the other myths about me.'

But however much Brando chose to ignore the tittle-tattle – there is not one word in his 468-page autobiography about his clashes with Richard Harris or problems on the set – there were strands of truth in the 'tapestry'. Brando was very protective of his lines and character, due partly to the way he had been sold the role of Fletcher Christian by Bounty's director. In late April 1789, following the Bounty's departure from Tahiti, Christian sparked the mutiny that overthrew the ship's captain and allowed the men to claim their Tahitian lovers. To Carol Reed, the master's mate was a hero and he wanted his star to play him that way. It was an unconventional and revisionist view, which angered the decision makers back in Hollywood. MGM, like most cinema fans, considered the original 1935 Oscar-winning version of Mutiny on the Bounty to be an authoritative account of history and Clark Gable – who hadn't even bothered to speak with an English accent – as the definitive Christian.

In his off-duty hours, Brando would sit alone, nursing a drink in the big hut that doubled as a reception area, dining room and bar, and study his fellow cast members with inscrutable precision. When he spoke it was direct and unnerving. At the film's New Year's Eve party, Brando was introduced to Elizabeth Harris. As they shook hands he asked, 'Are you faithful to Richard?'

'Yes,' she replied more than a little shocked.

'You can't be,' said Brando. 'You answered too quickly.'

'It is a question that doesn't require reflection,' said Elizabeth.

For the next hour or so Brando carefully watched Elizabeth as she drifted through the party. Eventually he cornered Harris. 'You're a lucky man,' he told his co-star. 'You've got a faithful wife.'

In January 1961, the unit returned to Hollywood to complete the indoor scenes. The studio helped find the Harrises a temporary home. It was on Bedford Drive and, until a few days earlier, had been rented by Lauren Bacall and Jason Robards, whom Harris had beaten to the lead in *The Ginger Man*. For Damian Harris, not yet three, the transition from the clammy heat of the South Pacific to the air-conditioned luxury of a Beverly Hills mansion, complete with cook and servants, was too swift to seem permanent. When Marlon Brando asked the toddler where he lived, Damian told him, 'In an aeroplane.'

On its release almost a year later, the *Daily Mail* heralded *Mutiny on the Bounty* 'a masterpiece'. The *Daily Sketch* thought it 'stupendous entertainment'. Across Britain and America cinema posters featured a picture of HMS *Bounty* and the faces of Marlon Brando and Trevor Howard. Above the title were the names of all three stars. But among the brotherhood of Hollywood there was one unanswered question: 'Who the fuck is Richard Harris?'

Lindsay Anderson heard nothing from his future star. Harris, caught up in the Hollywood bloodletting, was too preoccupied to comment on the *Shooting Life* script he eventually received sometime in February 1961. After ten weeks, Anderson could wait no more. He telephoned Harris in Tahiti and listened eagerly as the Irishman related the latest *Mutiny* tally: Carol Reed had finally been replaced by Lewis Milestone; the ninth writer was about to start work on salvaging the original Eric Ambler script; and everyone had been warned that they could still be in the Pacific until the summer. Why didn't Anderson fly out to discuss *This Sporting Life* in person?

On the way out Anderson stopped over in Los Angeles to spend a few days with his old friend and future biographer, Gavin Lambert. 'I suspect Richard Harris has reservations about the script,' admitted the director. 'So do I, but I also have no idea what to do about it ... Of course, it may never happen.' A week later Anderson landed in Tahiti and fell instantly and hopelessly in love – with Richard Harris.

Harris, 'all warmth and ardour', was still enthusiastic about the project, but feared the *Mutiny* delays might force it to move on without him. The director reassured Harris that the *This Sporting Life* lead was his if he wanted it and agreed to hold the start of shooting until the next year. All very businesslike and proper. But, inside, Anderson recognised the old signs – signs he could only secretly confide to his diary. Harris, he wrote, was

> so attractive that I found I responded to him with a wholeheartedness that made me tremble ... Richard has his work, and his wife and children [sic]. Is there room for anything else? I am beginning to think this is a mere fantasy: in fact I dare not hope otherwise, except under my breath so to speak.

Anderson returned to London and called an immediate script conference. Having first read the book, Harris complained that the screenplay lacked the focus and intensity of the novel. Part of the problem was that David Storey had written a conventional linear script, without the book's flashback scenes. It was agreed that the film should follow the original structure. Storey also accepted another Harris suggestion: that Machin's first name should be changed from Arthur to Frank. There was still one person who had reservations about the script.

John Trevelyan took over as secretary of the British Board of Film Censors in the late 1950s after seven years as an examiner. His signature on the certificates that were flashed up on screens before the opening titles was familiar to thousands of cinemagoers. Guiding the film industry through a period of enormous public liberalisation and change, he was fast earning himself a reputation as an enlightened censor who deeply cared about films and freedom of expression. When Trevelyan read the *Sporting Life* script, he still had grave misgivings.

'There are scenes of men in showers and changing rooms,' the censor warned Anderson. 'We do not want any censorable nudity and even full-length back-view shots should be few and discreet.' Trevelyan was more concerned with the near-rape scene between Machin and his landlady. 'We would not want to see him moving his hands over Mrs Hammond, bearing down on her and lying on top of her, and we would not want what I imagine would be the visual described by the phrase, "Their bodies are suddenly in spasm."'

While Lindsay Anderson was defending his script, his star was busy preparing himself for the role's physical demands. The rugby sequences were to be shot at a club in Wakefield, just south of Leeds. To get himself 'match fit', Harris signed on with Richmond Rugby Union Club. 'I suppose I could have played with the London Irish,' Harris commented. 'But I thought that if I played with a toffee-nosed club I wouldn't be noticed. I was right. Nobody on the team spoke to me.'

At school he had been a respectable goal kicker, but that was almost ten years previously. To get back into the game, Harris persuaded the club's top-scoring goal kicker to give him nightly lessons. Each morning the actor would spend two hours in a gym weight-training to strengthen his leg muscles. And each evening for six weeks before filming started he reported to the Richmond ground to sharpen his rugby technique.

On the first day of the northern shoot, Anderson arranged his cameras around the Wakefield pitch, and the club's professional players, hired as extras but looking more like gorillas in striped jerseys, trotted on to the field and began to warm up. 'Is this what you do all day?' Harris called to the nearest Neanderthal. 'Kick this little ball over that little bar?'

'Ay, bloody 'ell you've got to, lad,' the gathering team mumbled in unison.

'That's a simple kick,' taunted Harris. 'Give us a kick, then.'

The ball was scooped up and placed about forty yards from the goal line.

By now Harris was enjoying himself. He picked up the ball and repositioned it. The Wakefield players winked at each other. Harris took a couple of steps back before returning to the ball. This time he wanted a smudge of mud removed. Smirks and wide toothless grins.

As he paced backwards to take the kick, Harris closed his eyes and said a little prayer inside his head. 'If there's a God in heaven,' he pleaded, 'put wings on that ball and carry it over.' The entire ground fell silent, rising to collective cheer as the ball flew over and through the goalposts.

To Colin Blakely, who was acting the part of Maurice Braithwaite and who had never previously worked with the Irishman, Harris's meticulous approach earned him the actor's lifelong respect. 'He simply lived the role of Frank Machin,' recalled Blakely. 'On the rugby field he looked like one of those big Wakefield forwards capable of gobbling you up. He couldn't miss with an approach like that.'

There was still the question of the female lead. Heading the list to play Machin's widowed landlady, with whom he has an affair, was the stage actress Mary Ure. When she declined, the pair approached Rachel Roberts, whose list of credits was overshadowed by her increasingly public affair with Rex Harrison.

Like so many early 1960s actresses, Rachel Roberts was a star out of work: British film makers remained timid about using women whose strength of character displaced conventional physical beauty. Her career was not without distinction. She had already won the Clarence Derwent award for Best Supporting Actress in *Platonov* at the Royal Court Theatre and, more recently, the British Film Academy had named her Best Actress for her part in *Saturday Night and Sunday Morning*. An informal reading of *This Sporting Life* was arranged, but when Rex Harrison arrived to collect his lover it was obvious he disapproved of the character she was being asked to play. Confronting Anderson and Karel Reisz – whom he privately called the 'little twits' – Harrison loudly announced that he did not consider dressing up in 'dirty clothes and pretending to be working-class' something that show-business stars should do.

When the director rejected Harrison's suggestion that stunt doubles should be used for the 'dirty' rugby scenes, the star spluttered into a rage. 'The actors will have to rough it on the field,' Anderson insisted, obviously enjoying the reaction he was getting. 'Do them good to get a few hard knocks in life.'

'Little man,' said Harrison, puffing himself up to his impressive six foot two. 'If you were the last film director in the world, I wouldn't work with you.'

Before she left, and out of Harrison's hearing, Roberts agreed to a film test the following week. A sound stage and crew were booked at Beaconsfield Studios but the actress failed to make an appearance. Harrison, determined to thwart his girlfriend's enthusiasm, had whisked her off to Italy.

The search for 'Mrs Hammond' continued. Four other actresses were tested. 'None of them made us think they'd be as good as we now were convinced Rachel Roberts could be,' admitted Anderson. This time it was Roberts who protested. 'I'm too Welsh,' she told the director. 'I'm too emotional.'

'Rachel,' Anderson pleaded, 'I want all the emotions you have, but I want you to keep them bottled up inside you and make us feel the force that this woman uses to suppress all that's natural in life.' With Roberts under contract and Richard Harris at last free of his Hollywood commitments, shooting for *This Sporting Life* was scheduled for the first week of March 1962.

Meanwhile, Anderson's infatuation with Richard Harris was becoming more public and still more obsessive. Throughout his life he would fall repeatedly in love, usually with heterosexual married actors, including

Albert Finney, Malcolm McDowell and Frank Grimes. For the moment Anderson was focusing all his passion, sexual frustration and repressed anger on Richard Harris. 'Lindsay was always enamoured of the situation of highly talented men with families,' explains David Storey. 'It made him even lonelier, and if he was in love with the person, it fed his appetite for the loved one.'

On 23 April 1962, Anderson noted in his diary:

> From a certain point of view, this [Richard Harris] is a personality too big by far for me to cope with. Emotionally his warmth and wilfulness can sabotage me in a moment. And of course instinctively he knows this and exploits it. I ought to be calm and detached with him. Instead I am impulsive. We embrace and fight like lovers. His mixture of tenderness and sympathy with violence and cruelty is astonishing.

The first two weeks of shooting were a near-disaster. Trouble with the camera crew and on-set friction between Anderson and his principal actor failed to produce the magic everyone hoped. At one time the rushes (or dailies) were so 'appalling' that Julian Wintle ordered Karel Reisz to sack Anderson and take over. It was the crisis Anderson's paranoia needed, and his outbursts were now aimed at Reisz.

It is evident from reading Anderson's diary that he felt any studio aggression was generated by his unrequited lover: 'The storms of his temperament have been fierce and shattering. How can I be expected to resist? Whether he is embracing me physically, like some big warm dog, or ordering me to "heel" – I am at his service completely.'

On the set Anderson also noticed an 'uncomfortable feel' between his two leading players. Back in the late 1950s the pair had both worked at the Theatre Royal, Harris a resident actor and Roberts as the Theatre Workshop's first guest performer. Anderson later explained:

> Richard was a bit awed by Rachel. You see, she lacked self-confidence until she began to act the part. Then she was totally secure in it. She could acquit herself with a first-rate reading in just a couple of takes. Richard took a few more to feel he had got it right.'

Anderson's response to the sacking threat – and partly to keep himself away from the multitude of irritating on-set tasks and decisions he was expected to make – was to revert to the traditional theatre method of rehearsals. This he did, not following the shooting schedule but working sequentially through the script. Rehearsals went on long into the night and over the weekends and allowed Anderson not only to 'find' his film, but Harris and Roberts to 'become' their characters.

For Harris the real catalyst for getting 'it right' came when he eventually met the book's author, David Storey, and his brother. 'He was very uncommunicative,' explained the actor, 'and his brother had this wonderful dark brooding look and I somehow put them together. Their emotions were so raw and simple and unpretentious and the lostness of the character touched me emotionally.'

But what came instinctively to Harris was a grinding slog for Rachel Roberts, who devoted hours to preparing for her part. Sybil Christopher, the actress's International Creative Management agent, called in her client's dressing room. Christopher recalls:

She wasn't there, but the script was on a table. I picked it up to have a look and out dropped a whole sheaf of notes that Rachel had written about the Mrs Hammond character. She was a tenaciously academic actress. She had obviously talked to herself about 'this woman I'm playing', figuring her out, and not pushing herself in front of the role lest she obscured it. And then she had also written an essay about the woman's life.

One evening, soon after shooting had started, Richard Harris, Rachel Roberts, Lindsay Anderson and the film's producer, Karel Reisz, returned to the studio to discuss the script and rehearse the next day's scenes. They had been drinking heavily and Harris and Anderson were soon locked in artistic argument. Roberts was obviously irritated by the passionate discussion.

'Look, when you bloody kids have finished, do let me know,' said Roberts, stomping off to her dressing room. The disagreement continued and the trio forgot about the missing actress. She didn't return.

The next morning Reisz cornered Roberts to find out where she had gone. Her reply was typically bawdy and direct. 'Oh, I went into my room and locked the door and sat on the lavatory,' explained Roberts, 'and my arse got cold and I said to myself, "They're not going to treat the future Mrs Rex Harrison like this!" So I pulled up my knickers and went home.'

A few days later Roberts disappeared again. During a few days' unexpected break in the production schedule she flew back to Italy. On 21 March 1962, at Genoa City Hall, Rachel Roberts became the fourth Mrs Rex Harrison.

For Harris, working with Lindsay Anderson brought its own surprises. The director had evolved his own trial-and-error approach, not only in rehearsals but on set with the camera rolling. If the performance he got from his actors felt 'real', then Anderson accepted it as 'an honest and essential reality'.

'This instinct helped Richard create a dynamic and extraordinarily varied performance, obsessive and ruthless in the rugby scenes, disturbing in the outbursts of violence he can't control, touching in the moments of loneliness he can't conceal,' explains Gavin Lambert in his memoir of the director, *Mainly About Lindsay Anderson*. There was another, more personal, catalyst:

A director in love with his leading actress or actor connects with the beloved on a deep subconscious level, and the visual intimacy of movies always reveals it. Consummation ([Georg Wilhelm] Pabst with Louise Brooks, [Josef] von Sternberg with [Marlene] Dietrich, [William] Wyler with Bette Davis) and sublimation (Marcel Carne with Jean Gabin, [Alfred] Hitchcock with Ingrid Bergman, [Luchino] Visconti with Alain Delon) have the same result. The shades of emotion that a director guides his actor to play, from fascination to confrontation, longing to despair, tenderness to cruelty, become extensions of his own, the camera mirrors everything in the beloved that attracts and obsesses him, and in movies for other directors the actor never reaches quite the same intensity.

David Storey has his own theory about the actor–director relationship. Through the camera lens – through his own vision – Anderson came to regard *Sporting Life* as partly autobiographical. 'In effect he was Mrs Hammond in the film,' adds Storey. But it was a more primitive and less mutually respectful relationship than that shared by two willing partners, and by now Harris was the master and Anderson the slave.

On set Harris would suddenly turn on Anderson. 'Stop smiling,' he would hiss through clenched teeth.

'I'll smile if I wish to.'

'You'll smile when I tell you,' Harris ordered, delivering a hefty punch to Anderson's upper arm. There was, admitted the director, a 'strange sado-masochistic element in our relationship'.

But Harris could be equally disarming. After one row, which rumbled through the studio from dressing room to set and back again, Harris sidled up to the director. 'Never mind, guv,' he said, putting his arm around Anderson's shoulders. 'In your next picture you might get Margaret Lockwood. She always hits her marks.'

At home, the noisy, door-slamming rows and the drunken, all-night parties were becoming a weekly event. At least for the other residents of Allen House. Pleas for quiet and polite deputations for restraint had little lasting effect. In desperation all but one of the apartment block's residents – a drinking buddy of Harris – signed a petition demanding the family's eviction. While Elizabeth attempted conciliation, her husband defiantly shrugged his shoulders. Both agreed it was time to move on, not as a concession to defeat, but simply because they would need the extra room now: Elizabeth was pregnant for the third time.

The Harrises turned their back on the 'righteous and pompous' residents of Allen House and took a short lease on a nearby furnished home. With Elizabeth's confinement drawing near, although she was still able to mastermind the arrangements, the family moved once again, this time to a narrow, five-storey Victorian town house in Bedford Gardens. The stairs were steep and dingy and the two rooms on each floor cramped and pokey. It had the smell of Dickensian London about it and the only flash of colour was from the blossom on the cherry trees in the front and back gardens.

There were benefits to Harris's recent success. For the first time he could help his widowed father back in Limerick. Ivan Harris had never recovered from the death of his wife. Nor could he truly excuse himself from the decline and forced sell-off of the family business empire. In a secret deal with Rank Flour Mills – to whom his father was forced to sell his quayside mill – Harris agreed to pump enough of his own cash into the plant to keep it operating until after his father's death. Not long after Ivan Harris died, Rank laid off the remaining workforce and closed the century-old mill.

During those last few months Harris visited his father whenever his filming commitments allowed. In Los Angeles he had got to know – or hear about – several Hollywood legends. Ivan Harris remained unimpressed by his son's name dropping. 'Did you meet Betty Grabble?' he asked, mispronouncing the name of Betty Grable.

'No, I didn't, Dad,' replied Harris.

'You know Betty Grabble was my hero, Dick, don't you?' said his father.

'I know, Dad,' said Harris.

The cast of *This Sporting Life* decided to celebrate the end of filming with a party. Rachel Roberts was at the celebration with her new husband Rex Harrison. It was only Elizabeth Harris's second close encounter with Harrison who, uncomfortably surrounded by men who showed him little regard or respect, deliberately held himself aloof. Harris greeted his co-star's husband with equal indifference. 'As I looked at them both I thought how they were totally different types of actors, different kinds of men,' recalls Elizabeth. 'They had nothing in common.'

With the end of the film and a release date set for the following summer, Anderson found himself facing an artistic and emotional void and with an 'absolute inability to think concretely on any project except in terms of Richard Harris'. In his diary he confessed, 'The "Discovery" of masturbation at the age of thirty has not helped.'

Anderson mooted several projects on which they might collaborate. One was a screen adaptation of *Wuthering Heights*. Another was a series of three plays: *Hamlet*, *Julius Caesar* and a version of Gogol's *Diary of a Madman*, all to be staged at the Royal Court Theatre in London.

Rehearsals for the Gogol play started early in 1963, while *This Sporting Life* was still being edited. Harris, naturally, would play Poprishkin, the depressive civil servant whose megalomaniac madness ends with his claiming to be the king of Spain. Some days it was all 'friendship and creativity', others it was 'resentment, fear and nervous bullying'. Late one night, shortly before the March opening, Anderson and Harris were alone on the Royal Court stage. Suddenly Harris stood on the director's foot and clamped his hand around his throat. It was an unprovoked and aggressive show of supremacy and for Anderson a 'hallucinating moment'. Perhaps Harris wanted to show he was still the master.

Still unaware of Harris's true potential, the critics tore into *Diary of a Madman* and its 'hysterical melodrama'. Herbert Kretzmer predicted that its only award was likely to be for being 'the most tedious theatrical entertainment of the season'. For Karel Reisz, who now considered himself a friend, it was simply a 'disaster'.

A few days later the press and the public were given their chance to pass judgment on *This Sporting Life*. But first the film – which many saw as the last of the English 'neo-realistic movies' and the end of kitchen-sink drama – needed the seal of approval from its backers. A prerelease screening for Rank executives concluded with a self-conscious silence. 'They were genuinely stirred and impressed,' recalled Anderson, 'but they didn't honestly know what to do with it, how to sell it or to whom.' Karel Reisz thought their film 'had a hard, intransigent, ruthless quality about it ... rightly charmless in the acting ... But people came away having been pained rather than cheered.'

Sadly, *Sporting Life*'s critical success in both Britain and America did not match its box-office returns. It was a film of desire and denial, of pain and violence, appreciated by most critics who applauded Richard Harris's and Rachel Roberts's performances. One of the best appraisals of their work came from Penelope Gilliatt, who wrote:

> The first time you see him [Harris] with his landlady ... you wonder what on earth the pressure is between them. This is the way it happens in life (and in Ibsen's plays), but hardly ever in the cinema ... There is something about her put-upon Englishwoman's silences that makes him behave like a pig, and he could boot her for the way she droops over the memory of her dead husband: but at the same time there is a kind of purity about her withdrawal that somehow ought to console him, although he does everything to wreck it ... The relationship thickens with hostility. Sometimes a love-making works, but she generally manages to make him feel that he has assaulted her. They begin to have a gruelling power over each other, but it is a power only to give pain; they make demands of each other that are cruel because they can't be met, can't be communicated, can't even be defined in themselves.

A more intuitive verdict on the film was delivered by the actor Kenneth Williams, who kept a secret and vitriolic record of his daily life. He was more gracious about his fellow actors than the film's director. On Saturday, 9 February 1963, Williams's diary notes:

> Went to see early showing of *This Sporting Life* with Rachel Roberts. She is marvellous. Richard Harris is superb in it too. He is unquestionably a star. I haven't seen it in him before. You really care. I didn't stay to the end tho' 'cos the direction of the film was so awful. Expect it will get rave notices from the posh critics in the Sundays.

Not just the Sundays. Lindsay Anderson was informed his film was to receive a prestige screening at that year's Cannes Film Festival and his leading man a Best Actor Palme d'Or.

Harris, however, had a more pressing engagement on his mind: the birth of his third child. On 15 May, the day of the award ceremony, an overdue Elizabeth finally went into labour. A few minutes after arriving at a London nursing home, she gave birth to an eight-and-a-half-pound baby boy, Jamie. There was just time for her husband to catch the late-afternoon flight to Nice. Thirty-seven years to the day later, and after his brief flirtation with rock music, Jamie Harris would also be praised by the Cannes judges for his part in a low-budget American film, *Fast Food Fast Women*.

For a while, at least, Harris was holding Hollywood at arm's length. A £100,000 offer from Anthony Mann to play Commodus opposite Alec Guinness's Marcus Aurelius in *The Fall of the Roman Empire* met with a tentative acceptance. There were hot-tempered and ill-mannered rows with the director, who surprisingly agreed to his star's demand that several of his scenes be rewritten. When the new pages arrived Harris was still not happy and walked off the picture. His place was fortuitously taken by Christopher Plummer, who would later replace Harris in his estranged wife's life.

One film Harris did make that summer was *The Red Desert*, a part he was offered only days after its director, Michelangelo Antonioni, had seen the *Sporting Life* premiere at Cannes. Financed as a French–Italian co-production, it would star Monica Vitti as Giuliana, a woman trying to cope with her neurosis in the face of a modernised and mechanical society. After a car crash, Giuliana is hospitalised with a nervous breakdown and attempts suicide. Her engineer husband fails to notice or understand her inner suffering and his wife finally seeks solace in the arms of a businessman, Corrado Zeller, played by Harris.

Italy was a bigger disappointment than Tahiti. When Harris arrived in Rome he was unaware that Antonioni spoke little English and he faced the unique experience of being directed with a series of mimes and guttural Italian expletives. Another distraction was Antonioni's habit of arriving on set with an 'actor' he had recruited on a street corner or whose face fascinated him across a restaurant and whom he insisted on including in a previously rehearsed scene. Through his disillusion, Harris conceded that the director was a autocratic genius, 'but quite mad'. Elizabeth, who arrived a month later, found Antonioni fascinating for quite a different reason: 'His skin was the colour of parchment. His whole personality reminded me of old parchment. It was as if all life had dried up within him.'

Working on *The Red Desert* was frustrating and boring, and Harris sought excitement elsewhere in the Italian capital. One evening in Rome the boredom of the day's filming appeared to be resisting Harris's usual attempts at obliteration. The drink just wasn't working. Someone was handing round LSD and the actor swilled down a pill with another glass of whisky. The urge to 'fly' over to the Vatican and visit the Pope was suddenly all that mattered, but first Harris needed somewhere from which to 'take off' – like the top of the city's Piazza Trevvi fountain.

Early the next morning, hung over from the booze and still scrambled from the drug, Harris staggered into his bathroom. A worn, red-eyed and puffy face glared aggressively back at him from the mirror. Harris let him have it right between the eyes. And then on the jaw. And another to the nose. The bastard had disappeared in a spray of glass splinters and pumping blood.

CHAPTER SIX

Harris had finally swapped the dirty brown and cream paintwork and the greasy net curtains of Stratford East's Café L'Ange for the likes of Leicester Square's Pickwick Club. His generation of actors was finally coming of age. And, when they tired of the glitz and the publicity, there was always a backroom of the Salisbury pub in St Martin's Lane. Some nights there would be as many as five of Britain's leading young actors, all riding their own particular wave and doing their best to get drunk.

Harris was determined to live the life of the stars he was now drinking with – even though it frequently meant losing the respect of those he employed. The minimum £100,000 fee his agent was now demanding for each of his client's films required a suitably impressive wardrobe and lifestyle, including a succession of chauffeur-driven Rolls-Royces. His drivers could cope with Harris's habit of kissing them goodnight. But the flurry of early morning epithets and obscenities – invariably followed by a kick up the arse when they failed to open the car door fast enough – proved too much. Most lasted no more than a month.

CHAPTER SIX

In Europe an actor is an artist. In Hollywood, if he isn't working, he's a bum.

— Anthony Quinn

The telephone rang in Bedford Gardens. From what seemed like the far end of a long cardboard tube, a man's voice said: 'Richard has collapsed, he's in hospital.'

It took a second or two for Elizabeth Harris to understand what Jerry Bresler was saying: 'Richard collapsed with severe exhaustion and was rushed to hospital,' explained the producer of *Major Dundee*. Harris had flown to Hollywood to meet the cast and start rehearsals, unaware just how debilitating the drink and drugs and the five-thousand-mile flight could be. 'Don't worry, he's been sedated and he's sleeping like a baby. He'll be fine in a couple of days.'

There was no need for Elizabeth to be with her husband, reassured Bresler. She could meet him as planned when the crew moved to Mexico the following month.

A few minutes later, the telephone rang again. This time it was Harris calling from his Californian hospital bed. 'Why haven't you called to see how I am?' he demanded.

'But I've only just heard,' said Elizabeth, taken aback by her husband's fury and obscene abuse.

'Well it isn't fucking good enough,' bellowed Harris. 'It isn't fucking good enough at all.'

The ten-week shooting schedule for *Major Dundee* was already running late and under pressure, not all of it down to Harris's late arrival from Italy and his subsequent hospitalisation. There were serious problems with the script. 'If we can't get it right after five and a half months in the typewriter,' complained the film's star, Charlton Heston, 'then how are we going to get it right in front of the camera?'

Part of the problem was Heston's clout. As one of Hollywood's top five bankable stars, he was readily granted the final say by Columbia Studios over the script and cast, and even the choice of director. It was Heston who championed Harris for the role of the flamboyant Confederate cavalry captain Benjamin Tyreen and who demanded Sam Peckinpah as director. He would find himself at odds with both men, but at script stage he was clashing with Peckinpah over the director's 'artistic interpretation' of the story.

Dundee was conceived as a rough and ready Western, which follows an attempt by a US cavalry detachment to track down and annihilate a band of marauding Indians. Peckinpah continued to believe he was making a movie that dealt with the back issues of the American Civil War; his employers at Columbia wanted nothing more than a 'money-making cowboy-and-Indian story'; Heston, forever the technician, thought the story was just too complicated.

When the cast finally assembled in Los Angeles, Peckinpah decided to claw back a little time by rehearsing the script with stage-style readthroughs. Only Harris and James Coburn had performed in the theatre. Heston found the rehearsals 'a little like masturbation – pleasant enough, but not much use'.

Major Dundee was not only Harris's first Western, but was also the first time he would be forced to spend weeks in the saddle. The expected discomfort failed to surface and the actor's laid-back attitude increasingly began to irritate Heston. Heston insisted his fellow actors – 'arrive on time, be ready, and just bloody well do it'. Sick of Heston's perpetual clock-watching, Harris hung an alarm clock around his neck and set it to go off just as he stepped on to the set.

As ever, Heston was keeping a diary. After one particularly exasperating day's filming he wrote of Harris, 'He is more professional Irishman than Irish professional.'

Several years later, in his autobiography, *In the Arena*, Heston attempted to make amends. 'All Irishmen, particularly the actors, are very good at being Irish,' he wrote. 'Richard is one of these. He is both witty and funny. (What's the difference? I'd say wit is a matter of brains, funny is attitude.) He also has a fine native gift, which he's honed consistently ever since he began, in a wide variety of roles, in both film and on stage – the best test of all. I've seen him on stage; he's an actor.'

Off set and out of earshot, Harris voiced his own view of his leading man: 'The trouble with Charlton is that he never thinks he is just another hired actor like the rest of us. He thinks he is the entire production.'

Another actor who found Heston's domineering attitude hard to take was James Coburn, whom Peckinpah had personally recommended for the part of Samuel Potts, the one-armed scout. 'I thought I was going to work with an icon,' admitted Coburn. 'Instead I found myself bullied by a tyrant.' Not surprisingly, Coburn found a ready friend in his rebellious Irish co-star, two years his junior.

There were other professional similarities that brought the two men together: they were both, early in their careers, dedicated Stanislavski students; they made their first film within six months of each other; and, six years later, they were both working on their tenth film. The breakthrough movie in both their careers had been World War Two epics: Harris with *The Guns of Navarone* and Coburn with *The Great Escape*. Privately, both men shared an impish sense of humour and a lust for retribution.

Harris and Coburn would spend hours thinking up devious plots to humiliate Heston. By the time each plan was perfected and suitable props acquired, it was outpaced by a still more dastardly scheme. When the pair started asking the crew where they could get hold of a rattlesnake it was time for their director to step in. Peckinpah summoned the two actors to his caravan. 'I was never much good at discipline and the thought of giving these guys, especially two men as tall and fit as Dickie and Jim, a dressing down filled me with dread,' recalled Peckinpah. Harris and Coburn shuffled in and stood side by side like naughty schoolboys. 'I started telling them how important Charlton Heston was to the picture and how they owed him some respect. Suddenly Jim flashed his famous grin at me and I knew I was in trouble. When Dickie started giggling it was all over. By the time I said, "Thank you, gentlemen. I'll see you on the set," they had collapsed on the floor, gasping for breath and with tears streaming down their faces.'

Elizabeth Harris flew out to join her husband in Mexico. During a spring break in filming the couple rented a house in Cuernavaca, 37 miles south of Mexico City and on the foothills of Mount Ajusco. It was not long before Elizabeth was introduced to James Coburn and primed for her first encounter with 'Chuckles', the pair's nickname for Heston.

One day Coburn suggested he treat the Harrises to an afternoon at a Mexico City bullfight. Before the trio took their seats in the whitewashed and slightly grubby Plaza de Toros, Harris insisted on buying a bag of boiled sweets. 'The first bullfight was a disaster,' recalled Coburn. 'The bull was enormous and angry and the matador turned coward and fled the ring followed by everything the crowd could throw at him: food, fruit, cushions from the seats; even personal things like hats and shoes and handbags.' To the three nonaficionados the display of disapproval was chaotic and comical. Not so the man in front of us, adds Coburn. In response to their laughter, 'he turned round and ranted something about not showing the fight enough respect.'

When the laughter continued the Mexican took aim at Harris's bag of sweets, scattering its contents. 'Did you see that?' An indignant Harris appealed to the crowd around him. 'Did you see what that fellow has done to my sweets?'

Sympathy among the spectators was divided. The Mexican's abuse and Harris's demands for an apology and a new bag of sweets were met with equal support and scepticism. The stalemate was finally broken, adds Coburn, when Harris landed a 'perfect right-hander' on the Mexican's chin and the crowd roared with approval.

Back at Cuernavaca, the rest of the holiday progressed more peacefully. The weather was cool and pleasant and Harris seemed to be making an honest effort to spend time with his family.

In England, and buoyed by the critical if not financial success of *This Sporting Life*, Lindsay Anderson persuaded David Storey to start work on *Wuthering Heights*. United Artists read the first draft and backed off. But Harris's Hollywood credit rating was rising fast. While he was working on *Major Dundee*, the Academy of Motion Picture Arts and Sciences announced that both Harris and Rachel Roberts had been nominated for a 1964 Oscar for their parts in *This Sporting Life*. In March Arthur Krim at United Artists telephoned Anderson and asked if the script to *Wuthering Heights* was still available. The Englishman immediately flew to New York and shook hands on the deal.

Anderson's voice bubbled with excitement as he telephoned the news to the holidaying Harris, who immediately invited him down to Mexico to celebrate. The flight from New York only rarefied Anderson's enthusiasm. Harris greeted him at the airport with open arms and a slap on the back. That night when the director retired to his Cuernavaca guestroom he found a handwritten note on his pillow: 'I am Heathcliff.'

For the next two weeks Harris concentrated on relaxing while Anderson attempted to get him to do 'a bit of work' on the script. The pair also discussed the stage production of *Julius Caesar*, with Harris as Mark Antony, which had already been booked into the Royal Court for that coming November.

When Harris's break was over he left for Hollywood to complete the final scenes for *Major Dundee* and start work on a John Huston epic, *The Bible*. Funded by American and Italian money, *The Bible* (subtitled *In the Beginning*) promised, at least at its inception, to be an exciting and imaginative project. Eleven Old Testament stories would be scripted by different writers and directed by a host of smart names: Cartier Bresson for the Creation, followed by Visconti, Welles, Fellini, *et al*. In the end it turned out to be an Old Testament epic like any other with John Huston directing the entire film and reading the narration and making an appearance as Noah. Most critics could not wait for it to end. 'The episodes are diffusely long, tediously slow, and depressingly reverent,' reported the British Film Institute, adding, 'The Cain episode at least derives a certain bizarre quality from Richard Harris's epileptic acting.'

Anderson had flown back to England with 'marks of emotional fatigue clearly showing under the eyes'. In London he fretted over Harris's extended absence and his apparent coolness for the second of the Royal Court trilogies. Over the next few months Harris repeatedly refused to sign a contract or make a firm commitment. Anderson pressed ahead and opened auditions for *Julius Caesar* on the same September day his star landed at Heathrow. Two weeks into rehearsals Harris quit. He was taking up a Hollywood offer of a part in the George Roy Hill-directed *Hawaii*.

Heartbroken and betrayed, Anderson locked himself away and refused to speak to anyone. 'Richard's departure was a shattering blow for Lindsay,' recalls the stage director Anthony Page. 'He even asked me to drive him past Richard's London house one night to see if the lights were on and Richard was at home.' Harris was eventually replaced by Nicol Williamson.

Anderson's infatuation with Harris, like the star's interest in *Wuthering Heights*, was all but dead. 'Richard didn't really want to work with Lindsay again,' concluded David Storey. 'And it was probably a good thing the film was never made – could any producer have coped with the two of them?'

Reading the Daniel Taradash and Dalton Trumbo script for *Hawaii*, Richard Harris found himself fascinated by the conceit and vain self-importance of his character. 'Rafer Hoxworth embraces and lives life in style,' said Harris. 'Living life to the fullest because you only have it once.' It was *The Ginger Man* all over again. For Harris the making of *Hawaii* was unlike any other film he had worked on. For Elizabeth Harris the paradise of the Pacific islands would become a boozy and bloody ordeal.

Based on a third of James A Michener's immense novel of the same name, the action spans twenty years and follows the life of a pious Yale divinity student who attempts to convert the natives of the Hawaiian

Islands to Christianity. Ironically, United Artists offered the part of the Protestant missionary Abner Hale to the Swedish actor Max von Sydow – who had just finished playing Christ in the four-hour epic *The Greatest Story Ever Told*. Hale's arranged and unwilling wife is played by Julie Andrews, anxious to shed her goody-goody Mary Poppins image with a serious, nonmusical role, and whose character is secretly in love with Harris's Rafer Hoxworth, a rugged New England sea captain. To her dismay, the only song Andrews agreed to sing – the lullaby 'My Wishing Doll' – was nominated for a Best Song Oscar.

To save money and cut back on the actors' contractual time, most films are shot out of sequence and edited and completed weeks or months later. Hawaii would be shot page by page according to the script and more or less chronologically as the twenty-year story unfolded. The majority of the movie would be filmed in Honolulu during the summer of 1965.

Location shooting began almost eight thousand miles away in Sturbridge Village, a reconstructed 1800s town-museum in southwestern Massachusetts. The film company paid $10,000 a day to keep the public off the site. It needn't have bothered. A late winter snowstorm brought New England to a standstill, forcing the cast and crew to crawl north from New York in a fleet of cars and lorries.

To Elizabeth, with her three young children and their nanny in tow, it seemed she had been living the life of a glorified camp follower. After weeks of hotel suites she could, at last, look forward to a couple of months of unhurried luxury.

By late April, they were on their way to Honolulu after a brief Hollywood stopover. The fashionable mansion United Artists hired for the Harrises was on Diamond Head Road at the far end of Waikiki. It had its own tennis courts and swimming pool and a small army of attentive servants. None of this seemed to impress Harris, whose drunken moods – fuelled by Mai Tais, a lethal local cocktail of rum, Cointreau and Grenadine – arrived home each day as predictably as the late-afternoon clouds over the nearby Diamond Head Crater.

Roger Hutchinson, the British-born manager of a nearby hotel, recalls the frightening experience of watching the star lose control. 'Any attempt to suggest he might have had enough was met with a vicious and embarrassing torrent of offensive oaths,' says Hutchinson. 'Once, when Harris could not even stand up, I offered to help him to his car. He took a swing at me. After that I contacted the film company and asked them to inform Mr Harris he was not welcome any more.'

There were other fights and other bans and, as one member of the cast remembers, 'Richard was not the most pleasant person to be with.' When Harris's patience with the film – or with his wife's evident reluctance to fight back – snapped, he had a unique and dangerous way of venting his frustration.

A few years earlier in Spain a drunken Harris had leaped from a taxi and, after dodging traffic on a main road, attacked a solid oak door with his fists and feet. The assault momentarily slackened when an elderly resident opened the door, dragged out a chair, relocked the door, and sat down to watch this apparently demented stranger smash his extremities to a bloody pulp.

In Honolulu the nearest target was a stream of oncoming traffic on Diamond Head Road. Drivers brave enough to approach too close were sworn at and abused and their cars pummelled and punched. When the demon within was eventually exhausted Harris would drag himself back to Elizabeth, his skinned knuckles and gashed hands dripping with blood.

One night an exhausted Harris returned to the mansion to find his wife on the telephone. 'What the fuck are you up to?' he demanded. Elizabeth was pleading with a local hospital to send a doctor and an ambulance without notifying the police. His face tightened. With each step towards her, Harris clenched and unclenched his fists. Elizabeth was saved from yet another beating only when Frank Harper, Harris's film stand-in, managed to get between the couple. Blinded by rage, the actor lashed out at his one-time drinking companion. It was an uneven fight. Harper fought back the best he could, knowing that any damage he caused to Harris's face would almost certainly lead to his dismissal from the film.

On more than one occasion, Elizabeth thought of flying home. 'I felt we were being irrevocably forced apart by emotional chaos,' she later admitted. 'My own grip on any emotion except fear was tentative.' Their relationship, just when the ambition and hard work were paying off, was, at least for Elizabeth, taking on nightmare proportions. 'Richard had success and fame,' she said. 'We had money. We had three healthy children. Yet my only thought was how I could keep out of his way.'

Things were also going wrong on the set of *Hawaii*. After five months the $12 million picture was weeks over schedule and seriously over budget. Part of the problem was that director, George Roy Hill, was unintentionally neglecting his stars by spending too much time coaching and rehearsing the untrained Polynesian extras. To resolve the problem Walter Mirisch, the producer, flew out from Hollywood and ended up firing Hill. The final weeks of shooting were directed by Arthur Hiller.

A couple of years later Harris would also make a 'silent' appearance in *The Hawaiians*, a film based on the second half of Michener's generation novel and sequel to *Hawaii*: in the second film, Harris's character's grandson is played by Charlton Heston and a portrait of his ancestor – modelled on Harris – hangs in one of the interior sets.

Ben Fisz ran his fingers along the line of books. He was searching the biography section of the public library in London's South Audley Street for material on Orde Wingate, the maverick World War Two general. What caught his eye was the spine of a book called *Skis Against the Atom*.

The producer flipped through the pages. With each paragraph Fisz became more convinced he was making the wrong film. *Skis Against the Atom* was written by Norwegian Knut Haukelid, who took part in the World War Two raids that destroyed Hitler's chances of producing the first atom bomb. Two previous raids on the hydroelectric plant at Rjukan by British commandos and American bombers had failed. Haukelid's story was a first-person account of a sabotage mission in which a handful of resistance fighters succeeded in blowing up the German supply of heavy water, an essential component in early nuclear reactors.

Himself a World War Two Polish air force fighter ace, Ben Fisz was accustomed to backing long shots and overcoming setbacks. He quietly bought the film rights to the book from its author, still a serving officer in the Norwegian army, and hired a writer to work up a screen treatment. On the day the typescript was delivered, Fisz walked into a nearby bookshop to discover that a new book on the guerrilla action – *But For These Men* – was about to be published. Worse still, the film rights to the new book had already been sold to Walt Disney.

By chance, Walt Disney arrived in London a week or so later. Fisz arranged a meeting at the American movie mogul's hotel. 'Disney said that as I had already put so much time and money into the project, he would relinquish his rights,' recalled Fisz. 'It was an extremely rare and gracious thing to do.'

The next step was to find a director. In Madrid, and putting the finishing touches to *The Fall of the Roman Empire* was Anthony Mann. After serving as an assistant director to the brilliant Preston Sturges on *Sullivan's Travels*, Mann spent the 1940s and early 1950s making cheap B-movie dramas, thrillers and musicals, most of which Harris would watch from the front row circle of Limerick's Savoy, Carlton and Grand cinemas. A copy of both books and the initial treatment were sent out to Spain, where the director declared himself 'thrilled at the project's potential' – but dubious at just how 'such a story could be filmed'.

With tentative offers of finance from the Rank Organisation and Allied Artists, Mann and screenwriter Ben Barzman set off for Rjukan, a hundred and fifty miles from Oslo. 'The place had hardly changed since the war,' said Mann. 'The factory was almost buried in the mountains in a huge gorge, like an eagle's eyrie. A suspension bridge, the only link between the factory and civilisation, had been built after the American bombing. The river beneath it flowed down to Lake Tinnsjo where the ferry carried the heavy water on its way to Germany.

'At that moment I knew we could film the story. I could see it all photographed,' added Mann. The expedition also gave him a title – *The Heroes of Telemark*.

The Norwegian government gave Mann permission to shoot inside the massive factory, still in operation and selling heavy water to a carefully guarded list of customers. Even the mountain huts, used by the saboteurs to hide from German ski troops, were still in use by the local reindeer hunters.

Mann returned to London to discover that Allied Artists, the film's US distributor, had pulled out of the deal. With his cases still packed from Norway, he caught the next flight to New York and persuaded Columbia Pictures to step in.

Even before the £2 million film became a certainty, Fisz and Mann agreed on the two actors they wanted to head the cast. 'There really was no argument about Richard Harris,' said the producer. 'We both had Richard in mind even before we admitted it to each other. He was big and brash and looked as though he might well have been a war hero given the chance.' Harris would play Knut Straud, the leader of the demolition party. To take on the role of Dr Rolf Pedersen, the Norwegian scientist who first warned the Allies against the Nazi atomic threat, the pair approached Kirk Douglas. The 49-year-old actor immediately accepted, despite a preshooting 'artistic clash' six years earlier, which ended with Mann's sacking as first-choice director of the Oscar-winning *Spartacus*.

The pairing of two such well-known actors attracted the inevitable press speculation and their alleged clashes have since passed into show-business mythology. Harris, whose boundary lines on his personal map of truth and falsehood were never marked with flapping flags, quoted their first meeting in the lounge of a Los Angeles hotel. The film's executives and stars were gathering prior to the unit's departure for Norway. When Douglas caught the Irishman studying him across the room, he mentally chewed over Harris's hard-man reputation and called out, 'Don't believe a word of it.' Harris claimed he rose to his feet and hollered back, 'Hold it, Kirk! Do you want it now, or shall we step across the river into Texas?'

Harris's memory appears to have been as suspect as his geography. In fact, in an unpublished interview not long before his sudden death in 1967, Anthony Mann claimed Harris and Douglas did not exchange their 'hard and chilly' handshake until the hundred-strong cast and crew assembled in Oslo. The next eight weeks, recalled the director, were like 'working on the slopes of an angry volcano'. There were no squabbles over close-ups, no demands for script rewrites, and no nose-to-nose stand-offs. Both actors completed the film with 'professional respect and mutual distrust', said Mann. 'They did not meet socially. I don't think it would have occurred to either of them to spend time in each other's company. They were different animals.' Harris was less coy about Douglas: 'We just didn't get on.'

Late in 1965, *Nova* magazine proclaimed Harris to be 'the next of the big international stars. He could be the biggest of them all.' It was an accolade won mainly for his role in *Telemark* and a tribute that left him feeling wrong-footed and defensive. Harris had enjoyed the mountains and the snow-covered slopes and the physical demands of the Rjukan valley location and, best of all, playing the part of a real hero. But, he told *Nova*, he would much rather be playing Shakespeare or *Wuthering Heights* than be an action star. 'That's my Calvary,' he complained. 'That is where I am crucified as an actor, action films are the actor's burden. They drive you mad and they drive you to drink.'

It was a statement made purely for public consumption. Harris's passion for acting was being diluted by a new and far more hedonistic devotion – 'grabbing life by the balls and having fun'.

One of the first victims was his marriage. The Bedford Gardens house was fast becoming a drunken battleground of broken promises and empty, tearful nights. It was obvious to Elizabeth that her husband was seeing other women; there were sexual encounters and one-night stands too short to be dignified by calling them affairs. When she felt brave enough to confront her husband, Elizabeth could do little but allow his self-righteous anger to engulf first her, and then the house, like some dark and dangerous whirlwind. 'His wrath was short-lived while it lasted,' she recalls, 'but it was rough.'

A cold and lonely fear was filling the void between them. Like their

Earl's Court flat and then Allan House, their latest home was filling with faceless, annoying and ever-present strangers who paid neither Elizabeth nor her property the respect either of them deserved. 'So many of the people around Richard now were sycophants and cadgers,' said Elizabeth. 'Actors are surrounded by people who make a living out of them, it isn't surprising that actors sometimes lose sight of themselves.'

Harris had finally swapped the dirty brown and cream paintwork and the greasy net curtains of Stratford East's Café L'Ange for the likes of Leicester Square's Pickwick Club. His generation of actors was finally coming of age. 'We were all mates, raving it up around the pubs and clubs,' recalls Michael Caine. 'Everyone in my crowd seemed to be coming into prominence at about the same time.' And, when they tired of the glitz and the publicity, there was always a backroom of the Salisbury pub in St Martin's Lane. Some nights there would be as many as five of Britain's leading young actors, all riding their own particular wave and doing their best to get drunk: Harris, fêted for his Oscar-nominated performance in *This Sporting Life*; Peter O'Toole, who had earned his own Academy nomination for *Lawrence of Arabia*; Albert Finney, who was about to win a BAFTA for *Saturday Night and Sunday Morning*; Terence Stamp, another Oscar nominee for *Billy Budd*; and Michael Caine, whose appearance in *Zulu* launched his international career.

Harris was determined to live the life of the stars he was now drinking with – even though it frequently meant losing the respect of those he employed. The minimum £100,000 fee his agent was now demanding for each of his client's films required a suitably impressive wardrobe and lifestyle, including a succession of chauffeur-driven Rolls-Royces. His drivers could cope with Harris's habit of kissing them goodnight. But the flurry of early-morning epithets and obscenities – invariably followed by a kick up the arse when they failed to open the car door fast enough – proved too much. Most lasted no more than a month.

All this Elizabeth watched with growing disdain and disrespect. To his friends, or at least those who noticed her, she remained the devoted wife. Inside, her husband was no longer the 'priority in my life'.

There were flashes of guilt for Harris. Aware of the harm his drunken insensitivity was inflicting on his marriage, Harris would book himself into a London hotel. It was the physical and mental distance they needed. If he was away filming, they would fall into a polite telephone relationship, which centred on the children and gave hope of a new start. It never lasted.

No matter how hard Harris tried, their evenings out invariably ended in a ruckus or brawl. One night the Harrises were dining at Mirabelle's, the Mayfair restaurant. They were soon joined by the writer and film producer David Newman. When the conversation turned to politics, Harris and Newman exchanged a few verbal blows before going outside. Brandishing his damaged thumb, Harris would later say, 'I got that hitting David Newman. As he came at me I stepped aside and handed him off rugby style with my fist. He went down with a thud and I had to take him to the wash room to look after him.'

One night in January 1966, the Harrises attended a dinner party given by the writer Ivan Moffat. Among the guests was Princess Margaret. Another was Robin Douglas-Home, a nephew of the last Conservative prime minister before Labour came to power two years earlier. A rather foppish socialite, Robin Douglas-Home had written a well-received biography of Frank Sinatra and was currently earning a living – or at least enough to fund his compulsive gambling – as a newspaper columnist and playing piano in various nightclubs.

Elizabeth found herself drawn to this 'supreme advocate of Annabel's and Ascot'. When Douglas-Home invited her to tea at the Ritz, she agreed. After nine years of living in her husband's pocket, an illicit afternoon with a man whose appearance and values were so different seemed strangely exciting. 'He was,' recalls Elizabeth in her autobiography, 'amusing, attentive and what was more important he found me attractive – and wasn't afraid to say so.'

The pair were soon 'unsuitable' lovers, attempting to lead an 'unhappy' double life. If Harris had been out of the country or away filming, it would have been easier. The affair ended when Elizabeth lent her lover £2,000 to pay off his dangerously overdue debt to a London casino, but not before her husband's suspicions were aroused. Harris would demand to know where she was going and where she had been. The questions continued long after the relationship petered out. One day, when the pressure became unbearable and Harris demanded to know the truth, Elizabeth confessed.

CHAPTER SEVEN

'You know they want to film *Camelot*?' said Harris.

Laurence Harvey said he did. In fact he had wanted to play King Arthur on screen since Moss Hart, the American playwright, gave him a copy of TH White's novel *The Once and Future King*, on which the musical was based.

'I want the part,' said Harris, turning to face Harvey. 'Arthur, I want it. It's mine.'

Since the stage success of *Camelot*, Harvey had taken it for granted he would be first in line for the movie lead. He poured himself another glass of champagne, purposely ignoring his visitor. 'I didn't know you were interested,' he said.

'Well, I am,' snapped Harris. 'So keep your fucking hands off. King Arthur's mine.'

Before Harvey could protest, the dressing room door slammed shut. It was the last time Laurence Harvey and Richard Harris spoke, and one of the final times they were ever in the same room together.

CHAPTER SEVEN

Actors ought to be larger than life, you come across quite enough
ordinary, nondescript people in daily life and I don't see why you
should be subjected to them on the stage too.
                                                    – Donald Sinden

Laurence Harvey sat back in his dressing room armchair and lit a
cigarette. Beside him, on a small table, were the remains of two newly
laid hard-boiled eggs and a half-slice of dark rye bread. It was a ritual.
Three times a week between the matinée and evening performances of
Camelot, his chauffeur would deliver and serve the snack while the actor
prepared to greet his admirers.

The walls of Harvey's Drury Lane theatre dressing room were pasted
with good-luck notes and congratulatory messages. His favourite was
from Richard Burton. The telegram, which Harvey insisted on reading to
every visiting journalist, informed him that, had Burton been able to
name his successor to play King Arthur, it would have been Harvey.

The musical's London run was proving as successful as its Broadway
run. Ticket presales ensured its financial success, and Harvey, whose
gauche style of acting had been overtaken of late, found his flagging
career on the up. Acting luminaries – such as Noël Coward, Kirk
Douglas, Natalie Wood and the Romulus Films founders James and John
Woolf – had become regular callers at the Drury Lane dressing room.
One Wednesday, Harvey relaxed in his white towelling robe, unaware
that his confidence and reputation were about to be shattered – by one
of his closest friends.

Richard Harris did not wait for his knock to be answered. Harvey
greeted his friend with a smile and a glass of champagne. The pair had
remained close since *The Long and the Short and the Tall*. Their drinking
had also progressed considerably since their lunchtime sessions in the
Red Lion. One friend to both men recalls a game the pair would
frequently play which involved walking from bar to bar and downing a
different drink in each. There were only two rules: you were allowed to
order and knock back a particular type of drink only once, although
different types of beer – lager, bitter, stout – were allowed (cocktails were

forbidden); and you could not use any form of transport – the contestants must be capable of walking to the next pub or club or bar. The last man standing was the winner. Given Harris's ever-growing acquaintance with London drinking establishments, the challenge often ran well into the night, starting at regular pubs, moving on to nightclubs and, when they closed, to all-night drinking clubs. One marathon session started at lunchtime, went through the night and found the pair still drinking at dawn at one of Harris's old Covent Garden haunts.

Harris and Harvey had also developed a mental telepathy for mischief: the same mischievous thought would often occur to both men at the same time. Joan Cohn, who many years later would marry Laurence Harvey, remembers a Palm Springs Easter Eve party.

About twenty of us had gone out to dinner and returned to our house. I was wearing a yellow silk Givenchy dress and pearls and diamond earrings – in those days you wore the real thing. Larry and Richard were standing talking by the deep end of the pool. I went over to them and without a word to each other, or any kind of sign, they suddenly caught me and threw me in. On the way down I told myself, 'I mustn't come up angry.' Larry and Richard jumped in fully clothed and the three of us swam around the pool chatting.

In the Drury Lane dressing room, Harris suddenly became defensive. Turning his back on his friend, he began reading the wall of good-will messages. 'You know they want to film *Camelot*?' said Harris.

Harvey said he did. In fact he had wanted to play King Arthur on screen since Moss Hart, the American playwright, gave him a copy of TH White's novel *The Once and Future King*, on which the musical was based.

'I want the part,' said Harris, turning to face Harvey. 'Arthur, I want it. It's mine.'

Since the stage success of *Camelot*, Harvey had taken it for granted he would be first in line for the movie lead. He poured himself another glass of champagne, purposely ignoring his visitor. 'I didn't know you were interested,' he said.

'Well, I am,' snapped Harris. 'So keep your fucking hands off. King Arthur's mine.'

Before Harvey could protest, the dressing room door slammed shut. It was the last time Laurence Harvey and Richard Harris spoke, and one of the final times they were ever in the same room together.

Harris's pursuit of the Camelot role was obsessive and relentless. 'Camelot got under my skin,' he confessed.

To direct *Camelot*, Warner Bros hired Joshua Logan. One of the industry's most successful and gifted theatre directors, the 59-year-old American had made his first film in 1938, and had since earned two Academy Award nominations. He now specialised in musicals and had a string of Broadway hits to his name, including *South Pacific*, *Annie Get Your Gun* and *The World of Suzie Wong*. Although Logan was brilliantly sensitive to the needs and demands of his actors, his career would ultimately be blighted by his connection with three large-budget and unwieldy screen musicals. The first, in 1958, was *South Pacific*, in which Logan employed a series of colour filters that gave the overlong movie a sickly, jaundiced appearance. For the about-to-be-made *Camelot*, Logan's biggest fault would be his failure to rethink the Lerner and Loewe Broadway hit cinematically enough, leaving it irredeemably stagebound. Still a year away was his $17 million flop *Paint Your Wagon*.

Logan flew in to London to begin casting Camelot and was immediately contacted by Harris's agent. 'I had not seen anything in any of Richard's previous works to recommend him for the part of Arthur,' the director admitted. 'And I told his agent so.' The next morning a telegram was delivered to Logan's suite at Claridge's. It read, 'ONLY HARRIS FOR ARTHUR.'

The next morning the newspapers carried a story that Richard Burton, the original stage Arthur, was being tipped for the film role. By midday a second telegram had arrived: 'HARRIS BETTER THAN BURTON.'

White's novel – which retells the story of King Arthur and his Knights of the Round Table – is made up of four books. The rights to the opening book, *The Sword in the Stone*, had already been acquired by the Disney studio, so Lerner and Loewe bought the rights to the three remaining books. *Camelot*, which deals with Arthur's later years and the love triangle between the king, Queen Guinevere and Sir Lancelot, opened at Broadway's Majestic Theatre on 3 December 1960, with Richard Burton making his musical debut as King Arthur and Julie Andrews, a personal friend of TH White, as Guinevere. It closed little more than two years later after a run of 873 performances.

The film of *Camelot*, the latest $15 million Warner Bros musical, was being personally produced by Jack Warner who, four years earlier, had rejected Julie Andrews in favour of Audrey Hepburn for *My Fair Lady*. Warner let it be known he was seriously considering Andrews for the role of Guinevere. Along with the *Camelot*, script rumours reached Harris that Warner had also approached Richard Burton to play King Arthur. A second story, this time picked up by the trade press, claimed that to pay Warner back for his previous miscalculation Andrews was holding out for a reported $1,200,000 fee.

The pairing was not to be. Burton was in the middle of a succession of films with his wife Elizabeth Taylor and too busy to consider returning to *Camelot*. And Warner's interest in Julie Andrews was soon torpedoed by his own director. To transfer the musical from stage to screen, Logan had heavily reworked *Camelot* with its original creator, Alan Jay Lerner. When the producer voiced his preference for the female lead, Logan scoffed, 'Can you see two men and two armies going to war over Julie Andrews?'

Six days and as many telegrams later, Harris could stand it no more. Logan and his wife were about to sit down to breakfast when the Irishman burst into their suite. 'You've got to give me a test,' Harris demanded.

Unfazed, Logan took his place at the breakfast table. 'Look,' he said, tucking into his bacon and eggs. 'I don't want you. You wouldn't be right, so please go away.'

'Never,' said Harris.

The next evening, Logan was guest of honour at a cocktail party. Reaching out for a drink, he realised the waiter skilfully carrying the tray was Harris. 'Jesus,' Logan protested. 'Will you leave me alone, for Christ's sake?'

Harris politely handed him a drink. 'Never,' he said. 'Wherever you go, I'll be there. If you go to the toilet, I'll pop out of the bowl. If you catch a taxi, I'll jump in beside you. If you catch a plane, I'll be in the next seat. Just give me a test.'

Each morning the director took a pre-breakfast walk around London. The next morning he arrived in the Claridge's lobby to find Harris waiting for him. He looked as though he had been there all night. 'I'll tell you what,' offered the actor. 'I'll pay for my own test. It'll cost you nothing. Just test me.'

'OK,' conceded Logan. 'Now please go away.'

Richard and Elizabeth Harris were on everyone's 'must have' guest list. Those who didn't invite him as a friend or colleague did so hoping he might provide some unscheduled entertainment by disgracing himself. Although he never failed to make use of the bar or appreciate the fine wine, he was, more often than not, charming and respectful. A few days after his film test at Pinewood Studios the Harrises attended a dinner party hosted by the theatrical agent Joan Thring. The guest of honour was Thring's star client, Rudolf Nureyev, the 28-year-old Russian ballet dancer. It was not long before the couple were introduced to another guest, a flamboyantly dressed silver-haired man who, five years earlier, had given up accountancy to study astrology.

Patric Walker was urbane and intelligent and spoke with a refined New Jersey accent. He was, recalls Elizabeth, a 'man of volatile temperament and ricochet wit'. At various times gay or bisexual, Walker retrained as an astrologer after a warning from his fellow celestial interpreter Helene Hoskins that his life was 'on a downward spiral to hell'. He was surviving in London on what he could earn from private readings and the generosity of his lovers – among them Rudolf Nureyev.

But what really fascinated Harris was Walker's claim – unusual for an astrologer – that destiny did not exist, that everyone was capable of directing their own lives. Before the party broke up Harris made an appointment for a private consultation.

A *Camelot* offer had still not arrived from Joshua Logan. When Harris confided his doubt to Walker, the astrologer told him not to worry, that King Arthur was his. 'How do you know that?' Harris demanded.

'I'm telling you,' reassured Walker. 'Mr Logan will go with you.'

Harris thought for a minute. 'The odds are against it.'

'If you want odds go to Ladbrokes,' said Walker. 'I'm an astrologer, not a bookmaker. I only deal in predictions.'

A day or so later, Harris's agent telephoned with the news that the actor was on his way to Hollywood and *Camelot*. Harris promptly telephoned Walker to invite him to America as his personal astrologer. He was determined to arrive on the west coast in style. A beautiful wife on his arm and a celestial guide in tow would provide the suitable panache. All three would sail for New York on the ageing Cunard liner *Queen Mary* before flying on to Los Angeles a week later.

Twenty years later Walker's syndicated star column would attract more than a billion readers, but on his first night out of Southampton, though, he failed to predict one of his new benefactor's brutal and violent mood swings.

The trio sat down to dinner after drinks at the purser's cocktail party. Harris, already more than a little drunk, became increasingly aggressive with each course. He was still brooding over Elizabeth's recent admission of adultery, and nothing was going to mollify his bellicose indignation. Walker, sensing something was going to blow, excused himself and headed for his stateroom.

Attempting to distract her husband's darkening anger and increasingly blue language, Elizabeth steered him towards the bar for after-dinner drinks. The ploy failed. That 'familiar marbled look' appeared in Harris's eyes and Elizabeth braced herself for the inevitable verbal battering. The ferocity of his attack – she was a 'slut' and a 'cheat' and a 'whore' – shocked both the bar staff and other passengers. 'There was this awful, frenzied, animal-like tone in his voice,' recalls one cocktail waiter. 'At that moment he was probably the most dangerous drunk I have encountered in forty years on passenger liners.'

Elizabeth turned and fled to Patric Walker's cabin, where she found the astrologer sitting up in bed reading a copy of *Nicholas and Alexandra*. 'Please let me stay and talk for a while,' she pleaded. At that moment the stateroom door was kicked open and Harris snorted his way in. Grabbing the astrologer by the lapels of his silk pyjamas, Harris dragged Walker out of bed and threw him, several feet above the carpet, across the room and against the far wall. From furniture to flower vases, from silver-framed photographs to clothes and curtains, Harris slowly and deliberately destroyed every item in the room. It was the most frightening experience of his life, Walker would admit to a friend shortly before his 1995 death from salmonella poisoning.

In the mid-1960s, Bel Air was considered as good as it gets in southern California. The area contained some of Los Angeles' largest and most elegant estates situated on winding, hilly streets. The Villa Vesco was a palatial house built on the crest of its own hilltop estate with magnificent views of the Pacific Ocean. Inside, the scenery was equally stunning. Genuine and very expensive paintings hung on every wall and seventeenth-century imported Italian ceilings gave the rooms, including the vast ballroom, a regal feel. It was also a place, as Elizabeth Harris recalls, where reality was never allowed to intrude. A little way down the valley, in the 20th Century-Fox studio, Doris Day was attempting to keep her own kind of reality at bay.

The Beatles had successfully invaded America; the Motown phenomenon was rolling back across the Atlantic; miniskirts were measured in inches; and the sexual revolution had taken over from the civil rights movement as the cause of the decade. Amid all of this, the wholesome and 'virginal' Doris Day was still the world's favourite film star.

Universally derided by the critics, who considered her platinum hair and freckles too cutesy, the American actress still attracted massive and loyal box office support. Above all, she was a stars' star: her own films had elevated the careers of an equal numbers of actors and revived some considered past their best. 'To appear with Doris Day could make your career,' admitted James Garner.

By 1966, the 42-year-old Day had to choose her own films very carefully and she had grave doubts about *Caprice* – 'Thank God I don't have to make movies like that any more.' As an inducement, Day's producer husband Marty Melcher suggested Richard Harris, who's *Sporting Life* performance she had admired, as co-star. Day promised to reread the screenplay of the spy spoof. Co-written by Jay Jayson and its director Frank Tashkin, the original script cast Harris as the agent, Pat Foster, out to avenge the murder of his father, and Day as the double-agent Christina White, sent to trap him. Somewhere in the chaotic script the writers included industrial espionage and a plot to smuggle drugs in cosmetic face powder. Day relented, on one condition: that the roles be reversed. Pat was changed to Patricia and Christopher became Christina.

Shooting started, but was brought to an abrupt halt when Harris collapsed on the set complaining of severe pains in his arms and chest. His second Hollywood breakdown. Everyone feared a heart attack, and an ambulance ferried the stricken actor to the emergency room at the Cedars of Lebanon Hospital. After ruling out a coronary, the doctors remained baffled until two days of tests pinpointed an inflamed gullet and a scarred oesophagus. Recovery, he was informed, depended on a sensible stress-free lifestyle and a drastic reduction in his alcohol consumption. Harris celebrated his near escape by getting drunk.

Filming restarted, but by the end neither star saw it as one of their better efforts. Day herself lost no opportunity to inform 20th Century-Fox it had backed a loser, classing *Caprice* among her other stinkers, *Where Were You When the Lights Went Out?*, *Ballad of Josie* and *Do Not Disturb*. 'There were good actors like Rod Taylor, Peter Graves and Richard Harris cast in them,' commented Day, 'but these poor men were the pearls cast before the swine of their scripts.' Her fans did not agree and the film at least broke even.

Caprice won little praise from the critics, and one dubbed it 'The Spy Who Came in from the Cold Cream'. After sitting through the Radio City Music Hall premiere, Judith Crist informed American viewers watching the *Today* show that the actress looked like an ageing transvestite. *Village Voice* described it as 'a long Day journey into naught'. And the *New York Morning Telegraph* regretted the arrival of 'another Day, another Doris'.

On the other side of the Atlantic, Richard Harris fared only marginally better. His performance 'seems understandably ill-at-ease' commented the British Film Institute's review, which went on to say:

> The incoherent and indeed barely comprehensible plot, which apparently baffled even the distributor's synopsis writer, is merely an excuse to enable the stars to project their respective sex appeal against a high-gloss background – Paris and the Swiss Alps, and a succession of expensive apartments topped only by the villain's HQ, which is decorated like the Rhode Island boudoir of the heroine's daffy mother in a Thirties screwball comedy ... One wonders what the director could have done with the same story a few years ago with Jerry Lewis, in or out of drag.

Harris always guarded his own privacy and respected that of his fellow actors. He seldom commented – at least not with any reverence – on his working relationships. When the film critic and show business writer Eric Braun contacted Harris to ask for help with his biography of Doris Day the actor refused to talk about his time making *Caprice* unless Braun produced a letter of permission from Day.

Long before *Caprice* was ready for release, Harris received news that Joshua Logan – who remained in Britain looking for a woman capable of sparking a war, or at least 'worth losing England over' – had finally found an actress capable of playing Queen Guinevere. Vanessa Redgrave, the militant actress daughter of Sir Michael Redgrave and Rachel Kempson, arrived for her first meeting with the director clutching an album of her records. 'I knew instantly she was right for the part,' Logan later confessed. 'I was aware of her social campaigning and her fiery nature. That was the Guinevere I wanted. She was also very beautiful, which didn't hurt.'

None of this impressed Laurence Harvey. He marked the partnership of 'dirty Richard Harris and that female impersonator' by getting drunk and narrowly escaping a court appearance.

To announce his arrival in the land of hype and to celebrate his elevation to the Hollywood peerage, Harris demanded that his inaugural party out-glitz the season's best. Everything had to be perfect. Every detail double-checked. Every one of the 350 invitations re-evaluated daily to ensure the recipient's industry and star status placed him or her on the correct rung of the night's two-tier guest list. The party would start with a sit-down dinner for one hundred actors and actresses, directors and studio executives – the people the Irishman would need to work with and impress if his ascendancy was to continue. At midnight, the remaining guests would arrive for drinks and dancing and a champagne breakfast. To please their eye as they arrived on the Bel Air estate, Harris had every bloom in the vast rose beds dyed lilac. A twenty-piece orchestra – primed with appropriate film themes and personal favourites – wafted the diners to their seats. And a small army of chefs, kitchen staff, waiters and security staff ensured their safety and comfort.

Also in California were Rex Harrison and his wife Rachel Roberts. The couple were living in a rented mansion that once belonged to Greta Garbo on North Bedford Drive. Their dinner invitation had already caused problems. When word filtered back that Vanessa Redgrave refused to sit next to Harrison, his wife threatened equally humiliating retribution. And so the seating plan was hastily reshuffled. Far worse was to come.

As soon as they arrived, it was obvious that Roberts, wearing a sexy long black dress, had started celebrating several hours earlier. After dinner, and several more glasses of champagne, she floated unsteadily through the gathering until she spotted Harris's prize African lovebird. The pet was watching the boisterous proceedings from a large ornamental cage and, according to Harris's friend, Nancy Holmes, was so valuable 'you wouldn't be surprised to see it kept in a safe'.

'Don't you think birds should be free?' Roberts asked. Before anyone could stop her, she had unlatched the cage door. The bird hopped out, focused on an open window at the far end of the room and took off into the night. Harris, who claimed he shared part of his soul with the bird, exploded in anger and threatened to eject Roberts physically from the party.

'I didn't like to see any kind of creature caged up,' Roberts later explained when the incident hit the Hollywood gossip columns. 'I wasn't to know that Richard had very special feelings for that bird.' After scouring the West Coast pet shops for a replacement lovebird, Elizabeth eventually replaced the escapee with an Amazon parrot – 'but Richard never trusted the bird with his soul'.

Almost a decade before the rebellious Oliver Reed began dropping his trousers at drunken events, Rachel Roberts had taken to interrupting boring or pompous party monologues by transforming herself into a rabid Welsh corgi. Her target tonight was Robert Mitchum.

The veteran American actor, with whom Harris had worked on *A Terrible Beauty*, was informing a group of admirers how he contracted and survived leprosy while working in the Congo. Mitchum ignored the annoying tugs at his trouser leg. And the snarling growls. But when a circle of pain clamped itself on his calf he narrowed his famously slitty eyes and looked down. Roberts was on all fours. Having chewed her way through his expensive made-to-measure trousers she was now attempting to draw blood with her bared teeth. 'There, there,' said Mitchum, as if patting one of his favourite hounds, before finishing his story.

There were other parties. Some, when Harris was in the mood, were intimate, loving affairs in the mansion's candlelit dining room. Others, when he felt in need of more gregarious company, ranged through the house and invariably ended with a semi-naked romp in the pool. Rex Harrison remained unimpressed. 'What does Richard think he's doing?' he once demanded with squiffy self-importance. 'Who's he trying to impress? This is Old Hollywood. It's so passé now and twenty-five years out of date.'

There was another reason for Harrison's derision. 'I am,' he admitted at the time to an American friend, 'finding myself drawn to Elizabeth Harris.' Once he even used the word 'love'.

Elizabeth had, by now, lost the 'uncomfortable remoteness' she once felt in the actor's presence. Despite the difference in their ages – Elizabeth was almost thirty, Harrison in his mid-fifties – they shared a society background with its common standards and courtesies. At parties or more formal gatherings, they talked and danced and escaped in each other's company before returning to the hazards of their individual relationships. For Harrison the debris would be scattered in the full glare of Hollywood society.

After a late-night session at the Daisy Club, a favourite pub with British actors and actresses, Lionel Jeffries issued an open invitation for a nightcap at his rented villa. 'First Rex tells Michael Wilding he's never been able to understand a word he says,' recalls Harris's future *Camelot* co-star. 'Then he berates Margaret Leighton for falling into bed with a nancy boy like Laurence Harvey. Someone else he calls a phoney and says he could never credit how he came to be considered a celebrity . . . and so on. In the middle of this tirade, in marches Rachel, takes stock of the scene and announces she's going to put a Welsh curse on Rex. She shuts her eyes, makes a few cabalistic signs, crosses her fingers and directs a string of Welsh words at her husband, which at least shuts him up.'

The next morning Harrison telephoned Jeffries to apologise for his wife's behaviour.

Elizabeth, meanwhile, was forced to endure a far more lonely and painful destruction, driven equally by her husband's cruelty and her own persecution.

The Luau was a cosy Beverly Hills restaurant famous for its regular and rowdy expatriate parties. For no reason in particular Rex Harrison and Rachel Roberts decided to hire the entire venue and throw an all-comers party. It was gone midnight when Elizabeth steered her drunken husband towards their car. As she was driving home, Harris began hurling abuse at some unseen and threatening demon. By the time Elizabeth reached Sunset Boulevard her husband had set about destroying the inside of the Cadillac.

Elizabeth concentrated on driving while Harris tore apart the upholstery and trim and smashed the fascia panel. Spattered by the blood from her husband's ripped hands and gashed forehead, she felt no compulsion to stop the car and run. 'I didn't feel fear or hatred or even curiosity,' she recalls. It was all happening in another dimension.

She'd already had one failed suicide and Elizabeth felt her sense of helplessness slide into a hopeless breakdown. And the fault, she persuaded herself, was all her own. The passion she once enjoyed for Hollywood had somehow turned into a confused disgust for a place where movie fantasy ruled and the honest and truthful things no longer mattered. In the coming days Elizabeth would retreat more and more into her bedroom and herself, and a crippling paranoia. Her husband was spying on her: the telephone was bugged; there were listening devices in every vase and behind every painting; the staff had been bribed to report her every move. In Elizabeth's mind, 'Richard became my jailer, my inquisitor, my persecutor. His suspicion was relentless and grinding and vindictive.'

After days on all-fours crawling around the bedroom, hiding behind furniture and under tables, or sitting in a foetal ball with her back against the locked door, Elizabeth finally found the courage to announce she wanted to return to England and her children. Harris refused in an explosion of rage. Elizabeth pleaded. Finally, Harris ordered her to stay. He had fought long and hard to earn his place in Hollywood, he ranted. If she loved him, if she had any respect for him, she would remain by his side. It was expected. It was her duty.

And then one morning Harris tapped gently on his wife's bedroom door and whispered that he had booked her a ticket to London. Elizabeth scrambled to pack. The twelve-hour flight to Heathrow did not leave until late that afternoon. 'I'll come to the airport to see you off,' Harris told her.

The drive to Los Angeles International Airport was silent and nervous. Elizabeth was still not convinced this was not one of her husband's grotesque practical jokes. At the terminal she raced for the Pan American check-in and the protection of the departure lounge.

The Boeing's first-class cabin was comfortingly empty. As Elizabeth settled herself into her window seat, she was suddenly overtaken with exhaustion and a light-headed, almost drunken sense of freedom. She closed her eyes and waited for sleep to overtake her.

Someone edged into the seat next to her. 'A glass of champagne, thank you.' The voice was chillingly familiar. Elizabeth felt the man shift in his seat to face her. She could feel his breath on her cheek. She forced herself to open her eyes.

'You can't come with me,' she said. 'You won't be allowed into England without your passport.'

Harris emptied his glass of champagne. 'Yes,' he said. 'It's a long way to go just for free booze.'

The stewardess returned to refill Harris's glass. 'Sorry,' he said, standing up. 'I get off here.'

Elizabeth followed him to the still-open door. She was not going to be fooled a second time. Harris stepped off the plane and turned to face her. As the aircraft door hissed shut she saw one of his red and angry eyes watching her through the tiny peephole.

CHAPTER EIGHT

'I think the crew imagined I wasn't going to do it,' he admitted of the decision to take over direction on the $1.5 million *Bloomfield*. 'Or if I did it would be an actor's brief indulgence in direction.'

The pressure of directing and acting was immense, however, and an experience Harris vowed he would never repeat. There were lessons. Whenever the crew or technicians informed him an idea for a scene was impossible, Harris demanded to know why. Balancing the books was another revelation. 'I had never worked on such an inexpensive movie,' said Harris. 'My previous three films had cost $28 million between them, but once I began to go through the accounts on *Bloomfield* I realised the fantastic wastage in the industry.'

Harris was adamant he should see the *Bloomfield* project through to the end. 'I know famous directors who hand over their work when they've finished directing,' he later explained. 'They see the editor once a week and make suggestions while they're doing other jobs, and then they believe they have cut the movie. But you must be there every day and look at every frame. You must supervise the laying of the soundtrack and the dubbing of the music, otherwise you have no right to call it your movie.'

CHAPTER EIGHT

Every time I get a script it's a matter of trying to know what I could do with it. I see colours, imagery. It has to have a smell. It's like falling in love. You can't give a reason why.

— Lena Olin

Everything has its price. The months and years of obscurity and ambitious poverty were long over. So too were the days of integrity and fidelity and trust. Elizabeth was paying the price for her husband's fame with her own sanity – and she wanted out. She also wanted revenge.

David Jacobs was a lawyer and legal showman whose client list included some of the world's top entertainers. In 1959, he secured a six-figure libel settlement for the pianist Liberace against the *Daily Mirror* and its 'Cassandra' columnist William Connor. Four years later he was hired by the Beatles' manager Brian Epstein to act as the group's legal adviser and oversee its business affairs and, in one spectacularly inept deal, managed to give away 90 per cent of the Beatles' merchandising profits. When Elizabeth Harris telephoned to make an appointment to see Jacobs in the autumn of 1966, the solicitor instinctively knew he was about to be handed a high-profile and juicy matrimonial case.

The next day – her second day back in England – Elizabeth was shown into Jacobs's ultramodern and sparsely furnished London office. She wanted a divorce. But she was more afraid her husband was about to snatch their three sons and take them back with him to America. Elizabeth had no plans to return to Hollywood – with or without her children. Yet, she explained, less than 24 hours after her arrival in London, Pan-American had telephoned to confirm a family return ticket to Los Angeles for that coming weekend. Harris, the airline also confirmed, was flying into Heathrow the next day.

Jacobs was confident and reassuring. He would seek an immediate injunction. 'Your husband won't be able to contact you after that,' said the solicitor. 'And there will be no way he can take the children out of the country without your or the court's permission.' To allay Elizabeth's fears over the inevitable publicity, Jacobs promised to serve the injunction papers personally. The hearing, he said, would be presided over by a judge in chambers, safely out of earshot of the public and press.

The following afternoon, Jacobs got his hair cut, put on his best suit and headed down the A4 to Heathrow. His secretary had spent the morning tipping off every national newspaper and press agency in the book. When Harris emerged from the Terminal 3 customs hall, he found himself facing a conspiratorial and strangely silent wall of reporters and photographers. A small, dapper man approached the actor. Harris naïvely raised his right hand, into which Jacobs promptly slapped the court papers – before turning and smiling at the battery of flashbulbs.

Harris had arrived in England hoping – expecting – to persuade his wife and family to return to Hollywood. Rehearsals for *Camelot* were due to start the following Monday. Instead, he found himself with a High Court order forbidding any contact with his wife and banning him from removing his sons from her care or the country. An open court hearing to formalise the separation order was set for two weeks hence.

Elizabeth was horrified by the next morning's front-page coverage of the Heathrow ambush. Jacobs had not only lied to her, but had quite obviously treated the event as an exercise in self-publicity. Some time before dawn, a small army of journalists had set up camp outside the Bedford Gardens house. The telephone rang continually: news desks and newspapers from all over the world wanted to buy her story. Elizabeth made just one call of her own – to fire her solicitor.

Harris spent the night at London's Savoy Hotel, nursing his indignation and stoking his bitterness. He considered his wife's legal action a 'terrible betrayal'. His resentment, however, did not stop him from talking to the press. 'I am absolutely shattered by this divorce action,' he told one reporter. 'I have always tried to treat my wife like a delicate and beautiful flower. I flew here intending to give her a pleasant surprise.' He failed to mention either Elizabeth's agonising breakdown or his brutish behaviour. That night Harris flew back to America alone.

Throughout the weeks of readthroughs, rehearsals and costume fittings at Warners' Burbank Studio, Harris watched as *Camelot* took shape. It was a mammoth task with sets of breathtaking proportions. Modelled on the Castle of Coca near Segovia, King Arthur's castle and its adjoining courtyard covered seven acres of backlot and measured 450 by 300 feet. It was 100 feet from cobbles to turret top. At a cost of half a million dollars, it remains one of the biggest standing sets ever built in Hollywood. The interior sets were equally impressive. The largest, the

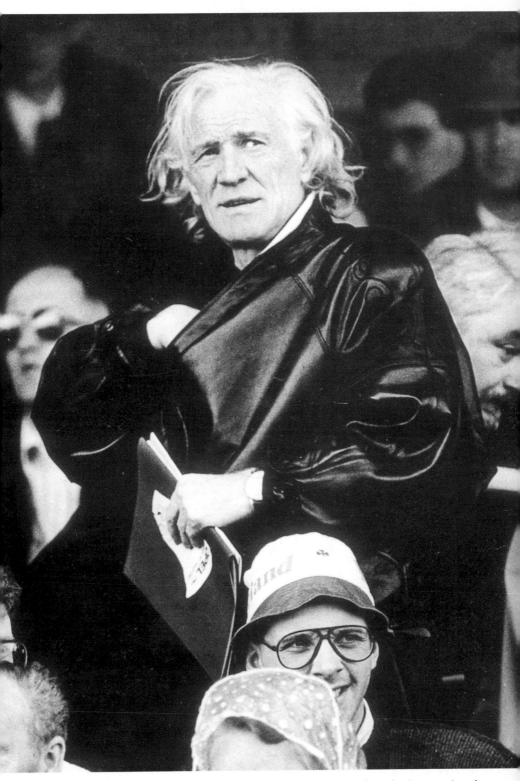

Richard Harris takes his place for a 1992 Lansdowne Road rugby international. His dreams of playing for Ireland were shattered when he contracted tuberculosis as a teenager. (© *Irish Times*)

Left 9 February 1957: Mr and Mrs Richard Harris leave the Church of Notre Dame de France, Leicester Place, on their way to a House of Lords reception. Twenty-year-old Elizabeth Rees-Williams met her future husband when she auditioned for a play he was producing and directing.

Below To his three sons – Damian, Jared and Jamie – Richard Harris was the perfect father who played football in the lounge and never complained when things got broken. To his wife Elizabeth he was fast becoming a womanising drunk.

Right As a teenage film fan Harris idolised Marlon Brando. The image soon faded – working with the American star on *Mutiny on the Bounty* turned an on-set tantrum into a lifetime feud. (© Tony Hillman Collection)

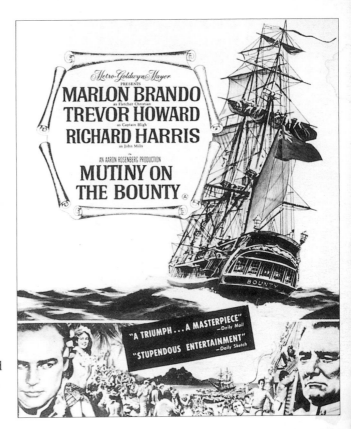

Below When Harris repeatedly arrived late on the set of *Major Dundee*, Charlton Heston ordered him to 'arrive on time, be ready, and just bloody do it'. The Irishman responded by hanging an alarm clock around his neck. (© Tony Hillman Collection)

Left Harris played Knut Straud in *The Heroes of Telemark*. (© Tony Hillman Collection)

Below During the filming Harris takes time out to check camera angles. It would be another four years before he directed his first film. (© Tony Hillman Collection)

Above left Harris was so convinced he was destined to play King Arthur he bombarded *Camelot*'s director Joshua Logan with a series of telegrams – 'Only Harris for King Arthur.' (© Tony Hillman Collection)

Above right Disillusioned with film-making Harris bought the stage rights to *Camelot* and, for almost ten years, toured the world with the musical. When it opened at London's Apollo Theatre in 1982 Fiona Fullerton took over as Queen Guinevere. (© Tony Hillman Collection)

Below Camelot: Anyone who missed the musical at the cinema could follow the adventures of Harris as King Arthur in a series of newspaper cartoon strips. (© Tony Hillman Collection)

Above In *The Molly Maguires* Harris played opposite Samantha Eggar, who said, 'He pours out so much energy that you simply have to try to match up to him.' (© Tony Hillman Collection)

Below *Man In The Wilderness* was set and filmed in Canada with Harris playing a fir trapper mauled and left for dead by a grizzly bear. One actor equally abandoned in the credits was Dennis Waterman. (© Tony Hillman Collection)

Great Hall and Throne Room, dwarfed anything undertaken at Burbank and overshadowed even the record-breaking Covent Garden set for *My Fair Lady*. But it would be Edward Carrere's accounting rather than his creative skills that would ultimately earn the art director Hollywood immortality. Carrere's budget for *Camelot* was $2,600,000. On the last day of shooting he smugly announced: 'I've spent $2,599,023 and 14 cents.'

For Harris, and probably the majority of cast and crew, *Camelot* would consume more time and mental energy than any other project of his career. Without overruns or unexpected delays, an entire nine months had been blanked off the studio calendar. Sustaining the emotional impetus day after day, six days a week, was very often more demanding than the physical filming. 'To cope,' admitted Harris, 'you needed to invent a kind of artificial emotion.' At other times the terror of a new experience provided a badly needed shot of adrenaline.

Unusually, the film had two musical directors: the 58-year-old Ken Darby and the still older Alfred Newman. A former child pianist, Newman had composed the music for almost 250 films in his forty-year career. It was Newman's responsibility to rehearse and conduct the movie's 96-piece backing orchestra and shepherd the actors through their individual recording sessions. Each song would then be played back on set with the actors miming the words. For Harris, who had never sung in public before, it was a daunting prospect.

The morning of his first recording session, Harris failed to appear. He was, claimed a message, suffering with a cold. Newman stood the orchestra down and drove out to the actor's Bel Air mansion. 'The only medical thing wrong with him,' recalled the veteran musician, 'was stage fright – and that had crippled him.' Harris was pacing the floor and doused in sweat. 'It wasn't that he did not want sing,' said Newman. 'He was more frightened of letting everyone down. Here was this strapping Irishman bulging with confidence and afraid, not that he would make a fool of himself, that never really bothered Richard, but that he might let me and the orchestra down.' The session was rescheduled for the next morning and, to ensure Harris's presence, Newman arranged to pick him up in his own car.

The ordeal was not over yet. The first song to be recorded was 'How To Handle a Woman' and, to ensure he came in on the right note, Harris asked the musical director to stab a finger in his direction. The orchestra played the introduction. Newman pointed. And Harris let out a panic-stricken gurgle.

For relaxation, there was always the omnipresent party invitation. One night, a clutch of celebrities descended on the legendary producer David O Selznick's former Bel Air home. Among the guests – invited and uninvited – were Jane Fonda, Roger Vadim, David Hemmings, Rex Harrison and his wife Rachel Roberts and Harris's *Camelot* co-star Vanessa Redgrave. The film's leading man did not arrive until three in the morning. For some reason David Hemmings began sparring with his fellow guests. Harris, still a few drinks behind, took exception and began remonstrating with the British actor, eventually demonstrating his own boxing prowess by landing a punch on Hemmings's jaw and splitting his lip. Watching the fracas, Redgrave burst into a flood of tears and announced she would never act with that Richard Harris again.

Like Associated British before it, Warner Bros, with the help of its publicity machine, was left to fend off the gossip-column enquiries, and coped with its star's off-screen behaviour the best it could. Harris's antics were getting almost as much exposure as the film itself and could hardly be ignored. 'He continues to be, to put it mildly, boisterous, uninhibited and exuberant,' admitted a souvenir brochure sold to *Camelot* cinema audiences around the world. 'He lives overwhelmingly. Almost everything he does is original. He challenges conformity every step of the way.'

News of Harris's marriage break-up began to spread, attracting offers of support from the most unlikely sources. While the actor was working on the *Camelot* set, he was told there was a telephone call for him. The voice was instantly recognisable. 'You know you can't make love long-distance,' suggested Frank Sinatra. And to support his theory the veteran American singer informed Harris his private jet was on standby at LAX to fly the Irishman back to Elizabeth.

Two weeks into filming, Harris made his own way back to London and into court. He arrived at the separation hearing suitably calm and surprisingly well dressed. In his mind, he later confided to a friend, he was still convinced Elizabeth simply needed a 'cooling-off period. That given a few weeks apart they would once again forgive each other'. Any hopes Harris may have nurtured were swiftly and legally destroyed.

Elizabeth Harris was, her new solicitor Joseph Jackson informed the court, afraid to return to her husband. His legendary 'drinking bouts' had led to violence in the past and there was no reason to suppose he might not seek 'physical revenge' on her in the future. A divorce petition had been filed that morning. And then there was the question of his influence on their three children, as Jackson explained:

Mr Harris is a man of considerable talent and exceptional success in his profession. His wife alleges that her husband drank – drinks – to excess and would then go berserk with whoever was in sight. Unfortunately, too, he is addicted to using foul language. Perhaps this is not the disgrace it was, but when there are children using four-letter Anglo-Saxon words the time has come, perhaps, for a halt.

For the second time in less than a month, Harris returned to America alone. The pressure on his marriage was relentless. Years later Harris would comment: 'Life is strewn with compromises and scars. In Elizabeth's and my case we needed more Band-Aids than most people.' The wounds were invariably of Harris's making. One evening, while Elizabeth was preparing dinner in their Earl's Court flat, her husband had announced he was popping out for a drink. What he had forgotten – deliberately or otherwise – to tell his wife was that the drink was in Dublin and he would be gone ten days. 'When that happened I used to worry so much,' she recalls. 'At first I would ring the hospitals and the police and the airports, but after a while I got used to it.'

Elizabeth, whose reaction to her husband's excesses had turned her almost teetotal, drove back to Bedford Gardens and celebrated her freedom with a drink. It was time, she decided, to make him pay. 'I had never been very good at turning the other cheek,' she confesses in *Love, Honour and Dismay*. 'Now I couldn't rest until I had evened the score. I lied to him, I double-crossed him, and I cheated. But I don't believe I fooled him for one moment. How could I? He taught me everything I knew.'

The studio security guard spread his arms in the air and waited for the car to stop. 'Please, Mr Harris, sir, stop. You've got to stop.'

'Go, go,' shouted the actor, ordering his chauffeur to aim the Cadillac at the Burbank gateman.

As the guard jumped for his life, his trouser pocket caught on the car's wing mirror, spinning him round to see a neat square of torn fabric flapping from the disappearing vehicle.

Harris was free at last. 'Fed up and tired' of *Camelot*, he was not leaving Hollywood without a souvenir or two. Wedged beside him in the back of the car was the bicycle the studio had given him to get around the vast backlot. As he had emptied his dressing room to leave on the last day of shooting, one of the film's associate producers spotted the bike –

but not King Arthur's gold crown hidden in the boot – and ordered the studio guards to stop the wayward Irishman and retrieve the stolen machine.

Harris drove straight to Malibu. Wheeling the bicycle on to the beach, he got on and waited for a suitably impressive wave. At the right moment he yelped and pedalled furiously down the sand and into the plunging surf.

Throughout the 1960s Harris's finances had roller-coastered out of control. He would think nothing of hiring a Learjet to whisk his friends – some at a day's acquaintance – off to Paris and happily pick up the bill for eighteen suites at the prestigious Georges V Hotel. Twice, his impending bankruptcy was averted only by judicious film offers.

In his quieter moments Harris remained haunted by the evaporation of his family's fortune. Where there might have been bitterness, there was just a determination to survive. 'I realised at the height of my career that one day it would all stop and I did not want to dwindle into looking for work on television and playing small parts,' he explained. An equal incentive was the British tax rate, which was skimming off 60 per cent of everything Harris earned. Moving to the income-tax-free Bahamas gave Harris enough spare cash to invest in his future – and pull off some legendary land deals.

His agent on the west coast of America informed Harris whenever an estate or tract of land came on the market. Harris would add a few more acres of California to his portfolio and sit back and forget about them. Twenty, or sometimes thirty, years later he was still selling off the land at a vast profit. One spectacular deal would involve a house and estate Harris bought for $400,000. In the late 1980s, he would sell on the property to the singer and actress Barbra Streisand – for $6.5 million.

But for the moment all he wanted was to return to London and see his children. At the end of June 1967, Elizabeth arranged for her estranged husband's possessions to be moved to his new home, a luxury flat in Chesham Place just off Belgrave Square. Not long after Harris had taken possession, he received a transatlantic telephone call from Warner Bros asking him if he knew anything about the missing crown, already on display on his sideboard. 'If you do find it, let me know,' he lied. 'Because I'd rather like to have it.'

The *Camelot* premiere was held at London's Warner Theatre. The first-night profits were shared between two charities: the Invalid Children's

Aid Association and the Zebra Trust, which gave financial assistance to African students studying in Britain. After the screening, the studio organised a Knightsbridge dinner. Princess Margaret and her husband Lord Snowdon represented the children's charity. Among the Zebra Trust guests were Elizabeth Harris and her new boyfriend, the Canadian-born actor Christopher Plummer.

The inevitable meeting came when Princess Margaret enquired whether Harris and Plummer knew each other. 'We share something in common,' said Harris. When the dinner party broke up Harris scooped up the couple and a dozen other guests and invited them back to his Chesham Place flat. 'The evening ended amicably enough,' recalls Elizabeth, 'with all of us gathered around the piano and with Christopher playing songs from *Camelot*.'

Despite its three Academy Awards and a fourth nomination – all for technical disciplines – the spark of the stage show somehow failed to transfer to the big screen. After sitting through the premiere, the critic John Simon described the experience as, 'three hours of unrelieved glossiness, meticulous inanity, desperate and charmless striving for charm'. *MFB* magazine wondered 'whether the fashion for musicals in which only the chorus can actually sing may be reaching its final stage'. The *New Yorker*, however, conceded that '... it does have good bits tucked in among the elaborate mistakes. It has a fascination; it's like a huge ruin that makes one wonder what the blueprint could possibly have indicated.' Harris's performance, added the critic Pauline Kael, 'was eccentric and unfathomable in the first half, but achieves some powerful moments later on'.

For Harris the premiere was a chance to revive his personal and professional association with Faye Dunaway, whose latest film *Bonnie and Clyde* had opened at the same cinema a few months earlier. The pair first met in New York in the early 1960s while Dunaway was taking part in a theatre workshop at the Lincoln Center. After the performance, Harris sought out the young actress and informed her she had a 'rare talent'. In Dunaway the Irish actor sensed a wildness, a crazy foolishness Harris was devoting much of his own time and energy to exploring. 'Faye, love,' he would tell her, 'just run the length of your wildness. Live whatever is in you.'

After the restrictions of *Camelot*, Harris was bursting with energy and ideas. 'We talked about many things,' Dunaway recalls. 'One of which was the idea of doing *Hamlet* together, first on the London stage, then on film. With me playing Ophelia to his prince. Richard became very dear to me and said if he was going to do the film, he wanted me to be part of it. Sadly, it just never happened.'

Another project that failed to materialise that year – at least for Harris – was a film version of the Alan Jay Lerner and Burton Lane musical *On a Clear Day*. Following the success of *The Sound of Music*, Hollywood had succumbed to a frenetic hunt for musical properties and, despite its financial failure on Broadway, Paramount Pictures paid $750,000 for the *Clear Day* film rights. The studio's vice-president in charge of production, Howard Koch, decided to produce the film personally and knew exactly who he wanted as leading lady.

Heavily pregnant, Barbra Streisand was in England shooting *Funny Girl* and claimed the last thing she wanted to think about was work. Koch approached Audrey Hepburn, who also turned him down, this time because she felt *On a Clear Day* – complete with naïve young woman and know-it-all professor – was too close to her role in *My Fair Lady*. Several other screen musicals, including *Camelot*, were by now clocking up serious box-office receipts. Koch was becoming desperate and once again contacted Streisand, whose postnatal business sense had returned sharper than ever. Her signature on the contract cost Paramount a $350,000 salary and the promise of full creative control.

Vincente Minnelli, director of Oscar-winning *Gigi*, had already agreed to direct and suggested Richard Harris might make an excellent professor. The Irishman liked the script and was close to signing but, according to Koch, 'walked out on it because he got a better deal on something else'.

The truth was a little more complicated. From the start, Harris insisted he should have as many musical numbers as his co-star. Then he got a call from Alan Jay Lerner inviting him to the lyricist's home. 'I knew something was afoot immediately,' recalled Harris, 'because Streisand wasn't there.'

Lerner sat down at his piano and started to play his way through the entire score. After playing five songs, he turned to Harris and said, 'And now here's one for you.'

Harris bit his tongue as he listened to the next five songs. 'And here's another one for you,' Lerner offered.

'Fuck this,' said Harris and stormed out.

Replacing Harris was not easy. Both Frank Sinatra and Gregory Peck turned down the role. Ironically, the part, originally written with the professor as a Frenchman, went to the French singer Yves Montand.

For someone who, up until eighteen months earlier, had never sung a note in public, Harris suddenly found he enjoyed singing – at least in a studio. 'I was never quite sure about an audience,' he admitted. 'At least in a studio you can stop and do it again and get it. If you get it badly wrong you can also lock the door and keep the producer at bay.'

One recording Harris got seriously right during the early summer of 1968 was a song that has since achieved mythical status. 'MacArthur Park' – in reality situated on the west side of Wilshire Boulevard between downtown Los Angeles and Santa Monica – was a doleful, cryptic, love lament written by the American songwriter Jimmy Webb and ideally suited to Harris's flaky voice. Originally issued as a track on an album called *A Tramp Shining*, the single proved strangely in tune with the times and peaked at No. 2 in the US *Billboard* charts and topped a twelve-week run in Britain by reaching No. 4.

The price of pop success would leave Harris explaining the lyric to successive generations of interviewers. 'Jimmy Webb was in love with a girl, and they went for a walk in MacArthur Park. She says, "Look, we have been together for a long time now; you have to marry me." She proposes. He says no. She meets somebody else that she was keen on. Now MacArthur Park is what? It's where he lost her. So he goes back and sees the old men playing checkers under the trees . . .'

> *I recall the yellow cotton dress*
> *Foaming like a wave*
> *On the ground around your knees*
> *The birds, like tender babies is in your hands*
> *And the old men playing checkers by the trees*

'. . . and the cake is the wedding cake . . .'

> *MacArthur's Park is melting in the dark*
> *All the sweet, green icing flowing down . . .*
> *Someone left the cake out in the rain*
> *I don't think that I can take it*
> *'Cause it took so long to bake it*
> *And I'll never have that recipe again . . .*

'. . . the wedding cake that he blew. It's melting in the rain. And he would never have that recipe again.' To Harris – and more so to Webb – it was all very logical. To the rest of the world it remained an indecipherable icon of the pot-hazed 1960s, selling more than 6 million copies.

Harris, who by now was also writing his own lyrics, had come to accept singing as a natural extension of his poetry. 'Acting is not enough,' he told the *TV Times* writer Robert Ottoway. 'Singing, especially if you've written the songs yourself, is a great form of expression.' But, he complained, only his acting and his brawling made the headlines. 'I was in New York recently to read some of my poems to the city's Poetry Society. It gave me the greatest creative satisfaction I've ever had. A few days later I went on a pub crawl, and *that's* what the papers covered. Not a mention of my poetry reading.'

His voice, as one critic described it, may have sounded 'like coal being shovelled' but at least it was something new. 'I'm prepared to try anything,' said Harris. 'At least that way I don't get bored.' Fortunately, there were two other projects to distract him that year.

The first was a stout-hearted war film called *Play Dirty*, co-written by Lotte Colin and Melvyn Bragg. The story involved a squad of ex-criminals given the job of destroying an enemy oil dump in North Africa. Harris, it was agreed, would co-star with Michael Caine. Less than a month before location shooting started, Harris announced he was quitting the film. Nigel Davenport was hired to replace him.

Warner Bros approached Harris, now back on the market, to play the drunken Indian living on a dilapidated reservation who declares a public-relations war on officialdom. The film would be called *Flap* in America – later renamed *The Last Warrior* for the British market – and directed by Carol Reed. The studio was so desperate to net Harris that it quickly gave in to his demand for a $325,000 salary, plus 20 per cent of the gross. With the deal in black and white and out in the open, Harris once again changed his mind. This time his place was taken by Anthony Quinn.

One idea that did manage to fire Harris's imagination – ultimately in more ways than he expected – was a low-budget sports film set in Israel. *Bloomfield* was conceived and written by Wolf Mankowitz and told the simple story of a ten-year-old boy who hitchhikes to Jaffa to see his soccer idol play his last match. Persuaded to invest more than a quarter of a million pounds of his own money in the production, Harris enthused over the 'autobiographical' storyline. 'It's pathetic,' he told the press before his departure for Israel. 'The man has put everything he has into his playing career and has given no thought to what will happen when he reaches forty and is finished. He doesn't care. He's existed only for sport. Everyone else sees what's going to happen to him. And everyone deserts him.'

Less than a year after Israel's victory in the Six Day War and with Yasser Arafat about to be elected leader of the Palestine Liberation Organisation, 1968 was not a good time to be in the Middle East to make a film. The political tension soon spread to the *Bloomfield* set. Ten days after shooting started, the Israeli director quit. Harris reluctantly agreed to take over; it was more than a decade since he had directed anything and LAMDA end-of-term extracts from *St Joan* were a long way from a $1.5-million movie. 'I think the crew imagined I wasn't going to do it,' he admitted. 'Or if I did it would be an actor's brief indulgence in direction.'

The schedule was rearranged to give the new director time to plan and rewrite the scenes. It was even suggested the sixteen-week shoot be divided in two to allow Harris time to return to England and honour his contract to play the title role in the Leslie Bricusse musical *Scrooge* – and collect his $600,000 fee. As a major investor, he decided to stay with *Bloomfield*. His part in the Dickens story was offered first to Rex Harrison and finally to Albert Finney.

The pressure of directing and acting was immense and an experience Harris vowed he would never repeat. There were lessons. Whenever the crew or technicians informed him an idea for a scene was impossible, Harris demanded to know why. Balancing the books was another revelation. 'I had never worked on such an inexpensive movie,' said Harris. 'My previous three films had cost $28 million between them, but once I began to go through the accounts on *Bloomfield* I realised the fantastic wastage in the industry.'

Harris was adamant he should see the *Bloomfield* project through to the end. 'I know famous directors who hand over their work when they've finished directing,' he later explained. 'They see the editor once a week and make suggestions while they're doing other jobs, and then they believe they have cut the movie. But you must be there every day and look at every frame. You must supervise the laying of the soundtrack and the dubbing of the music, otherwise you have no right to call it your movie.'

To carry out his responsibility and 'lay his head on the block', Harris flew to America. From a New York dubbing suite he searched the world for original soundtrack music. By chance, he was introduced to a young American musician who had just returned from Ireland, where he had taken part in a hippie wedding in Limerick's People's Park. Michael

O'Mahoney suggested the actor-turned-director listen to a demonstration tape written and produced by a teenage former pupil of Harris's old school.

Bill Whelan had graduated from Crescent College less than a year earlier. 'The next thing, I get a telephone call from Harris telling me my music was to be featured in a film he had just made,' recalls Whelan. 'I'll never forget that day. I was sitting in Limerick listening to the arrangement of my song being played over the telephone from America.'

The next day Harris flew to Ireland. In his Kilkee hotel suite the pair worked their way through the nineteen-year-old Whelan's other songs and tunes for the film. The score would eventually be completed and orchestrated in London by the movie's unrelated musical director Johnny Harris.

Never one of Harris's greatest admirers, the British Film Institute was scathingly critical. Reviewing *Bloomfield* in the Institute's monthly bulletin, David Wilson reported:

> Ambition gets the better of talent in this embarrassing debut by Richard Harris. Given a Wolf Mankowitz screenplay which recalls all the maudlin excesses of *A Kid for Two Farthings*, Harris responds with a piecemeal directing style crashingly out of key with the simple requirements of the material (and simple is the word). Synthetic lyricism, complete with sunset silhouettes and filtered slow motion, alternates with a variety of camera gymnastics which extends to a couple of scenes pointlessly shot from under a table. The stylistic whimsicality is matched by the story, a blend of sentimental moralising and thumping dramatic irony which plunges to an excruciating nadir in the last sequence as the camera turns away from Harris – fallen football idol – kneeling alone on a deserted pitch to the accompaniment from a soaring heavenly choir.

One evening in October 1968, Robin Douglas-Home telephoned Elizabeth Harris from his Sussex cottage. They had not seen each other or spoken for some time, although Elizabeth, like the rest of the country, was by now aware of his affair with Princess Margaret.

Douglas-Home and Margaret first met in the late 1950s, shortly before her marriage to Anthony Armstrong-Jones (who was created Earl of Snowdon in 1961). In 1966 the pair met once again – at a party attended by Richard and Elizabeth Harris – and immediately began a passionate month-long affair. The press soon picked up on the royal scandal, and on 25 March 1966 Margaret ended the relationship in a farewell letter: 'Our love has the passionate scent of new-mown grass and lilies about it. Not many people are lucky enough to have known any love like this.'

Douglas-Home never recovered from the rejection and began living the life of a near recluse. His casual invitation for Elizabeth to come down to Meadowbrook that October weekend turned more desperate. Each time she attempted to explain that it was impossible, Douglas-Home's pleas became more earnest. She had already made arrangements. No, she could not change them. Elizabeth's former lover said goodbye and hung up the phone. That night Robin Douglas-Home committed suicide.

CHAPTER NINE

Most obsessive drinkers use alcohol as an escape, as a catalyst to dull and ultimately obliterate the line between reality and fantasy. With Harris, there was an added complication. The majority of his life – at least his working life – was spent in a deliberate world of make-believe. Instead of staring into a looking glass and watching the image blur with each tumbler of vodka, Harris all too frequently found himself staggering through a fairground hall of mirrors – distorted and disoriented and never quite sure in which direction he was facing. The crunch, when it came, saved his life.

For five months Harris *lived* the life of Oliver Cromwell. One day towards the end of shooting he was shown a photograph of his co-star Alec Guinness, dressed and made up for his part as Charles I and about to face beheading. Harris ordered his secretary to halt the execution. When she tried to explain it was only a film and that Guinness was not a real king he began hurling dictatorial threats and then anything he could lay his hands on. It needed a doctor and a sedative shot to calm him down.

'I had finally crossed the line from sanity to madness,' Harris later admitted, 'and I realised it was all over.' The drinking had to stop.

CHAPTER NINE

This is not a tough job. You read a script. If you like the part and the money is OK, you do it. Then you remember your lines. You show up on time. You do what the director tells you to do. When you finish, you rest and then go on to the next part. That's it.

— Robert Mitchum

The telegram arrived just as Ken Hughes was finishing his breakfast. From the kitchen window of his Surrey home, the director watched the bright red GPO motorcycle and its rider turn on to the main road before ripping open the envelope.

I WANT TO PLAY THE PART OF CROMWELL STOP I'D LOVE TO DO THIS FILM STOP RICHARD HARRIS

A sudden chill rippled down Hughes's back. As one of Britain's leading film directors, he was aware of Harris's acting ability. He had also heard stories, some more accurate than others, of the lengths the actor went to in order to land a role. But it was Harris's off-screen image that worried him. 'The thought of being pursued and bullied into giving him the part was bad enough,' admitted Hughes. 'Giving in and then having to keep control of him while we made the film was too frightening to contemplate.'

Once informed Harris had been contracted for their film, directors would often add an extra week to the shooting schedule as an insurance against the drunken days he could not work. But Harris wasn't the worst culprit. When Richard Burton said yes to a movie they automatically added three weeks.

Harris, in Los Angeles to sign a film contract, had spotted a copy of the *Cromwell* script on a Hollywood producer's desk at Columbia Pictures. That evening he cabled Hughes. Part of the attraction was that the screenplay included several scenes covering Cromwell's ruthless 1649 campaign to suppress the Irish civil disobedience. Harris, like every Catholic pupil, learned about the sacking of Drogheda on the River Boyne and the bloody massacre of its inhabitants while at Crescent College. The telegram was followed by a number of transatlantic telephone calls. Unlike Joshua Logan on *Camelot*, Hughes agreed to meet Harris on his return from America. 'Although no self-respecting Irishman should play Cromwell,' declared Hughes, 'I had to admit he was perfect for the part.'

Cromwell's film adversary was an equally good fit. For Ken Hughes there was only one English actor with the 'stature and dignity' capable of playing the doomed King Charles I – Alec Guinness. The director approached the 55-year-old actor while he was appearing in *The Cocktail Party* at the Haymarket. Guinness admitted he felt the majority of his recent work lacked substance and, after reading the *Cromwell* script, conceded that the film might be 'the impossible something that would pull the best out of me'.

With both principal roles now cast, Hughes was only months away from a project he started almost a decade earlier.

Away from the film set, Ken Hughes liked to relax with a book. Years before, he had just finished reading two Ian Fleming thrillers in quick succession and, with another week of *The Trials of Oscar Wilde* to shoot, the director was a book short. Someone – he could never remember exactly who – offered him a biography of Oliver Cromwell.

Hughes was hooked. For the next nine years he read more than a hundred and twenty books on Britain's first and only revolutionary. In his spare time he toured England visiting historic sites and spent hours researching documents in museums and record offices. By 1967 he was ready to start work on a film script about Cromwell and his opposition to Charles I – 'a tragic drama that had all the haunting inevitability of a Greek tragedy'.

The following year, while directing *Chitty Chitty Bang Bang*, Hughes met another filmmaker who shared his obsession with Cromwell. Since his university days, Irving Allen had read almost as many books on the Protector as Hughes. Together – with Hughes as director and Allen as producer – they worked out a *Cromwell* project in which realism, not romance, would be the keynote and in which what *looked* right would at no time influence what *was* right.

By the time shooting started in the spring of 1969, the pair had masterminded one of the biggest filmmaking operations in history. Three months before the cast and crew arrived at Shepperton Studios, southwest of London, more than two hundred workmen began building the largest outdoor set ever constructed for a motion picture in England. Covering a little over two acres, it represented Parliament Square as it looked in 1642 and included the House of Commons, the

Palace of Westminster, the Great Banqueting Hall, Westminster Abbey and some fifty other buildings and houses. The wardrobe department undertook the design and manufacture of 3,851 Puritan and Royalist costumes – a feat that would ultimately earn them an Oscar – and ordered thousands of wigs from specialist suppliers across Europe. To dress the sets, the props manager needed no fewer than 16,000 separate items, ranging from quill pens and sanders to antique pocket watches and a king's tent.

Historical precision did have its drawbacks. On the first morning, Guinness unsettled the crew by stammering and apparently stumbling over his lines – until Hughes reassured them the king had indeed suffered from a similar speech impediment. And each morning before shooting started Richard Harris's make-up artist consulted a contemporary portrait of Cromwell to ensure the Puritan's famous warts were reattached in exactly the right place. It was only after several scenes had been shot that a continuity girl noticed a wart was missing – Hughes ordered the entire day's footage to be reshot.

From Shepperton, the cast and crew moved first to various Civil War battlefields in England and Ireland before setting up in Spain, the only country capable of supplying sufficient trained cavalry and soldiers for the full-scale battles.

Among *Cromwell's* star-studded credit list was 61-year-Robert Morley. Reading the script before accepting the role of the Parliamentary general the Earl of Manchester, the portly veteran actor was dismayed to find many of his scenes involved riding a horse, a species of animal he had never felt comfortable with, let alone sat upon. Morley confessed his misgivings to the director, who ordered the acquisition of a suitably well-built and passive beast. Shooting started with Harris and Morley arriving on horseback on the site of an impending battle. It was the cameraman who suddenly noticed an odd discrepancy. Despite their having started out on similar-sized horses, Harris would end each take a good head above his fellow actor. Someone then realised the pair were riding on soft ground and Morley's horse was slowly sinking up to its knees under its rider's weight. The horse was swapped for a carriage and Morley's line – 'Marston Moor, I see' – changed to set the location. 'I seem to have become a subtitle,' quipped Morley.

The film was taking its toll on Harris's health. Without his make-up, his complexion was sickly. He was run down and tired, but so high he couldn't sleep. He was also chasing dreams that, for the first time in his life, were so real he couldn't distinguish between fact and fiction.

Most obsessive drinkers use alcohol as an escape, as a catalyst to dull and ultimately obliterate the line between reality and fantasy. With Harris, there was an added complication. The majority of his life – at least his working life – was spent in a deliberate world of make-believe. Instead of staring into a looking glass and watching the image blur with each tumbler of vodka, Harris all too frequently found himself staggering through a fairground hall of mirrors – distorted and disoriented and never quite sure in which direction he was facing. The crunch, when it came, saved his life.

For five months Harris *lived* the life of Oliver Cromwell. One day towards the end of shooting he was shown a photograph of his co-star Alec Guinness, dressed and made up for his part as Charles I and about to face beheading. Harris ordered his secretary to halt the execution. When she tried to explain it was only a film and that Guinness was not a real king he began hurling dictatorial threats and then anything he could lay his hands on. It needed a doctor and a sedative shot to calm him down.

'I had finally crossed the line from sanity to madness,' Harris later admitted, 'and I realised it was all over.' The drinking had to stop.

As with everything else, Harris plunged head first and heedless into his own unsupervised aversion therapy: he filled every room, every cupboard, of his house with bottles of vodka. It wasn't simply a matter of doing – surviving – the 'cold turkey': for Harris it was a now a personal challenge, a matter of guts and willpower and blank stubbornness, and that was something he was supremely good at. 'Dickie never spared himself,' admits a fellow Irish actor and friend, Godfrey Quigley. 'I'm convinced it helped him survive.'

It was not that simple. To help him cope, to help distract him from the deliberate temptation, Harris needed something else to feed his cravings. First he tried cocaine; then heroin; then LSD. 'I tried them all, every drug I could lay my hands on. I didn't like it very much and my drug addiction, if that what it was, didn't last very long. I found alcohol much more satisfying and much less dangerous.'

The end of his experiment with drugs came when Harris overdosed on cocaine – 'maybe mixed with something else' – and, not for the first time, woke up in hospital. A priest was administering the last rites. He decided he would much rather die drunk or from a heart attack after making love to a beautiful woman.

Cromwell's London premiere produced some unexpected reviews. Writing in the *British Film Institute Bulletin*, Brenda Davies complained:

Ken Hughes' ... hopes for his long cherished project on *Cromwell* were perhaps unreasonably high. But this time Hughes, backed by a big American distributor, was clearly subject to all the pressures attached to the production of a wide-screen, all-star historical epic; inevitably these have caused an over-simplified approach to complex situations. Subtlety has given way to spectacle, and time which might have been spent on developing characters and relationships is given over to the confused crash-bang of battle. Simplification, however, cannot justify distortion of historical fact even in the service of dramatic effect.

It was an accurate verdict, even if Davies was passing sentence on the wrong culprit. With his 'historically accurate' film in the can, Hughes soon found himself under constant establishment pressure to edit – with commercialisation in mind. The biggest single cut ordered by Columbia was the sequence showing the destruction of Drogheda, the very scenes that had attracted Harris and that he considered 'among the best we shot'. At first Hughes refused to edit out the massacre, claiming it was both part of Irish history and vital to Cromwell's story. 'I felt audiences were being cheated by omitting the scenes and fought tooth and nail to keep them,' he said. Columbia refused to release the film until all its demands were met.

On Richard Harris's performance, Davies continued: 'He is encouraged to play at, and often beyond, the full pitch of his vocal power; within its own terms it is a performance of vitality, but as a serious study of Cromwell it is simply absurd.' In reality Harris had started each day's shooting by taking himself off and literally shouting himself hoarse – because Cromwell spoke with a flat, rasping voice.

By the late 1960s Richard Harris was a man of multiple contradictions. Capable of massive generosity – everyone employed on *Camelot*, even the technicians, received an expensive Tiffany silver gift – he repeatedly allowed imagined slights or unintentional behaviour to wreck friendships, some of many years' standing. While undeniably possessing an abundance of endurance and physical courage, he would carefully and carelessly cultivate the image of a hard-drinking, two-fisted brawler. A doting father and devoted womaniser, he seemed capable of striding free from the ruins of his marriage with the same casual brutality with which he left his affairs.

Elizabeth Harris was still living in Bedford Gardens. In her own words, 'The grand parties of Hollywood, the caviar and champagne and the private orchestras had given way to spaghetti and Italian plonk and record players.' She was, for the first time in her life, having to finance her own life while coping with three boisterous sons. Agreeing to a bizarre divorce settlement did not help. Against her solicitor's advice, Elizabeth's personal settlement – Harris had willingly accepted responsibility for his sons – was a one-off £3,000 shopping spree at Cordoba's, a Bond Street leather store.

To those who knew her, Elizabeth was the epitome of a relaxed 1960s young mother: bright and gay and very beautiful and instinctively charming. Guests at Bedford Gardens were made to feel welcome and comfortable. One frequent arrival was Rex Harrison. He was obviously in need of company – Rachel Roberts was appearing each night in a West End production of *Who's Afraid of Virginia Woolf?* – and Elizabeth poured the drinks and listened patiently to her uninvited guest.

'Elizabeth seemed to encompass all the attractive qualities of all the women I have met,' Harrison would later admit. 'She is very beautiful, she enjoys life, she is not competitive. She is divinely feminine, very lazy, and loathes exercise in God's fresh air. She is a strong person, mentally, and has strong convictions, which happily coincide with mine.' In his heart he had never really fallen out of love with Elizabeth.

They began to see more of each other. When Rachel Roberts took a small apartment in London's Eaton Square under her own name, the British papers soon picked up on an Easter visit Elizabeth and her three sons had made to Harrison's retreat near the Italian village of Portofino.

'I got to know all the right people with Rex and behaved like a clown,' Roberts reflected in her own book of memoirs, *No Bells on Sunday*. 'I felt equal to the rich and the beautiful and I wasn't. When he started to be too embarrassed by it all, I drank more and got louder. I still, unbelievably, thought I was a riot. I barked loudly like a dog at society functions. Drunk, of course. I couldn't see that my husband was publicly disowning me as he sat with pretty, blonde Elizabeth Harris at one table, leaving me interrupting conversations at another ... no secrets did I withhold from the world, no mystery looked in my eyes, just noisy, manic, uncontrolled behaviour.'

Roberts's career was, by now, being kept afloat by drugs and booze. When she wasn't working she was drinking and when she was drunk she brooded on her separation. She needed to know the truth and telephoned Elizabeth to ask her rival if she and Harrison were lovers. 'Yes,' confirmed Elizabeth.

There was a long pause until Rachel said simply, 'It happens.'

A few months later, the acceptance had faded and Roberts appeared at Bedford Gardens while Rex Harrison was visiting Elizabeth for the afternoon. Roberts glared first at Elizabeth and then at her estranged husband. 'Choose between us,' she demanded. 'Now!'

Harrison fell back on a comedy line that would have won him a matinée standing ovation. 'I'll take that,' he said pointing to Elizabeth's pet dog, which had just padded into the room, before departing.

On 1 October, 1970, Richard Harris was forty. He celebrated by buying himself a new home – complete with a family of ghosts.

Given an in-flight newspaper to read while flying back from the States, Harris noticed a short news story in the *Evening Standard* saying that Liberace, the American pianist and singer, had purchased Tower House in London's Knightsbridge. Back at his Chesham Place apartment, and with his bags still unpacked, he telephoned the agent handling the sale and demanded to be shown round.

Harris arrived at the Melbury Road property just as dawn was lifting. Waiting for the agent to arrive, he padded round the garden, peered through the windows and stood back to admire the building's eerie Gothic lines. Designed and built by the Victorian architect and eccentric William Burges as his private home, the house was exactly what Harris was looking for. The inside, which Burges had notoriously cluttered with furniture and his collection of *objets d'art* and *objets trouvés*, was even more impressive.

Harris assumed Liberace had already purchased Tower House and that he would have to pay over the odds to buy the property from the American entertainer. 'But Mr Liberace has not yet put down a deposit,' confessed the estate agent.

'How much is it?' demanded Harris.

The agent told him the price.

'Right,' said Harris, writing out a cheque for £75,000. 'I'll take it.'

Harris had just bought himself one of the biggest and most prestigious houses in Knightsbridge. Not only did the Melbury Road mansion come with some equally high-flying neighbours – one of his closest was the film director-cum-screenwriter Michael Winner – it was also home to several wayward spirits. Despite his friendship with the astrologer Patric Walker, he remained sceptical about all things astral: 'I don't believe in all this horoscope nonsense.' But ghosts were another matter. Apparitions and phantoms and banshees were part of his Irish inheritance and imagination. They could also be very useful, he would soon discover, in extricating himself from fruitless and boring affairs.

Harris's recent birthday was one he – and certainly some of his friends – never thought he would celebrate. Ten years earlier, and with some of his worst excesses still to come, an American trio of friends had bet him $25,000 each that the actor would not survive another decade. It was a close-run thing, but he collected his winnings.

To his surprise Harris had survived the 1960s. To those he had blustered or bullied or fought with he had clawed his way into a select list of obnoxious talents: Oliver Reed, Albert Finney, Peter O'Toole and Richard Burton. Years later, and in a more sober time, he tried to explain: 'What that group of actors had was a fine madness, a lyrical madness. We lived our lives with that madness and it was transmitted into our work. We had smiles on our faces and a sense that the world was mad. We weren't afraid to be different. So we were always dangerous. Dangerous to meet in the street, in a restaurant, and dangerous to see on stage or in a film.'

On each continent – in each country – Harris discovered, and staked his claim at, a favourite bar or restaurant. In his native Ireland it was McDaids, off Grafton Street, where Brendan Behan hung out and where Samuel Beckett used to go quietly through pints of Guinness, and where the IRA leader Michael Collins once trapped and murdered a British spy. In London, a hasty raincoat pulled over his pyjamas, Harris would head for the Green Room Club off the Strand in Adam Street. It was founded in 1876 by Fred Terry, Sir Henry Irving and Sir Herbert Beerbohm Tree as a haven for the acting profession – the club where they had been members had decided to kick out actors – and Harris would prop up the bar and discuss the finer points of rugby league with a selection of equally eccentrically dressed thespians.

After landing at Kennedy International Airport, Harris would always make his first stop PJ Clarke's classic mahogany and cut-glass saloon on New York's Third Avenue. Frank Sinatra drank there; Jackie and Aristotle Onassis used to people-watch from a window in the middle dining room; and the composer and lyricist Johnny Mercer had written 'One For My Baby' on a napkin at the bar. During the 1960s one of the actor's favourite barmen was called Vinny. Each time Harris walked in he would ask for his 'usual' and Vinny would line up six double vodkas on the bar. When

Harris related the story to a New York journalist, his interviewer was sceptical. 'That's a load of bull,' said the reporter. 'It's got to be one of your bullshit stories.'

Harris stood up. 'Right,' he said, 'call me a taxi.'

When the pair walked into PJ's, Harris caught the barman's eye. 'Vinny, my usual.' Seconds later, six double vodkas appeared on the bar.

Harris had always been a binge drinker rather than a slow and destructive alcoholic like Richard Burton. When the need drove him, he could remain sober for weeks on end. After a period of sobriety – 'I stayed sober just to make movies to get money for booze' – he would plunge headlong and happy into a massive bender. He saw no reason, other than work, to ease up. On one occasion Harris woke up in a police cell. The sergeant asked him if he knew why he'd been arrested. 'No,' admitted Harris, 'I haven't a fucking clue.'

His parties very soon earned him legendary status; so too did his retribution on grumpy sleep-deprived neighbours. One all-night Tower House shindig was brought to an abrupt 5 a.m. halt when his neighbours called the police. Harris promptly paid a man to walk up and down Melbury Road ringing a bell and wearing a sandwich board proclaiming: 'Love Thy Neighbour Harris!' That night he threw another party.

But the actor's health would soon cause him more problems, this time not through any self-indulgence. For some time Harris had been feeling off colour and tired; his joints ached and occasionally he would experience a dull, nagging pain in his chest. Blood tests confirmed he was suffering from haemochromatosis, an inherited disease in which excessive iron in the body accumulates in the liver and pancreas and in the skin cells, turning them a bronze colour. Triggered by a faulty gene, the condition leaves most sufferers ignorant of its presence, and, inadvertently, they feed the problem by eating meat and vegetables with a high iron content or even by taking iron supplements. If the condition is left untreated – and it is frequently misdiagnosed – a sufferer can experience life-threatening conditions such as cirrhosis, diabetes, liver cancer and even heart failure.

Not for the first time, Harris was warned that, unless he changed his eating habits, and drastically cut down his drinking, he would be dead within a year. It was a prediction that would come closer to fruition than Harris knew.

CHAPTER TEN

The take involved a 'friendly' football match between the striking miners. Harris as McParlan captained one team and Connery the other, and to beef up the action the director bussed in 25 professional New York and Philadelphia Gaelic League players. There were no rules and the match – a cross between rugby and soccer – produced as many casualties as goals. 'It was bloody murder on that pitch,' recalls Malachy McCourt, the Irish actor given the dubious task of refereeing the free-for-all and who earned himself a kick in the face after one disputed decision. 'Dickie Harris obviously thought he was back filming *This Sporting Life*.' By the end of the game the pitch was littered with groaning bodies. Connery limped off with a twisted right knee and a severely bruised shoulder and Harris, grinning like a happy raccoon with two black eyes, nursed a broken nose and several cracked ribs.

CHAPTER TEN

Remember this practical piece of advice: Never come into the theatre with mud on your feet. Leave your dust and dirt outside. Check your little worries, squabbles, petty difficulties with your outside clothing – all the things that ruin your life and draw your attention away from your art – at the door.
                                                    – Konstantin Stanislavski

In Northern Ireland the sectarian rivalry between Catholics and Protestants was building up pressure and about the explode. On 12 August 1969, a Protestant march to celebrate the 1689 Siege of Londonderry passed through Catholic areas of Belfast. By nightfall what started as stone throwing and name calling degenerated into a full-scale riot. Shops and commercial premises in the city's Bogside were looted and torched. The police, searching house by house to flush out the troublemakers, were attacked and shot at. The fragile peace that held Northern Ireland together had finally evaporated.

The Ulster troubles escalated as the Irish Republican Army resorted to mass terrorism to back its demands for the six counties to be incorporated into the Irish Republic. Loyalist extremists and hardliners were also arming. Assassinations and bombings triggered a vicious and bloody series of tit-for-tat murders until the police and politicians spoke openly of civil war.

And, at the end of 1970, the worst year so far for deaths and terrorist casualties, there appeared a movie about – but never eulogising – the IRA. *The Molly Maguires* was Harris's third Republican Army film: in the late 1950s he had accepted bit parts in *Shake Hands with the Devil* and *A Terrible Beauty*. On this one, though, he was the movie's star.

It was enough – intelligence, police and terrorist sources have confirmed for the first time – to put Harris near the top of a Loyalist hit list. For several weeks early in 1971 he would be just a telephone call away from death.

For the director Martin Ritt, *The Molly Maguires* was more than simply a chance to retell a darkly intriguing yet frequently mistold part of American history. Ritt himself was a victim of injustice – he was blacklisted during the McCarthy era – and this is his most overtly political film. To help him make his point Ritt chose as his leading men two Celts whose ancestry contained an equal portion of repression and subjugation.

The Molly Maguires was a secret organisation of immigrant coal miners supposedly responsible for a terrorist campaign in the anthracite coalfields of Pennsylvania and West Virginia between 1862 and 1876. The group named itself after a widow who led a band of Irish anti-landlord agitators from the 1840s. When poor working conditions and job discrimination led to acts of sabotage and terrorist assassinations by Irish–American miners twenty years later, the 'Mollies' were blamed. The pit owners contacted the Pinkerton National Detective Agency, which ordered one of its detectives, James McParlan, to infiltrate the group. His testimony led to the murder, conviction and execution of ten alleged 'Molly' members.

Although the story was previously used by Conan Doyle for his Sherlock Holmes novel *The Valley of Fear*, much of the script was based on Allan Pinkerton's own controversial book *The Molly Maguires and the Detectives*. 'This film had to be done on location, in a genuine atmosphere,' argued Ritt. 'Not only for the physical look of the movie, but also for the actors.' Studio bosses at Paramount were hesitant. In the end, they refused the director's demand to make the film in black and white, but allowed him to shoot on the sites where much of the original action had taken place.

Ritt recruited Richard Harris to play McParlan, the mole in the Irish camp, and Sean Connery as the leader of the striking miners. When they arrived on location the pair were soon overwhelmed by the oppressive summer heat and the director's bleak vision. The only Pennsylvania town that looked remotely as it had done a century earlier was the isolated community of Eckley. The sixty-odd homes and other buildings, roads and pithead gear were sprayed with thousands of gallons of slate-grey paint to make them appear more depressing. And, when trees and plants came into flower, gangs of local workers were hired to pick them bare. Many of the cast became scratchy and exhausted and Connery, recently released from the luxuries of his James Bond role, had to be treated for dehydration. It didn't affect his sense of humour. Asked by a mischievous journalist whether he minded that Harris was taking top billing, Connery replied, 'They're paying me a million dollars for this picture. For that kind of money they can put a mule ahead of me.'

Despite the high temperatures, and the obvious dangers, Harris and

Connery insisted on tackling most of their own stunts. One scene left both stars and a least a dozen extras – most of them professional football players – queuing for the unit's doctor.

The take involved a 'friendly' football match between the striking miners. Harris as McParlan captained one team and Connery the other, and to beef up the action the director bussed in 25 professional New York and Philadelphia Gaelic League players. There were no rules and the match – a cross between rugby and soccer – produced as many casualties as goals. 'It was bloody murder on that pitch,' recalls Malachy McCourt, the Irish actor given the dubious task of refereeing the free-for-all and who earned himself a kick in the face after one disputed decision. 'Dickie Harris obviously thought he was back filming *This Sporting Life*.' By the end of the game the pitch was littered with groaning bodies. Connery limped off with a twisted right knee and a severely bruised shoulder and Harris, grinning like a happy raccoon with two black eyes, nursed a broken nose and several cracked ribs.

Watching all this with a mixture of admiration and apprehension was the film's female star. Green-eyed and flame-haired Samantha Eggar, the daughter of an army officer and a Dutch–Portuguese mother, was a late theatrical starter, abandoning her convent education to make her acting debut alongside Donald Wolfit and Mona Washbourne in a Cecil Beaton play at the Dublin Theatre Festival. Seasons at the Oxford Playhouse and the Royal Court were quickly followed by offers of film work, and in 1965 Eggar was named as best actress at the Cannes Film Festival for her part in *The Collector*.

Eggar's 'glowing beauty and professionalism' took time to surface. She was, remembered Harris, terribly suspicious of the film's two stars. 'Her background made her very proud, very proper, and not able communicate openly at first,' he explained. 'She adopted this stand-off quality as a defence mechanism. After about ten days she relaxed and once we got to know her she became the darling of the crew. They adored her.'

Because the actress had rented a nearby house for herself and her two young children, Egger never witnessed her co-star's off-duty alcoholic excesses. On the set she found herself exhilarated by his enthusiasm. 'Mad as Richard was,' says Eggar, 'he poured out so much energy that you simply had to try to match up to him.'

Paramount's concern over Ritt's interpretation of the Walter Bernstein script heightened. For more than a year the studio remained uncertain about cashing in on its $11 million investment. *The Molly Maguires* was eventually released on both sides of the Atlantic in 1970 and, as the director later conceded, immediately 'landed on its ass'.

There were various reasons, both financial and personal, for the film's failure to attract cinema audiences. Years later, when his duty to promote *The Molly Maguires* was over, Harris admitted that making the film was a 'heartbreaking experience. It was not the movie I agreed to make.'

Harris readily identified with Martin Ritt's motives for making the film and sympathised with the director after his mauling by the studio executives. 'Ritt took the story and related it to those people who had betrayed his own kind during the McCarthy witch hunt,' Harris explained. 'He was very bitter about this period and wanted to make the film as a personal statement. He was also attempting something even more subtle: he was exposing the treachery on which America exists and the men who climb any kind of ladder to reach the top.'

Watching the first rough-cut version, Harris found the film 'shattering and intellectually brutal'. Sean Connery, sitting through a screening with scriptwriter and co-producer Walter Bernstein, was also disappointed. 'I told him I thought he'd missed it,' said the Scotsman. 'It was well intentioned and a good film, but it never caught fire. One reason was the fear that humour might creep in, when it can actually enhance a situation.'

The American critics in particular respected the artistry, but did little to encourage cinemagoers to go out of their way to watch a 'well-mounted but sluggish drama'. The *New Yorker* branded it a failure, 'yet an impressive failure ... too sombre and portentous for the rather dubious story it carries'.

British press interviews about the film invariably came round to the subject of Northern Ireland, which had exploded during the movie's first weeks on release. 'For God's sake,' Harris told one national newspaper, 'let's all learn to live in peace.' More often he was misquoted and misunderstood. Whenever he spoke of 'Irish nationalism' the media branded him an IRA sympathiser. In reality he had never taken sides and had even written and released a peace poem. It did not help when he informed the *Sunday Times*, 'I'm proud to be called an Irishman. Why not? I'm not ashamed.'

The week before Christmas 1970 Harris's name appeared in an intelligence report generated in Northern Ireland. A copy of the top-secret report was sent to the Metropolitan Police Special Branch. It warned that a hardline Loyalist group was searching for high-profile Irish-born assassination targets in mainland Britain.

Over the next six weeks, intelligence from both Royal Ulster Constabulary and military sources claimed Loyalist extremists had sanctioned a hit on the actor and ordered one of its London-based cells to reconnoitre and plan the attack. A former member of the terrorist group has now confirmed this: 'Richard Harris, as [a supposed] IRA sympathiser, was seen as a legitimate target.'

The police and Home Office were equally aware that the murder of an Irish national in the heart of London, especially one as internationally well known as Harris, would have opened a new front on the war against terrorism. Only the IRA had so far carried out mainland attacks, and then had targeted only the English. The Special Branch was ordered to keep watch on Harris's new Tower House home.

Records of the surveillance operation have never been released to the public. But it is almost certain that contact was made with members of the cell – confirmed by at least one former antiterrorist officer – and a decision taken to track the gang. An arrest operation would be mounted only when Harris's life was 'under imminent threat'.

The plan was for a single member of the gang to approach and shoot Harris as he returned to Tower House late one night. If he managed to survive and somehow escape, two other gunmen would be waiting at either end of Melbury Road. Everything was in place. So, too, were the police.

Mysteriously, the assassination was abandoned. In less than twelve hours all members of the cell disappeared. Two later served prison sentences in Northern Ireland for terrorism-related offences; one of the men has since claimed the attack was aborted for 'political reasons'. Police officers who worked on the case are convinced the gang received a high-level tip-off, from either Belfast or Dublin. No one felt it necessary to warn Harris of the danger he was in.

His time making *The Molly Maguires* with Sean Connery produced one of Harris's few lasting friendships with a fellow actor. There was little in their backgrounds – one the descendent of a wealthy milling family, the other a labourer's son whose grandfather had scratched a living as a tinker – that brought them together, but they talked easily and listened to each other's confessions. During lunch on the *Molly Maguires* set Harris suddenly announced, 'I am a very religious man.'

'Oh, yeah?' said Connery.

'Yes,' said Harris, taking another mouthful, 'but I don't believe in God.'

If I regret anything I've done then I'll forgive myself. I'm not going to confess my sins to someone else.'

'I know the feeling,' said Connery. 'Have you got any regrets?'

Harris thought for a few seconds, and then admitted that his biggest miscalculation had been in the choice of the parts he had accepted and declined. 'I turned down *The Ipcress File*, which went to Michael Caine, but I did *Caprice* with Doris Day. I once walked off an aeroplane when I learned *Caprice* was being shown. *The Red Desert* was also a miserable experience. Antonioni completely misrepresented the project. If he had not made a career in the motion-picture business, he would surely have been head of the Mafia. And then there was *Mutiny on the Bounty*: it looked terrific with Brando and was a total fucking disaster.'

Harris and Connery never made another film together, although they did fleetingly pass on the set of *Robin and Marian*. 'I don't like actors,' Harris would confess to the *Sunday Times*. 'I find them fucking boring. Sean Connery is my only genuine friend, the only one I've asked to my house. I'd spend an evening with O'Toole, Roger Moore and maybe Richard Burton, but I can't be bothered with the rest of them.'

Living in the divorce minefield that lay between her former husband and present lover, Elizabeth found life exciting and exasperating in equal measure. Although he had no control over his former spouse, Harris still possessed legal rights over his three sons – and insisted on exercising them at every opportunity.

When Elizabeth informed Harris she, and her brother Morgan and his girlfriend, had been invited to cruise the Yugoslav and Italian coast with Rex Harrison, Trevor Howard and his wife Helen Cherry, the Irish actor was determined to stop the boys from holidaying with Harrison. The High Court backed his application that his three sons should not be allowed to live or stay with Elizabeth and her lover until Harrison's divorce from Rachel Roberts was finalised. Soon after the decree absolute, the Harris discovered that Harrison was planning to fly the boys on holiday to France, tourist class. Harris's solicitor fired off a stiff letter 'ordering' they travel first class.

Harrison, who held little regard for Harris as either a man or an actor, had taken to calling his lover's ex-husband 'that bloody Irishman'. Mention of Harris's name would send Harrison into an obscene rage. On one occasion he toured the cabins of his yacht, scooping up every copy of Harris's records before confining them to the depths of the Mediterranean.

After starring in *My Fair Lady* for two years in New York and a third in London, Harrison, to the public and professionals alike, would for ever be Henry Higgins. He belonged, wrote Alexander Walker, to a totally different scene.

He was part – an essential, valued part – of the theatre of comfort, the theatre of nostalgia and the theatre of classical revivalism. He stood for the star system, the showcase production, the clappable scenery, the matinée audience, the nine-month run and, above all, the phenomenon he himself seemed to be – an apotheosis of the celebrity whose reputation courses through the veins of any performance he gives like blue blood.

So many things about Harris irritated the Englishman. Harris was disrespectful. His breath stank of liquor. He frequently looked as though he had slept in his clothes and not bathed in weeks. In short he never *looked* like an actor, like a member of a profession Harrison still held sacred.

One sartorial habit that particularly disgusted Harrison was Harris's habit of wearing 'thirty-bob-a-time' rugby shirts. He bought them by the score and threw them away when they needed washing. Preparing for a few days away, or a long weekend watching an international match in Dublin, he would scoop up three or four rugby shirts and hurl them into an overnight bag. Even that was not without its dangers.

Sitting next to an inquisitive fellow passenger on an Aer Lingus flight to Ireland, Harris explained his preference for rugby tops.

'Oh, I see,' said the passenger. 'But don't you think you've picked the wrong colours for this trip?'

Harris looked down to discover he was wearing the national colours of the visiting team. Sidling to the toilet, he stripped off the red, white and blue shirt and put on his raincoat. A few minutes later he arrived at Dublin bare-chested – but for ever loyal to Ireland.

For Harris's three sons it was also a time of confusion. At school Jared Harris's surname prompted more enquiries about Rolf Harris – the Australian singer, painter and humorist – than it did his real parent. 'In the end I sort of wished he *was* Rolf Harris,' admitted Jared years later. The transformation from a father – 'the big character who filled up every room he entered' and 'played soccer in the living room using the lamps as goal posts' – to famous actor came only after Jared sat through a West End stage performance of *Camelot*.

The experience of watching his estranged wife's increasingly public affair with Christopher Plummer – 'I was determined to make Richard pay' – had only added sulphur to the atmosphere between them. When Harris heard she now intended to marry her new lover, that 'has-been' Harrison, he was seized with an impotent anger.

Richard and Elizabeth Harris were formally divorced at 3.45 p.m. on 25 July 1969. They had been married for twelve years. Harris openly confessed he still loved his ex-wife. To mark Elizabeth's impending marriage to Rex Harrison, he organised a hellraising weekend of celebration – A Honeymoon without a Bride.

Among the six guests were Harris's long-time acting friend Malachy McCourt, and one of the few journalists he considered 'trustworthy'. Harris's Rolls-Royce toured London picking up his fellow travellers and greeting each guest with a glass of champagne. At Heathrow they piled aboard a chartered eight-seat Falcon executive jet and downed more drinks while they discussed where to go. For the next 72 hours they swooped in and out of Europe's liveliest cities, visiting nightclubs and strip clubs and refuelling at every bar they passed. For the reporter on board, 'Days were to scream crazily into nights and nights were to belch horribly back into days.'

Rex Harrison and Elizabeth Harris were married at Alan Jay Lerner's Long Island home on 26 August 1971. Rex described the day as a 'festive occasion', but for most of the time he was on the telephone to the BBC in London, preoccupied with the final cut of a television play about to receive its American screening.

'By the time it was all over Richard was too exhausted to get worked up about Elizabeth's new marriage,' explains McCourt. 'It was the tonic he needed. The "honeymoon" allowed him to forget the most painful part of his divorce.'

When it was all over Harris jetted off again, this time to Spain, where he teamed up with the villain-turned-actor John Bindon. For the producers of Man in the Wilderness, it would prove a costly and time-wasting partnership.

Bindon was a flamboyant London criminal who, at the age of eleven, earned himself his first stretch behind bars for selling live ammunition to would-be bank robbers. By the mid-1960s – when Bindon was in his early twenties – he graduated to fencing high-class items through his legitimate antiques business, and as 'recreation' delivered punishment beatings to errant members of several city gangs. Bindon was holding court one night in a Fulham pub when

Ken Loach walked in. The director, renowned for using amateurs in his films, was about to start casting Nell Dunn's working-class drama *Poor Cow* and thought the charismatic Bindon 'absolutely right' for one of the male leads. Not content with his burgeoning film career, Bindon was soon heading a network of protection rackets. One police report claimed he was earning at least £10,000 a month on top of his legitimate movie fees.

As a violent drunk, drug addict and sexual exhibitionist, John Bindon – whose underworld nickname was 'Biffo' because of his fondness for using his fists – could leave Richard Harris in the shade. When a young man in a Chelsea pub inadvertently said something to offend Bindon, he was dragged outside, beaten semiconscious and bundled into the boot of a car. The victim was driven to Putney Common, where Bindon ordered him to dig his own grave. The threatened execution was only minutes away when the effects of drink and drugs finally took over and Bindon collapsed.

In 1968 Bindon met Vicki Hodge, a baronet's-daughter-turned-fashion-model, who introduced him to polite society and, despite their long-term relationship, a string of celebrity lovers, including Christine Keeler and Angie Barnett, the future wife of the pop star David Bowie. Good looks and charm were not his only attraction – his party piece involved hanging five half-pint beer mugs on his erect penis. On holiday in Mustique, Hodge introduced her lover to Princess Margaret. The Queen's sister demanded immediate and personal proof of Bindon's mug-carrying capacity.

All this fascinated Harris, who quickly took to sharing his off-set hours with his wayward co-star. *Man in the Wilderness* was inspired by Harris's previous endurance melodrama *A Man Called Horse*. Both films were written by Jack de Witt. This time, de Witt cast Harris as a Canadian fur trapper who survives a mauling by a grizzly bear and sets out for revenge. Bindon arrived in Spain with a contract promising him third billing after Harris and the ageing actor–director John Huston, and a script that saw his character survive most of the film. On his first night, Bindon celebrated by getting drunk. The next evening he was escorted back to his hotel by the police. The filming was eventually halted to allow the healing of cuts and bruises Harris and Bindon suffered in a drunken brawl that had ended with both men fighting at the bottom of a roadside ditch. The director Richard Sarafian decided the Londoner 'had to go'. A hastily convened script conference resulted in Bindon's 'premature and suitably painful' screen death and his equally rapid departure from the Spanish location.

Harris and John Bindon, who also claimed Irish ancestry, remained friends and invariably met to celebrate St Patrick's Day. 'It took them the rest of the year to recover,' according to Hodge. But Bindon's acting career was already in decline. By 1976 he was declared bankrupt and two years later faced trail for the contract killing of an out-of-control gangster named Johnnie Darke. 'When Bob Hoskins agreed to speak as a character witness I knew I would get away with it,' Bindon later admitted. He died penniless of AIDS in 1993.

Harris had his own theory about women: they should have lots of opinions, but also the good sense never to express them. The only time you miss a woman, he would trot out to television interviewers and feature writers alike, was when you hadn't got one. But acquiring new female company was never Harris's problem. 'What I like about love is the tragedy of it all,' he said. 'If the relationship shows the slightest signs of not becoming tragic, I make it. As soon as I meet a girl, even before we have our first date, I've already worked out how it will end.' After just a few months at Tower House, he discovered a unique and frightening way of turning on the tragedy.

A week or ten days into a relationship, Harris would start to get bored. It was then that he would slip the ghosts that frequented Tower House into a conversation. The next day, over breakfast or while dressing for work, he would inform his girlfriend that he would be back around eight or nine o'clock that evening to collect her for dinner. He never showed. Irritated by his nonappearance and alone in the Knightsbridge mansion the woman would find her imagination taking over. By the early hours of the morning, with the house creaking and contracting in the cold night air, they invariably fled. Harris would return, having slept and breakfasted at the Savoy, to find a note: 'Sorry Richard, I can't live here any more.'

One of Tower House's numerous spirits could often be heard playing a one-fingered tune on the piano. During the making of one of Harris's albums the songwriter Johnnie Harrison was staying with the actor-turned-singer. One night the composer decided to go out and Harris went to bed.

He awoke to the sound of melodious but erratic music. It sounded as though the musician were creating and exploring chords. 'Johnnie,' Harris called as he descended the stairs, 'are you there?' No answer. The music continued and he listened for a few seconds from the downstairs hallway. Suddenly, Harris realised there was no light coming from under the music room door. As he slid back the door and reached for the light switch, the chords stopped. The room was cold and deserted – and the keyboard lid was down.

There were, quite often, witnesses to the hauntings. Harold Shirley, an American record-company executive whom Harris befriended one night in a restaurant, was invited back to Tower House for breakfast. He was due to fly back to the States later that morning. It was still dark when the pair arrived. Harris went off to change, leaving his guest to explore the house. Behind him Shirley heard a woman approaching; he is convinced she was wearing a nightdress or dressing gown. 'I had heard that sound a thousand times before,' explains the businessman. 'It was the sound my wife and daughters made walking round my own house: the swoosh of material. I assumed Richard had an unexpected house guest and I turned to say "hello".' The kitchen was empty. When Harris returned a few minutes later he confirmed that the two men were alone in the house.

'Oh, that,' said Harris, shrugging off the mysterious female. 'That's just one of my ghosts.'

But his own experiences with the spirits – and he claimed there were at least four – could be just as frightening.

Harris was in bed with a girlfriend. The couple were dozing when the woman heard someone running up and down the stairs. The footfalls were light and agile, as if the person were running on tiptoe. The woman nudged Harris awake. 'Quick,' she whispered, 'there's someone in the house.'

At that moment the door to the *en suite* bathroom began to rattle violently. It was not the sound of someone trying to break in, more as if the door had jammed and someone were pushing at it to get out. The bathroom was self-contained and there was no way anyone could have entered it without first crossing the bedroom.

Harris and his girlfriend sat up in bed. The commotion in the bathroom stopped. Now the handle on the bedroom door began to turn. The door swung silently open. Standing a foot or so back from the doorway was a woman dressed entirely in black with long, waist-length hair. 'Richard,' said the apparition. 'Are you alone?'

'Who are you?' demanded Harris.

There was no reply.

At that Harris leaped from the bed, slammed the door shut and switched on every light he could find. He and his girlfriend searched every room and cupboard in the house. Every window was bolted and every outside door locked.

In 1972 Harris returned to Spain to film *Riata*, an ill-conceived revenge Western in which a sheriff stalks the outlaws who killed his wife and son. The director, Samuel Fuller, had sold his own storyline to Warner Bros and recruited both Harris and Rod Taylor to play the male leads. Five weeks into filming, things were going so badly that the studio called a halt to the shoot and demanded all the rushes be sent back to Hollywood. Unwilling to lose its investment, Warner dispatched a new director, Barry Shear, to the Iberian peninsular and promptly renamed the project *The Deadly Trackers*. It was not enough. When the film was released the following year the *New Yorker* wrote it off as 'an incoherent, blood-soaked chase story'.

In Hollywood John Frankenheimer was having trouble casting his new movie, a violent 1940s gangster comedy with the wacky title *99 and 44/100 Per Cent Dead*. Richard Harris had already agreed to take the lead, but few actresses were willing to tackle the offbeat script or work with the notoriously difficult Irishman. When Jacqueline Bisset refused the role, Frankenheimer decided it was time to approach a newcomer. 'You're not going to wean an unknown actress?' protested Harris.

But watching the screen-test footage, Harris admitted he might have been wrong. Ann Turkel was possibly the most confident and self-possessed 'unknown' he had seen in a long time. Face to face, she was certainly the most beautiful.

Born into a Jewish middle-class family and raised in Manhattan, Ann Turkel was a precocious child whose grandmother quickly spotted and encouraged her gift for entertaining. By her sixteenth birthday, she had already studied at the Musical Theater Academy and the Neighborhood Playhouse under some of New York's most distinguished acting coaches, including Sandy Meisner and Philip Burton, the foster parent of Richard Burton. Still undecided whether her career lay in music or acting, Turkel attempted both. The summer of 1964 was spent acting with the Berkshire Playhouse in Stockbridge, Massachusetts, and followed by an autumn and winter singing with a rock band.

The group was booked to entertain at a fashion show, but one member of the audience was more impressed with Ann's stunning good looks than her singing voice. The *Vogue* editor Gloria Schiff introduced her discovery to the magazine's editor-in-chief Diana Vreeland, and within a week the sixteen-year-old was shooting her first *Vogue* cover. The 'new face of the

Sixties' was soon in demand around the world, gracing the covers of top fashion magazines, modelling in Europe and Japan and advertising cosmetics for Chanel and Fabergé. Less than ten years after quitting high school, she was already a millionaire and engaged to David Niven Jr.

The readthroughs and rehearsals went well. Harris remained coolly professional and began – touch-by-touch, glance-by-glance – to dispel the hellraiser reputation that Ann's friends and associates had warned her against. The effect was inevitable. 'I fell passionately in love with him,' she admitted. 'We fell in love before we'd ever gone to bed with each other.'

Despite attempts to keep their affair secret, the Hollywood press pack quickly scented a story – and possible disaster. 'If I believed all the wild stories I wouldn't be going out with Richard,' Ann told one columnist. 'Besides, there's no need to tame him: he's more of a lamb than a lion. What went on before doesn't worry me. It's the future that counts.'

One of Ann's closest friends at that time, who admits she had never personally met Harris, vainly attempted to refocus the model-turned-actress's usually faultless taste in men. 'She was impossible. She was obsessed by him and everything he did and everything he said,' recalls the friend. 'The fact that he was eighteen years older than her and treated his women like shit meant nothing. Ann was in love and Ann knew best.'

It was Harris's honesty about his past that not only deepened his lover's passion, but also won over her 'broad-minded' parents. 'They accepted that I needed to live with a man to get to know him better,' Ann later explained. 'It was all right as long as we eventually married, and I was determined to marry Richard Harris.'

CHAPTER ELEVEN

Once again, Harris was attempting to cut back his daily two and a half bottles of vodka by substituting cocaine. It was a lethal combination. After a month of punishment, his body gave up and the actor collapsed and was rushed to the Cedars of Lebanon hospital in Los Angeles. Emergency-room doctors were so concerned by his condition that they informed his family there was little hope for his survival, and a priest performed the last rites. Having been transferred to intensive care, Harris was now on a life-support machine and newspaper and television newsrooms around the world began compiling Richard Harris obituaries. In London two papers, the *Sun* and the *Daily Mirror*, even got as far as laying out a front page announcing his death.

It was not to be. From somewhere deep inside, Harris found the strength to recover. When he eventually returned home, he headed straight for the toilet – and flushed away his £4,000 stash of cocaine.

CHAPTER ELEVEN

I mean, the question actors most often get asked is how they can bear saying the same things over and over again, night after night, but God knows the answer to that is, don't we all anyway: might as well get paid for it.

                                     – Elaine Dundy

'*Harris!*' the voice hissed menacingly. 'The next time I see you I'm going to kick the shit out of you and I'm going to stamp on your face and break both your arms.'

'Where are you?' demanded Richard Harris.

'El Pedrino's.'

'Don't move.'

Harris arrived at the Los Angeles bar a few minutes later. 'Do I start with you?' he asked the muscle-bound bodyguard standing at his master's shoulder. 'Or do I begin with Oliver?'

'Me.' The man waved away his advancing minder and slowly stood up.

Gasps of recognition rippled through the lounge. In the silence Richard Harris and Oliver Reed glared at each other nose to nose. Ego to ego.

'Drink?'

'Don't mind if I do.'

After more than ten years of mischievous pranks and manufactured animosity it was only the second time the two actors had met. With the handshakes and backslapping over, they settled down to some serious drinking. 'Sober, he was a great guy,' recalled Oliver Reed. 'Drunk, he was even better.'

Since their brief Elstree encounter in 1960, Harris had been increasingly aware of the Wimbledon-born star's growing reputation, both as an actor and a hellraiser. But, while reading newspaper accounts of his own dimly remembered exploits, he considered Reed's antics 'childish and boring'. Nor was Reed a particularly dangerous professional rival: he picked up three leading roles only after Harris had turned them down. And unlike the Irishman, whose formative years were spent at drama school and as one of Joan Littlewood's 'little eggs', Reed had deliberately shunned the theatre. He remains one of the few film stars never to have given a single stage performance.

In 1969 Reed delivered a masterful and groundbreaking performance – opposite Alan Bates and the future Labour MP Glenda Jackson – in Ken Russell's adaptation of *Women in Love*. Amid the excess of praise and platitudes, Harris impishly sent Reed a pair of crutches – one inscribed 'Ken Russell', the other 'Glenda Jackson'.

By the early 1970s, Harris found himself more than a little irritated by Reed's self-proclamations. With his patriotism at its blustering height, Reed had taken to calling himself 'Mr England', and claimed to be 'the biggest star this country has got'. This time, Harris posted Reed a copy of his recently published poems, *I, In the Membership of My Days*. On the flyleaf he wrote, 'To Oliver – Mr England. Since you have not yet attained superstar status and salary and therefore cannot afford to buy this book, here is a free copy. Richard – Mr Ireland.' And on the endpaper Harris added, 'You are the only person I know who would go out of his way to claim an affinity with a bankrupt nation.'

The slim volume would remain one of the Reed's lifelong treasures. For several years he would treat his houseguests to an after-dinner Harris poem. 'Isn't that marvellous?' he would pronounce. 'Isn't that fucking beautiful?'

At first the taunting was nothing more than a private joke but it soon became a crucial part of both actors' publicity machine. 'Harris often made outrageous statements about me to reporters,' explained Reed. 'But we were both sensible and professional enough to know they were manufactured entirely for the benefit of the press.' And it would continue for years to come.

In 1975 Reed made the western *The Great Scout and Cathouse Thursday* with the fast-ailing alcoholic Lee Marvin. He made sure Harris got a mention: 'Lee Marvin is the roughest, toughest movie star in the business – and the hardest drinker. He'd make Richard Harris look like a half-pint of stale Guinness and Dean Martin a wet Martini.' The chance of another sideswipe came two years later, while Reed was making *The Prince and the Pauper*. One of Reed's co-stars – with whom he was orchestrating another well-publicised personality clash – was Raquel Welch. A telegram arrived at Harris's London home inviting the Irishman to take over a sex scene with Welch – 'providing your wig doesn't fall off'.

It had been a physically demanding and confidence-draining twelve months for Harris. He was in Los Angeles to recuperate from the rigours and critical mauling of an international concert tour, and his Los Angeles encounter with Oliver Reed came as badly needed fillip. Musically, his achievements since the 1968 success of 'MacArthur Park' were considerable: he had released three long-playing records and turned several of the individual tracks into hit singles (at one time he had no fewer than six records in the American Top 100); he had performed on pop-music programmes around the world, including the BBC's prestigious *Top of the Pops*; he had earned himself two gold discs; he'd written or collaborated on dozens of his own songs, most of which started life as a tune hummed into a tape recorder; and all this time he was collecting the royalties on the million-selling pop classic 'MacArthur Park'.

And, when he wasn't in a studio recording or editing or scribbling flashes of poetry, he was working on his first – and only – novel. *Flanney at 1.10* was about a man who refuses to be born – 'He'd rather spend the rest of his life in his mother's womb, with a butler to look after him, than face the outside world.' Harris found the process of writing 'absorbing'. He would wake in the early hours with an idea buzzing in his head and spend the rest of the night writing. He was, complained his friends, in serious danger of becoming a workaholic.

Harris had long since discovered the Queen's Elm, a Chelsea pub popular with émigré Irish. Another of the Elm's regulars was Phil Coulter. Twelve years younger than Harris, the Ulster-born musician spent the 1960s in London playing piano on stage for Tom Jones, Van Morrison and the Rolling Stones to supplement his songwriting ambitions. Success eventually came when he teamed up with an outlandish Scot called Bill Martin. In 1967 the pair clocked up their first major hit with Sandie Shaw's 'Puppet on a String', which won the Eurovision Song Contest for the UK and went on to be recorded by more than a hundred different artists. The following year they almost pulled off the double when Cliff Richard sang 'Congratulations'.

Over a Guinness at the Elm, Harris confessed his musical ambitions. 'I don't just want to sing a few songs,' he told Coulter. 'That's not an evening's entertainment. I think audiences will expect and deserve something a bit different from me. Even if they just want me to talk.'

Coulter was impressed, but more interested in Harris's idea of an album of songs charting a man's life from teenage love at first sight through marriage to eventual divorce. It was a heavily autobiographical project, which, by his own admission, cost Harris more than a few tears. One track, 'All the Broken Children', concerned the break-up of a marriage and how it affects the children. Another, 'Why Did You Leave Me?', was clearly a question aimed at Elizabeth. By October 1971, the Coulter-produced album was complete and Harris decided to release his favourite track, 'My Boy', as a single. An appearance on *Top of the Pops* guaranteed another hit.

Backed by the thirty-piece Coulter Orchestra, Harris started rehearsals for an eight-week concert tour of Britain and America. For one showcase performance he would be accompanied by the London Symphony Orchestra. Tickets sold well, but once again Harris was savaged by the press.

One of the hardest hitters was the *Guardian's* Robin Denselow, who suggested the two-hour theatre show was more suited to nightclubs and cabaret venues like the Talk of the Town.

Is it conceit or sheer self-deception? Why should a first-rate actor parade himself like a shambling tenth-rate Sinatra? True, he has handled a musical successfully, and gone on to record a series of albums, but when it comes to a full solo concert, there is no hiding behind a name or studio techniques. He tried to play it straight and just couldn't do it ... The Harris myth of the glossy record sleeves collapsed fast, but then for a few minutes, a more real Harris was allowed to look in, telling Irish bar jokes and stories showing mistakes from his films, and putting on a delightfully funny cabaret turn.

The tour moved to the States for its opening run in New Orleans, where one critic described Harris as 'the greatest entertainer the city has seen in the last decade'.

Coulter is reticent about his memories of working with Harris. It was hilarious and enjoyable, he claims, but 'I can't remember a lot about the tour, and the bits I can remember you don't want to hear about – trust me.'

On the final day of the *Sporting Life* shoot, Lindsay Anderson had turned to Richard Harris and said, 'Well, Richard, you're never going to get another part as good as *Sporting Life* again, nor a movie like *Sporting Life*. From now on your career is downhill.' From Anderson's lips it was nothing more than a light-hearted and deliberately pessimistic prophesy. When Harris attempted to capitalise on his director's words the results would prove predictably disastrous.

'Lindsay Anderson was wrong,' Harris informed an *Echoes of a Summer* pre-filming press conference. 'This wonderful film has come along and I have turned down four other pictures to be able to make it – I think I would probably have turned down the remake of *Ben-Hur*.' The US–Canadian-financed film, which tells the story of a dying eleven-year-old girl's last summer on holiday with her family, would be shot on location on the western shore of Nova Scotia and directed by Don Taylor. Not only was Harris confident enough to take on the lead role, he also co-produced the project and composed and sang the main theme.

Despite its launch poster campaign claiming *Echoes* was 'The most beautiful love story since *Love Story*', the result was excruciating. The *New York Post*'s appropriately named critic, Frank Rich, summed it all up when he declared, 'The only honest thing about this movie is its desire to make a buck.'

The new year started with a flurry of rumours. Newspaper columnists who claimed Harris's relationship with Ann Turkel would not last attempted to further the prediction by alleging they were continually quarrelling and about to split. Others, tipped off that Elizabeth's unhappy marriage to Rex Harrison was already in trouble, resurrected Harris's past proclamation that he would never remarry. The truth, when it came, took everyone by surprise. About to set off on his concert tour, Harris called a press conference to announce officially his engagement to the American actress. They were, Ann beamed, 'madly in love' and intended to marry in April. It was the first time Ann and Harris, already committed to his concert tour – followed, within days, by a new film – could both be sure of a week off.

Throughout late February and March, two new experiences were added to Harris's career. The first was that he made his first film with Richard Lester, a director renowned for his easygoing and incredibly rapid shooting schedule. *Juggernaut* would also be his first movie shot almost entirely afloat and the combination would elicit one of Harris's best performances in years.

United Artists and its co-producers hired a Russian cruise ship, suitably disguised and renamed the *Britannic*, as the setting for its latest suspense thriller. The plot was simple: seven steel drums, each containing a half-ton charge of the explosive amatol, had been placed on board the liner prior to its departure from Southampton. Masterminding an extortion attempt from his semidetached suburban home, the terrorist bomber – using the code word 'Juggernaut' and played by the veteran English actor Freddie Jones – demands £500,000 to save the ship and its passengers. The job of beating the 22-hour deadline is given to Harris (as Fallon) and his Royal Navy bomb-disposal team, whose mission begins with a mid-Atlantic parachute drop. In reality the *Britannic* got no further than the Irish Sea, where the late-winter storms caused havoc among the cast and crew and the hundreds of passenger extras.

Harris later admitted he 'greatly enjoyed' Richard Lester's 'easygoing style of direction'. Another of the film's stars appreciated Lester's frenetic style. 'He was an incredibly fast worker,' says Anthony Hopkins. 'Smash-bang. Four cameras and you're finished in a week. The actors would meet on the set. "Stand by, action." He'd do one take, then say to us, "Right, do you want to do another?" No, we'd say. "OK, on we go." '

With the *Britannic* bobbing about somewhere in the middle of a make-believe Atlantic, the film's critics were largely divided by the same ocean. The *New Yorker* panned the thriller as 'jaunty, cynical slapstick', while the British and European press sided with American Jonathan Rosenbaum, who declared, 'However unoriginal its basic ingredients, *Juggernaut* hardly ever slackens its pace or diverts attention from its central premise.' Part of the reason was probably that Britain was itself in the middle of a deadly Irish Republican Army bombing campaign. In 1974 – the year of the film's release – the IRA detonated bombs at the Tower of London, Westminster Hall and Harrods, and bungled an attempt to assassinate the leader of the opposition. These were events the Americans experienced only from the safety of their television screens.

As a concession to married life, Harris agreed to sell Tower House. His bachelor home – not that he was ever truly alone with its domestic staff and constant visitors – went on the market for £275,000 and sold within days, netting him a cool four-year profit of £200,000.

Harris and Ann still, therefore, needed somewhere to live. He was talking one day to Kevin McClory, the former sound-technician-turned-*Thunderball*-producer, when the 48-year-old Irishman suggested the Bahamas. Harris flew out to examine the real estate and found the house of his dreams on the suitably named Paradise Island.

Once owned by the American millionaire businessman Huntingdon Hartford – who still owned the entire island – the house was built on a sea spit and appealed to Harris's isolationist nature and dishevelled lifestyle. Surrounded by untidy gardens, it had somehow been

Left Though yet to make his appearance as a bomb disposal expert in *Juggernaut*, Harris took on the booby-trapped Kathrine Baumann in *99 and 44/100 Per Cent Dead* ... (© Tony Hillman Collection)

Below ... with mixed results. The film was later retitled and reissued as *Call Harry Crown*. (© Tony Hillman Collection)

Above In 1976 Harris made a brief appearance in the Richard Lester-directed *Robin and Marian*. His co-star was Sean Connery, one of the few actors Harris enjoyed meeting off the set. (© Tony Hillman Collection)

Right Rex Harrison: When Elizabeth Harris announced she was intending to marry the veteran actor, Harris embarked on a long, boozy 'honeymoon without a bride', which included ferrying his guests around the nightspots of Europe in a private jet. (© Tony Hillman Collection)

Left It was during the making of *99 and 44/100 Per Cent Dead* that Harris met Ann Turkel. The couple married within a year.

Below Two women in one film: in *The Cassandra Crossing* Harris had the dubious pleasure of co-starring with his second wife, Ann Turkel, while ending up in bed with Sophia Loren. (© Tony Hillman Collection)

Above Off duty on the set of *The Wild Geese:* Richard Burton, Roger Moore and Richard Harris – and their wives. (© Tony Hillman Collection)

Below While filming *The Wild Geese* Richard Burton asked his friend what the worst part of his past was. Harris thought for a moment and then replied, 'What I can't remember and what other people have enjoyed.' (© Tony Hillman Collection)

Above Filmed on location at Newmarket Racecourse, *King of the Wind* included some of Britain's top stars. Appearing with Harris (seated in chair) were Melvyn Hayes, Glenda Jackson, Joan Hickson, Anthony Quayle, Ralph Bates and Jenny Agutter. (© Tony Hillman Collection)

Below left and right After turning his back on the cinema for more than a decade, Harris made a critically acclaimed comeback as Bull McCabe in *The Field*. His co-stars included Sean Bean and John Hurt. (both © Tony Hillman Collection)

Above More than thirty years after his first Republican film, *Shake Hands with the Devil,* one of Harris's films once again involved IRA terrorism. This time the film was *Patriot Games* and his co-star was Harrison Ford. (© Tony Hillman Collection)

Below In the same year, 1992, Harris appeared in the award-winning Clint Eastwood film, *Unforgiven,* as the bounty hunter English Bob. (© Tony Hillman Collection)

Left Harris – who bore a striking resemblance to the murdered conservationist George Adamson – admitted that the big cats were the only members of the *To Walk With Lions* cast he missed. (© Tony Hillman Collection)

Below In the last few years of his life, Richard Harris's film career experienced a revival, starting with the multi-award-winning *Gladiator*, in which he played Emperor Marcus Aurelius opposite Russell Crowe as the eponymous gladiator. (© DreamWorks SKG)

Left The part of headmaster Albus Dumbledore in the first two films of JK Rowling's *Harry Potter* series made Harris beloved of children the world over. (© Warner Brothers)

Below Richard Harris: 'I gave it all I got.' (© *Irish Times*)

overlooked by Paradise Island's relentless development of luxury tourist hotels and casinos. The island itself, which sheltered Nassau's natural harbour, was connected to the Bahamian capital by a toll bridge. Ann was not enthusiastic about the ten bedrooms, plain blue walls and peeling paintwork and set about redecorating.

The wedding, originally arranged for 7 April, was mysteriously postponed. Once again, there were rumours of bitter tearful rows and a permanent separation. Those who claimed to be in the know blamed Ann's single-minded mission to transform their Paradise Island home into a chintzy film set. Harris fielded the gossip by saying he was too busy working. The Beverly Hills ceremony eventually took place in June.

Richard Harris's sense of quality was out of kilter – 'I just hired them my body and my voice' – but it did not stop him making some groundbreaking movies.

Gulliver's Travels, berated today for the quality of its animation, was in fact the first film in cinema history to combine human actors, three-dimensional miniature sets and cartoons. For Harris it was a painful new experience. During rehearsals he delivered his lines to an army of model Lilliputians. Before the cameras rolled the figures were removed and Harris was expected to direct each line to an exact spot, frequently 'talking' to three or four invisible characters in the same shot. To re-create Swift's famous scene in which Lemuel Gulliver is captured and festooned with tiny ropes, Harris was forced to spend day after day stretched out on a Pinewood studio floor, first while the ropes and nails and the trolley on which he is transported were measured and made, and finally while the scene was actually shot.

Harris's next movie was doomed from the start. Unknown to the Irish actor, the project was generating its own ever-thickening cloud of hopelessness. One summer morning in 1974, Richard Lester was sitting in his Twickenham Studios office when he was informed that the Columbia executive Peter Guber had flown in from Hollywood to see him. Guber spread seven three-by-five-inch cards on the director's desk. 'Each card has a story idea that Columbia owns,' Guber announced. 'Pick the one you want and make it for us. I'm not leaving this office until you agree.'

Lester read each card in turn. On the seventh card he found what he was looking for. 'That's what I'd like to do,' he said. Typed on the card were six words: 'Robin Hood as an Older Man'.

'You got it,' assured Guber.

Despite a handshake-and-dinner deal, it took a year of legal wrangling before shooting started. To Lester's dismay, the project had also changed title and direction. The original dashing concept of the death of Robin Hood had somehow transmuted into the $5 million comic romance of Robin Hood and Maid Marian; derring-do had turned to cynicism and fitness had given way to flab. Filming – 'six weeks under a Spanish tree' – began in the Plain of Urbaza near Pamplona, the same Iberian location Lester had used for his highly successful *The Three Musketeers*.

Making a brief appearance as King Richard, Harris not only found himself under the direction of Lester for the second time in two years but also was delighted to be working on his second film with his friend Sean Connery as the ageing Robin. 'The bones creak a bit in the film and in my legs,' confessed the 46-year-old Connery. 'This Robin is trying to be a young revolutionary at the age of fifty, and it doesn't work.'

Another cast member with doubts was Audrey Hepburn, coaxed out of semi-retirement to play Marian. 'I am the only Wendy among the Lost Boys of Sherwood Forest,' she said. Her 'Lost Boys' included Nicol Williamson as Prince John, Denholm Elliott as Will Scarlet, Robert Shaw as the Sheriff of Nottingham and the comedian Ronnie Barker as Friar Tuck. The finished product was, as one magazine proclaimed, 'as close to perfection as it's possible to get'.

Unlike the critics, however, the general public failed to respond and *Robin and Marian* never made a profit. Its director is adamant where the blame lay. 'The title should have been left as *The Death of Robin Hood*,' says Lester. 'To me the movie was not a "comedy adventure". People kept asking me where the jokes were. *Robin and Marian* was straight. I always saw it like that and because of the connotations of the changed title, it prompted the wrong reaction.'

Harris had spent most of December 1969 in Mexico making *A Man Called Horse*. 'I count it among my best half-dozen movies,' he later claimed. 'It was simply different.'

A year earlier, in 1968, Ken Russell's *Women in Love* passed a 'milestone in censorship' by including a scene showing Oliver Reed and Alan Bates wrestling naked. *Horse* went still further by presenting male nudity as a fact of life, with no sexual undertones or innuendo. Harris plays a pre-Victorian English aristocrat captured by Yellow Hand American Indians while on a hunting trip. His wealth and social status mean nothing and he is stripped naked and used as a slave. It was, claimed the actor, a breakthrough in the cinema's treatment of nudity.

'This is the unclothed body used to make a valid dramatic point, in keeping with the story's primitive setting.'

Six years to the day that shooting ended on the first *Horse* epic, Harris was back in Mexico to start work on a sequel, appropriately named *The Return of a Man Called Horse*. This time as co-producer with Sandy Howard, the star insisted on polishing the Jack de Witt script personally. 'After the first film I felt I knew the role so well that I had to contribute directly to his character on some level other than just interpretation.'

As co-producer, Harris kept his location drinking in check. He got round his four-pack-a-day addiction to nicotine by hiring a diminutive Mexican called Alfonso as keeper of the cigarettes. The ritual was enacted forty or fifty times a day. Each time the director, Irvin Kershner, shouted 'cut', Alfonso would race towards his employer with a cigarette in one hand and a lighter in the other. Harris was forced to bend nearly double to reach the flame and as he straightened up exhaling he would say, 'Thank you, Alfonso, for once more contributing to my destruction.' The tiny Mexican – who did not speak a word of English – would smile and bow and return to his place behind the camera.

The plot of *The Return of a Man Called Horse*, like the shooting schedule, picked up from the day after the prequel ends. In England, John Morgan (Harris) is unsettled living as a lord and decides to return for a year to the Yellow Hand tribe. He finds the sacred ground where the village once stood bare and lifeless. Eventually, he finds the remnants of the tribe and leads them in a war of revenge against the trappers who betrayed and cheated them. *Return*, which was shot in England and South Dakota, was also a casting coup for Harris and his fellow executives. The trio persuaded Gale Sondergaard – who, forty years earlier, had won the first Oscar awarded to a Best Supporting Actress – out of retirement to play Elk Woman, one of the moving spiritual forces of the Yellow Hand tribe.

'I would never do an action movie that didn't operate on some other level,' Harris informed a preshooting press conference (for him, the script had undertones of both his family's and his nation's exploitation by the English). 'What also makes this movie interesting is that it deals with man's inability to adjust to his own culture and his search for deeper meanings in life.'

Sadly, it was an insight lost on the majority of cinemagoers, although it did turn a profit in the United States, where the plight of the Native American was becoming a popular and just cause. The critics found its record-breaking seventeen-minute pre-title sequence unique and unusual while the torture scenes proved too realistic for the general public. 'It maintains a tidy balance between nausea and boredom,' reported the television critic Judith Crist.

In 1982, after yet another six-year interval, Harris would appear in the final film in the *Horse* trilogy, *Triumphs of a Man Called Horse*. This time the ageing John Morgan dies early, leaving the rest of the action to his son, played by Michael Beck.

But back to 1977 Harris had spent the last eighteen months making *Golden Rendezvous, Orca: Killer Whale* and *The Cassandra Crossing*. Three films; three stinkers. It was also the year Harris survived a bizarre *déjà vu* brush with death.

Once again, he was attempting to cut back his daily two and a half bottles of vodka by substituting cocaine. It was a lethal combination. After a month of punishment, his body gave up and the actor collapsed and was rushed to the Cedars of Lebanon hospital in Los Angeles. Emergency-room doctors were so concerned by his condition that they informed his family there was little hope for his survival, and a priest performed the last rites. Having been transferred to intensive care, Harris was now on a life-support machine and newspaper and television newsrooms around the world began compiling Richard Harris obituaries. In London two papers, the *Sun* and the *Daily Mirror*, even got as far as laying out a front page announcing his death.

It was not to be. From somewhere deep inside, Harris found the strength to recover. When he eventually returned home, he headed straight for the toilet – and flushed away his £4,000 stash of cocaine.

The hundred-degree daytime temperatures in the Northern Transvaal were the least of the producer's worries. Getting two of his stars to the South African province was, however, a task that demanded a unique blend of diplomacy and bullying from Euan Lloyd.

The Wild Geese was a $10 million all-action adventure adapted from the novel of the same name and itself loosely based on the life of the former soldier 'Mad' Mike Hoare, who had organised and led a mercenary raid to free an imprisoned African leader. To play the part of Hoare – renamed and only thinly disguised as Colonel Faulkner – Lloyd recruited Richard Burton. The screenplay had skilfully merged two characters from the original book into the easygoing Shawn Fynn, a role immediately accepted by Roger Moore. But, if Lloyd's choice of Burton had raised a few industry eyebrows, his final signing produced splutters of surprise. The role of Rafer Janders had been offered to Burt Lancaster. When contractual obligations forced the American actor to withdraw, Lloyd successfully approached Richard Harris.

There were two problems to overcome before the film's insurers would allow Burton and Harris on the same set. But it was the Welshman's niggling back injury that caused more concern. 'It was so bad, so severe, that we couldn't get any insurance on him,' recalls Euan Lloyd. 'It was a very strenuous movie, jumping on planes and fights all the way, and if his back went we would be finished. In the end we all wanted him, so we took the risk.' Despite his obvious agony, Burton lost just one day's shooting when a specialist was helicoptered in to give him painkilling injections.

Harris was equally dedicated to the film. The Irishman, like Burton, had sworn off the drink for the duration of the shoot. To underline his commitment Harris also agreed to put half his fee 'in trust' – to be withheld if he drank.

In the late autumn of 1977 the cast and crew descended on the tiny South African health spa of Tshipise. Only a few miles south of the Rhodesian (now Zimbabwean) border, the town had once earned its living as the last stop for stagecoaches making the run between Johannesburg and Salisbury. Now it was a modern holiday resort that attracted thousands of visitors to its mineral baths. The production company hired an entire complex of more than a hundred native roundhouses, with the most luxurious, Rondavels, going to the film's top stars.

Harris came close to losing the second half of his salary cheque just once. Each evening the cast and crew gathered in a Tshipise township shack they had converted to a bar and dubbed the Red Ox. As the film progressed the producer became progressively more relaxed as Burton religiously stuck to cans of Tab and Harris rehydrated his body with equally innocuous nonalcoholic drinks. One night Lloyd noticed that Harris was unusually boisterous. The soft drinks had been replaced by shorts and the pitch of the star's voice was rising with each double. Lloyd panicked. 'Time, gentlemen, please,' he announced, sweeping the drinkers out the makeshift pub. 'Time, please. Come on, everyone out.'

The next morning Harris, nursing a hangover, gingerly tapped on the producer's door. 'I'm sorry, Governor,' he apologised. 'It won't happen again.' This time he kept his promise.

During a break in filming, the 47-year-old Harris found himself sitting in the sand next to Richard Burton. 'We were like two old men,' he remembered. 'Once the greatest hellraisers in the world, we were now too tired to stand up and pee. After two hours of philosophical discussion, we came to the conclusion that the tragedy of our lives was the amount of it we don't remember, because we were too drunk to remember.'

Two years later Euan Lloyd attempted to reunite his three *Wild Geese* stars – Harris, Burton and Moore – and its director for another military adventure. This time, the action would take place in India. In his book *The Boarding Party*, James Leasor told the story of how the bored and ageing former members of the Calcutta Light Horse, all of whom had seen action in the Boer War, took on and silenced a German World War Two spy ship. Adapted for the screen as *The Sea Wolves*, the film, to Lloyd's surprise, found little Hollywood enthusiasm. Although *The Wild Geese* was well received in Britain, it had failed to make any respectable returns in the United States. To forestall a similar loss, Lloyd's backers were insisting on the inclusion of a star already 'bankable' in America. After a terse refusal by Charlton Heston, the producer managed to persuade Gregory Peck to join the cast. But the money men who had welcomed the 63-year-old Peck refused even to consider Richard Harris. At 49, he was deemed too young. Harris's place as Colonel Bill Grice was eventually taken by David Niven.

It was near the end of filming *The Wild Geese* that Harris was approached by a producer–director partnership with a script for what sounded an equally ambitious and dangerous project. As it turned out, the fictional threat of arrest Harris faced as a mercenary in *The Wild Geese* very nearly became a reality with *Golden Rendezvous*.

Andre Pieterse and the director Ashley Lazarus first teamed up first for the highly successful *E Lollypop*. Their second collaboration was to be loosely based on an Alistair MacLean bestseller. Pieterse was a former property developer and one-time MGM vice-president with an eye for potential publicity. Not only did he want Harris – who would play John Carter, a ship's first officer, who suspects that a multimillion-dollar heist is about to take place on the high seas – but the deal also included a co-starring role for Harris's wife Ann Turkel. Other passengers and crew aboard the cargo-ship-turned-floating-casino would include Burgess Meredith, David Janssen, Gordon Jackson and the seventy-year-old John Carradine. What really convinced Harris of the film's potential was the producer's determination to avoid studio tanks and models and, instead, to shoot the entire film at sea. He had already chartered an Italian-owned cargo liner and a 120-ton South African coaster and was in the process of converting them into floating studios.

Golden Rendezvous was the third film the couple would make together and the second MacLean-based movie for Harris (eighteen years earlier he had made a brief appearance in *Guns of Navarone*). It would not be the last time they visited the Republic of South Africa. Within a year they were back – but it would be Harris who would make newspaper front pages around the world, and not his new film.

By 1978 Southern Rhodesia was in its thirteenth year of unilaterally declared independence and struggling to survive a bloody guerrilla war. Sanction-busting businessmen were funding and arming the white rebels, exactly the role Harris would play in *A Game for Vultures* the following year.

During a break in shooting, the Harrises returned to the South African capital and he found himself at the heart of a government slush-fund scandal and about to be arrested. *Golden Rendezvous's* producer, Andre Pieterse, was claiming that the film's £1 million loss had come about because of delays caused by his star's location drinking sessions. Unknown to Harris, the project was partly financed with almost £500,000 from a secret South African fund, and when the government demanded its investment back the producer pointed the finger at Harris. To stop the Irishman leaving the country – which he had no intention of doing in the middle of a picture – a commission of inquiry ordered his arrest.

With his hotel besieged by the international press, Harris lashed out, claiming he was the 'perfect scapegoat'. 'I worked on that movie seven days a week, eighteen hours a day,' said the actor, who ensured that every news photograph was posed with a soft drink in his hand. 'Mr Pieterse asked me on four occasions to take over the direction. Would he have asked someone who was drunk and incapable?'

Harder to swallow was Harris's claim that he had been dry 'for almost a year', but whatever the truth of the matter, Harris immediately issued a £14 million writ for defamation. The inquiry, not wishing to get caught in a lengthy legal crossfire, withdrew its summons; Harris therefore abandoned the writ.

The Ravagers was the last film Harris would make with Ann. The marriage, at least that glossy part of it disclosed in a campaign book for the recently released *Golden Rendezvous*, was hectic and pleasurable:

What is it like to be married to such a dynamic man as Harris? 'The hellraiser image is all wrong,' says Ann. 'They don't know that he is a very serious person, very strong, very brilliant. We never sit around doing nothing. If we are not working, Richard is writing and I have my hobbies of photography and singing. Life is never dull.' The couple live, with their family, in a large rambling house at Nassau, in the Bahamas, when they are not travelling the world on far-flung movie safaris. Richard's future plans are to produce and direct three more films, all starring his wife.

'She bullies me,' jokes Harris. 'All the women I've had in my life I've treated badly. Ann is not a carbon copy of anyone. She's a true original – and a very talented actress.'

Ann had accepted her husband's three sons with equanimity and love. Their stays on Paradise Island were boisterous and noisy times, and somehow always managed to ground the static between their father and stepmother. Despite her restlessness and single-minded determination to advance her career, Ann wanted the couple to have a child of their own. Not long into their marriage, she announced she was pregnant. Tragically, their joy ended when she miscarried at 32,000 feet and 600 miles an hour while on a flight home. 'We never seemed to bother after that,' said Harris. 'Something was always missing between us.'

In private the compliments were increasingly rare, and both husband and wife were preparing themselves for the inevitable. The emotional stress of the break-up, when it came, weakened Harris and a viral infection forced him to pull out of *The Serpent's Egg*, a circus tragedy written and produced by Ingmar Bergman. Harris's place as an American trapeze artist working in Berlin and persecuted during Hitler's rise to power was taken by David Carradine.

Harris retreated to Paradise Island. A few days before he left London, he was given a scuff-edged and tattered Catholic Mass card. The name on the card was Rosie Harty – the name of a distant relative of his mother who had died at the age of twelve in 1912. The woman who gave Harris the card explained she was a medium and psychic. After finding it, she claimed to have been contacted by Rosie Harty, and that the little girl was now 'with' the actor.

'You will always be protected,' the woman told Harris. 'Rosie is on your shoulder for ever.'

Harris was taking no chances. His career, like his personal life, appeared to be going nowhere. He slipped the card into his wallet, where it religiously remained for the rest of his life.

Harris's interest in death took a macabre and bizarre twist after his mother's fatal cancer and his father's subsequent decline. In the early 1960s he founded the 65 Club, whose select membership – for no logical reason – believed the world would end sometime in 1965. Among those who accepted the actor's prophesy of doom were the recently fêted Irish novelist Edna O'Brien and the cabaret singer Georgia Brown. To give authority, if not credence, to its belief, members were supplied with official writing paper headed 'The 65 Club' in heavy Gothic type.

His fascination with death went even further. For years Harris would play a ghoulish game of announcing his own death. Disguising his voice, he would telephone his first wife or close friends claiming to be a policeman and announce gravely that 'Mr Richard Harris, actor' had been killed in a particularly gruesome accident.

CHAPTER TWELVE

Though Harris had forsaken drugs and forbidden himself alcohol, he had no intention of adding sex to the list of prohibited pleasures. That he continued to gulp down with equal style.

While in New York he exchanged telephone numbers with a beautiful young woman. A few days later, and back in England, Harris decided he would like to get to know her a little better and dialled the number scribbled on a slip of paper. It was 8 a.m. in London, around three o'clock in the morning on the eastern seaboard of America. 'How about lunch?' he said. 'Today, at the 21 Club?' By 10.30 a.m. (London time) he was on board Concorde and at 9.30 a.m. (New York time) was on his way to the woman's apartment. The rest of the day went just as Harris had planned: sex before and after lunch and back in London in time for dinner.

CHAPTER TWELVE

I'm disappointed in acting as a craft. I want everything to go back to Orson Welles and fake noses and changing your voice. It's become so much about personality.

— Skeet Ulrich

At the end of his first marriage, Richard Harris descended into a spree of pointless and celebrated excess: he drank; he screwed around; he craved excitement; he made films no one would pay to see; he woke up on planes he didn't want to be on and going to places he didn't want to visit; and he bought homes he had no intention of living in. 'I was numb,' he confessed, 'and it didn't seem to matter.'

In contrast, his parting from Ann Turkel triggered a deep and almost spiritual self-analysis. A notional Catholic, Harris dedicated himself to a near-Hindu cleansing of his mind and possessions. He would spend the rest of his life with the minimum personal baggage and with an accountability only to himself – if he had no responsibilities, he could do no harm and hurt no one.

Harris began with the closure of his second marriage, 'sexuality converted into possession,' he explained to the *Daily Telegraph*. 'You say, "I'm having great sex with this lady. I want no one else to have it. So I'll own her. No one else shall touch her now. She's mine." It's a horrible attitude. Horrible.'

One of the first physical assets to go was a Cape Cod-style, four-bedroom mansion in Malibu. Harris had bought the house as an investment before leasing it to the billionaire financier Kirk Kerkorian. From there Harris systematically worked his way through his acres of land and houses until only his Paradise Island beach house and a few first editions remained. The process took more than ten years, but by the late 1990s he at last considered himself 'free and unburdened'.

On the way, there were a few forgotten culs-de-sac. In 1997 he came across a photograph of himself standing beside a Rolls-Royce Phantom Five. The picture was 25 years old and he couldn't remember owning the car. Harris telephoned Elizabeth, by now long divorced from Rex Harrison, and asked, 'Did I own a Rolls?' She assured him he had and

Harris telephoned his Los Angeles accountant to find out what had become of it. The car, by now a classic, was mothballed in a Californian garage. For more than two decades Harris had been paying a $400-a-week storage charge. He hadn't noticed because he never checked his bills. The Rolls-Royce was shipped to England, restored by the makers and put up for auction. He could not stand the thought of driving around 'like Michael Caine' in such a posh car.

'The trouble with everyone these days is they want constant sensation, to live on the peaks of existence,' Peter O'Toole once observed. 'But the trudge is also an important part of life. You have to have the lows.'

By 1981 Richard Harris's personal life was as low as it could get. The glory days of his drinking – 'I adored getting drunk and I adored reading in the papers what I had done the night before' – were over. Some of his worst offences were never made public. Like the time he staggered into a hotel bedroom, unhitched his trousers and kicked them across the floor. His shirt and underpants and socks followed them into the darkness. He snuggled under the quilt, drunkenly oblivious of the two bodies already occupying the double bed.

'Oi!' a man's voice hissed in his ear. 'What's the big idea, mate?'

'I don't have one,' Harris replied, sensing that his other bed guest was a woman. 'But if one occurs to you by all means wake me up.'

For years the actor habitually downed two bottles of vodka a day. 'That would take me up to seven in the evening, then I'd break open a bottle of brandy and a bottle of port and mix the two.' But it was not simply the intoxication that hooked Harris. As an Irishman, he thrived on social contact and when Harris arrived in a bar everyone wanted to be his friend. 'It was anybody I could pick on,' he has explained. 'Anybody who could last the course. That was the great virtue of boozing, to go into a pub by yourself and end of with fifteen mates just for the night. Men, not women. Boozing is a man's world. You can't have women there. You have too many obligations.'

But Harris was finding it increasingly difficult to 'last the course'. His heartbeat had been irregular for some time and there were moments when he found it difficult to focus his mind. He put it down to exhaustion and reached for a drink. And then one night he collapsed on set. A few days later he keeled over in the street. When he lost consciousness during a dinner with friends he finally accepted that something serious might be wrong and consulted a doctor.

What Harris had dismissed as overwork blackouts were in fact comas triggered by functional hypoglycaemia – his pancreas was producing excessive and dangerous amounts of insulin. The prognosis was simple: if he didn't reform his diet and lifestyle and drastically cut down on his alcohol intake, he would die.

The end – at least the public end – to his drinking came one summer evening in 1981. On 11 August Harris walked into Washington's Jockey Club and studied the wine list. He ordered two bottles of Château Margaux '57 at $300 each and sat down to slowly and deliberately drink the lot. At 11.20 p.m. he swallowed his last glass of wine. 'I treated those two bottles with great reverence,' he said. 'I treated them like you'd treat making love to the most gorgeous woman in the world. If you only knew you had one orgasm left, you'd say, "I'm holding it up, babe, because I don't want this to end." '

But, if Harris had forsaken drugs and forbidden himself alcohol, he had no intention of adding sex to the list of prohibited pleasures. That he continued to gulp down with equal style.

While in New York he exchanged telephone numbers with a beautiful young woman. A few days later, and back in England, Harris decided he would like to get to know her a little better and dialled the number scribbled on a slip of paper. It was 8 a.m. in London, around three in the morning on the eastern seaboard of America. 'How about lunch?' he said. 'Today, at the 21 Club?' By 10.30 a.m. (London time) he was on board Concorde and at 9.30 a.m. (New York time) was on his way to the woman's apartment. The rest of the day went just as Harris had planned: sex before and after lunch and back in London in time for dinner.

Harris shows a gentlemanly reluctance to add names to his stories of brief affairs and even quicker sex. Nor did he elaborate on his publicly acknowledged relationships with a string of beautiful lovers, including Vanessa Redgrave, Sophia Loren and Ava Gardner. Not so an after-party fling with the 1940s leading lady Merle Oberon, with whom Harris had been on intimate terms since his teenage years. 'I'd masturbate about her all night,' he admitted. 'With the lights off, so God couldn't see me.'

The pair finally made contact at a Hollywood party. By now Oberon – nineteen years Harris's senior – was still an attractive fifty-something and had just completed a film appropriately entitled, *Of Love and Desire*. 'Have we met?' the actress asked.

'Many times,' confessed Harris.

Four times married and romantically linked to a catalogue of leading men, Oberon led the way first to her apartment and then to her bed. When she turned off the light Harris whispered, 'Merle, if we make love in the dark, I may as well be back in Limerick playing with myself.' That night they made love with the light on.

Some women he could not lure to bed. With these he flirted, an activity he considered a 'much underrated art form'. During a visit to New York he was being interviewed for radio by the journalist Cindy Adams. Under the studio table their knees touched. A light came on in Harris's eyes. 'You married?' asked the actor, ignoring the ON AIR sign.

'Well, yes,' fumbled Adams. 'Yes, I am.'

'Are you a fanatic about it?' teased Harris.

To a seasoned publicist like David Kramer, the egos and idiosyncrasies of Hollywood stars were no longer surprising. Through his forty-year career he has served a melting pot of clientele, including Ryan O'Neal, Leonard Nimoy, Farrah Fawcett, Carol Burnett, Eva Marie Saint and Dan Aykroyd. Among his other 'charges' were the entire 1970s and 1980s comedy output of Paramount Pictures Television including *Cheers* and *Happy Days*. 'In the early 1980s I met the first actor to bring home the sheer joy of my profession,' Kramer admits. That actor was Richard Harris.

Kramer volunteered to escort Harris to the NBC studios for an appearance on *The Tonight Show*. The two men were walking by a schedule board, which listed the show's other guests. Upon seeing Robert Mitchum's name on the board, Harris turned to Kramer and asked if he could see the legendary American actor.

'I knew Mitchum,' explains Kramer, 'but I didn't know they had already worked together and were acquainted. We went into Mitchum's dressing room and there was Harris leaning against the wall and finally on his knees looking up adoringly as Mitchum told story after story.' For more than half an hour the publicist silently watched as the stars swapped stories and caught up on the missing years.

Among his fellow actors, Harris's reputation was as solid as it had ever been but, especially in the years bridging the 1970s and 1980s, his name was fast slipping from the public memory. A trio of Canadian disasters did not help.

The optimistically named *Highpoint* – which got its title from its finale filmed on the top of Toronto's CN Tower – saw Harris as an out-of-work accountant pursued by both the Mafia and the CIA. The original version was so bad that the producers refused to allow its release and agreed to spend an extra $2 million on re-editing. It was eventually reviewed by the press in 1984, five years after filming. A second movie – *The Burning Bush*

– co-starring Christopher Plummer and David Warner, was shelved and then cancelled.

Tarzan the Ape Man was the 32nd film to be based on Edgar Rice Burroughs's character. For Harris it was an excruciating experience. After two months filming with the semi-naked Bo Derek as Jane – 'the most exciting pair in the jungle!' according to the movie's publicity machine – Harris realised he had had enough of films and filmmaking. Between 1974 and 1980 he had made more than fifteen films, most in quick succession and nearly all on alternating sides of the globe. 'It was horrendously bad time,' he recalls. 'It was all studio, travel, studio and I lost interest in the movies in a big way.'

As ever, Harris kept a daily journal. During the *Tarzan* shoot. 'I caught myself marking forty-four days left, forty-three days left, and I said, "Wait a minute, what are you doing with your life?" There's going to be a time when you want those forty-three days back and you've wasted them . . .'

Part of the problem was Harris's total commitment to – total immersion in – his character. He had never forgotten Joan Littlewood's advice that to deliver a good performance an actor must expose both his body and his mind, but the constant stripping bare of his own soul was leaving him exhausted and guilty. 'When I take up a character, I overpower the part,' he said. 'Come the end of the film, I never want to see the cast and crew again.'

'I consider half of my career a total failure,' admitted Harris. 'I went after the wrong things and picked pictures that were way below my talent, just to have fun.' By now the fun had stopped. Although they would remain good and close friends, his marriage to Ann Turkel was grinding towards its official end. It would be another seven years before Harris could bring himself to talk openly and frankly about his relationship with women in general and his two failed marriages in particular. In an interview for the Irish magazine *Hot Press*, Harris admitted:

I had a very bad second marriage. Not through any fault of Ann's. It was a bad time in my life. It was like Burton and Taylor, an all-consuming relationship. Look at me now, full of energy, right? If Ann Turkel called now and I spoke to her for ten minutes, I'd have to say 'the interview is over, Joe, call you Tuesday'. She'd drain everything out of me. She fed on it. She couldn't help it. It was something you couldn't extradite yourself from, it was just there. You'd try to solve it, get out – you couldn't.

Q: The darkness in a relationship like that can be attractive to some people.

A: There had to be some kind of attraction in all that, yes, otherwise I wouldn't have stuck with it so long.

Q: Do you think we learn from the failure of a first marriage – or do we make the same mistakes all over again?

A: This is interesting. I broke up my first marriage because I was totally selfish, right? The second one broke up because I was selfless. I did everything. I was like a nursemaid. I was a father, uncle, lover, doctor, psychiatrist, occasional husband, father-confessor in her eyes. It broke up because I couldn't take that any more. I gave too much because the first one was an absolute catastrophic fuck-up because of my behaviour – and so I tried to over-compensate in the second.

Q: Atoning for your sins, reacting to the then rather than the now?

A: Exactly, and that was disastrous.

Q: Is that what has left you so bitter about marriage?

A: I'm not bitter.

Q: 'Marriage is a custom thought up by women where they proceed to live off men ... eating them away like poison fungus on a tree.'

A: (Laughs) Did I say that? That's lovely, isn't it?

Q: But is it how you feel?

A: I don't feel bitter or angry. That there is a perfect description by a man who's been through it all, who says 'This is what it is.' Coolly, calmly, simply.

Q: Did you ever regard any woman as your equal?

A: I got carried away there (laughs). If I worked with Vanessa Redgrave again I'd consider us as equals, absolutely. She is a tremendous woman. And Joan Littlewood, who started me out in theatre. She was superior and would be today. So women like that, people like that, yes.

Q: So you accept that there are women and men on different levels in different capacities, who are you superiors?

A: My God you have to. How else could we learn? I'm a better actor than a lot of people and many – well, a few – are better than me (laughs). But as a human being how am I to know – or rather who am I to say?

Harris was grounded enough to realise he was not famous but notorious, and that is quite a different thing. When you are notorious you are news. When you are famous you have become solid and rooted in the landscape and people take you seriously. Early in 1981 Richard Burton would give him the chance, at least for a little while, to make the transformation.

After the horrors of the Sri Lankan jungle, Harris was determined to take at least a year off. He was recuperating in his Savoy Hotel suite before retreating to Paradise Island, when he took a telephone call from his agent. Burton, who had been persuaded to resurrect his early 1960s *Camelot* success with a tour of America, was dropping out. The niggling injury to his spine needed surgery. After crisscrossing the States, the musical had reached Los Angeles, where it was booked for three months.

Harris was nervous but eager to accept. It would be his first stage appearance in fifteen years. It didn't stop him driving a hard bargain: to take on the role he demanded £25,000 a week, plus a share of the box-office receipts; he also insisted the director Frank Dunlop fly with him to California to help him sharpen up his performance.

On tour the audiences came to see Burton, not the musical; ticket sales were disappointing and the houses half full. After the April 1981 sell-out opening night, they came to see Harris, who 'devoured the part of Arthur like a hungry dog who had been thrown a prime rib'. It was, proclaimed Jack Viertel, of the Los Angeles *Herald Examiner*, a triumph. 'Harris has pulled off an astonishing feat in stepping into Burton's shoes and delivering a performance that looks like it had months of thought and preparation poured into it.' The theatregoers agreed. In one week the production grossed half a million dollars, setting a new US record.

In the autumn, the musical resumed its tour of major cities. Back on the road, Harris found the experience exhausting and dangerous. In Detroit he was admitted to hospital with severe chest pains; a feared heart attack was ruled out. During the winter he was dogged by colds.

And when he injured his back during a stage fight he contracted a spinal infection and was forced to lose another week. In May the following year he escaped death when a diving stagehand bundled him clear of a rapidly descending one-ton set.

Despite their impending divorce Ann was a frequent backstage visitor. It was clear they still loved each other, but were equally determined to live separate lives. 'Annie is now free to do whatever she wants,' declared Harris. 'And so am I.'

Their 'separate lives' did not stop Ann from sharing his Savoy suite in the autumn of 1982 while he prepared for *Camelot*'s London opening. 'We probably have the most perfect relationship in the world,' said Ann, denying rumours of a remarriage. 'Richard is a genius.'

Neither the UK critics nor the public quite saw it that way. Reporting on the show's opening night at the Apollo Victoria, Milton Shulman informed *Evening Standard* readers, 'Back in 1964 I assessed *Camelot* as wholesome, pretty and empty. Seeing it again I felt it had been caught in a time warp. It is still wholesome, pretty and empty.' So, too, were the majority of seats. Harris demanded 'major surgery' to several scenes. He also offered to forgo his fixed salary until the musical was back in profit. It was not enough. By late January – after less than eight weeks of a planned twelve-month run – *Camelot* closed.

The fault, a disappointed Harris concluded, lay with the audiences and not the show. *Camelot* meant something quite different on the other side of the Atlantic. *Camelot* – both the word and the stage show – had long occupied a special place in American affection. *Camelot* was the favourite musical of the assassinated president John F Kennedy, whose name is frequently linked with the words, 'Don't let it be forgot that once there was a spot for one brief shining moment that was known as "*Camelot*".' It was also the secret service code name for the White House during Kennedy's presidency.

So, in 1983, Harris purchased the stage rights to *Camelot* and spent the next six years directing his own stage version of the musical and touring North America . By 1987 the production had grossed $92 million – 'And I didn't need to earn another penny . . . ever.'

There were times, however, when it felt as though he were earning every single dollar. As a pre-tour taster, Harris negotiated a multimillion-dollar deal with a US cable company for a television production of *Camelot*. The 'artistic and accounting' differences between Harris and the show's producer sparked daily disagreements. After one confrontation the actor stormed off the set and out of the studio, followed by the ever-bellowing producer. In the street outside, and surrounded by a gathering crowd, Harris taunted, 'You want me to hit you, don't you?'

There were other, sadder, distractions. In 1984, shortly after Richard Burton's death, Harris was asked to take part in a Hollywood memorial tribute. He decided to start his eulogy with a quotation from *Richard II*. He got as far as, 'let us sit upon the ground . . .' when he broke down and left the podium. Out of sight of the Wilshire Theater audience, he wept uncontrollably, but forced himself to continue the Shakespeare line, '. . . and tell sad stories of the death of Kings.' A few minutes later Harris returned to the stage and admitted, 'If Richard could have seen me a moment ago he would have been howling with laughter.'

During the early summer of 1985 *Camelot* was on the road again, crisscrossing America and playing to sell-out houses. In June the show, with many of the original Broadway cast supporting Harris as King Arthur, arrived in Colorado. While the crew were unloading and setting up the scenery at the Denver Auditorium Theater, Harris checked in to the nearby Brown Palace Hotel. The luxurious red-granite and sandstone establishment had catered for emperors and presidents and show-business royalty during its 93-year history and Harris's special instructions, wired ahead of his arrival, were accepted without question. All the windows of Room 840 – dubbed the Beatles Suite, after the group's August 1964 visit – had been draped with heavy blackout curtains. In the kitchen, cartons of the actor's own 'private' soup had arrived by courier with special instructions on how it was to be heated and served.

Dermot Harris was not only Harris's younger brother, but was also his best friend. The motivating power behind a profitable London music company, Dermot had, for several years, masterminded his brother's business affairs. Together they rented a country house in the Cotswolds and, when Harris was away filming or living abroad, Dermot would dutifully video and post every Ireland international rugby match. He was a natural choice as producer for *Camelot*'s extended tour.

The show had reached Chicago by early 1986. Harris was waiting in the wings for his opening cue. 'Dick, I don't feel too good,' Dermot told his brother. 'I think I'll go and lie down.'

'Look after yourself,' said Harris over his shoulder, striding on to the stage. By the end of the show Dermot Harris was dead.

Harris was devastated but philosophical. 'The great mystery was solved,' he admitted, 'when I saw him on a slab in the hospital, his face purple from a massive heart attack. And that's what it's all about, isn't it? Here and gone.'

Determined that his brother's name should not be forgotten, Harris arranged with the University of Scranton, where Dermot had lectured as a guest professor on its theatre-arts course since the early 1980s, for the establishment of the Dermot Harris Foundation. Each year the foundation, funded by the actor's own money, would pay for a student to study at the Pennsylvania academy. The university reciprocated in the only way it could, by awarding Richard Harris an honorary doctorate.

To cope with the strain of touring on his larynx, Harris spent two hours every day doing vocal exercises to 'consolidate' his voice. He claims to have enjoyed the travelling and the repetition, another actor's nightmare, of performing the same piece week after week. The therapy of constant work was also helping him come to terms with his brother's death.

It was an exhausting tour and, by the time the musical had concluded its run on Broadway, the majority of the cast were showing signs of mental and physical exhaustion. 'Let me describe Richard Harris to you,' offered one opening-night reviewer. 'For those who may not have seen his movies, from his neck down he's built like an Adonis, but from the neck up he looks like a dried-out prune.'

During the last scene of the show, King Arthur talks to a young child, telling him to remember the glory days of Camelot. Arthur's scripted lines were, 'What is your name, child?' What came out was, 'What is your name, Devon?'

The young actor fielded the slip like a true professional. 'Devon, sir,' he said.

Harris, realising he had muffed his line, stumbled on. The boy was supposed to inform the king, 'I'm Devon of Gloucester, sir.' Instead Harris announced: 'Well, Devon, I suppose you're from Gloucester.'

There was no way the young actor was going to miss a chance of upstaging an old pro like Harris. 'I had no idea that kings were so wise, sir,' he ad-libbed.

Harris's appeal was not simply that he was a natural and gifted stage actor, more that he somehow teased his audience through a two-way mirror so that they not only identified with the character he was playing but could still see and love the man beneath. When things went wrong it was easy – instinctive – for Harris to appeal directly to his audience for forgiveness. Once, during a twice-a-day, seven-month tour of Camelot, Harris forgot the words to a short song. He stopped in mid-stride, halted the orchestra and walked to the edge of the stage. 'Four-hundred and twenty-eight performances,' he confessed to the sell-out audience, 'and I forgot the lyrics! Would you believe it?' Somebody cued him on the words, the orchestra started again, and he finished the song to a standing ovation.

Harris's gaunt appearance was causing concern. He was visibly losing weight and in considerable pain, often doubling up in the middle of a conversation. Routine medical checks for his other conditions failed to spot anything serious. When he could not longer keep down the meagre and specially prepared food he was forced to eat, his doctor insisted on more tests. The results were not good. Harris was suffering from stomach cancer and needed immediate surgery. The sell-out tour was postponed because of its star's 'exhaustion' as Harris insisted his long battle with cancer remain a family secret.

By 1987 Georges Simenon was more concerned with his financial empire than his literary reputation. 'There isn't enough money you can pay me for the television rights,' the 85-year-old Belgium-born writer abruptly informed Arthur Weingarten.

It was only after years of pestering and a personal introduction from the novelist Graham Greene that the producer was granted a business meeting with Simenon. 'He really wasn't anxious to do a deal,' recalled Weingarten. Money, as far as Simenon was concerned, was an incidental: he was already worth more than $115 million and grossing at least $8 million a year in royalties. The clincher was Weingarten's promise of an American television deal for his new *Maigret* series.

'His eyes lit up at that,' said Weingarten, who already knew his quarry considered his annual US sales of $300,000 disappointing. 'Once we had made the agreement he didn't want to know what stories we would do or how we would film them, or even what changes we proposed to make.'

As the meeting broke up, Simenon asked, 'Who are you getting to play Maigret?'

'Richard Harris,' the producer replied.

'I would never have thought of him in a million years,' said Simenon. 'And how will he look?'

Weingarten explained that he intended to dress the police inspector in rumpled old clothes with a duffel coat and a hat without a stiffener inside.

Twenty-five years earlier Simenon had personally blessed the BBC's choice of actor to play his legendary Paris detective. When the best-selling writer was first introduced to Rupert Davies, he was amazed at how close the actor was to the Maigret of his imagination. Davies, like creator and creation, was an inveterate pipe smoker with a collection of more than forty pipes. The 52 *Maigret* episodes turned Davies into a celebrity. At the height of his popularity he was paid £10,000 for a single Dubonnet commercial – an advertising-industry record for the time.

In fact Harris was not Weingarten's first choice for Maigret. Richard Burton had accepted the role and was working his way through the 75 *Maigret* novels and 28 short stories when he died suddenly in August 1984. The producer approached Harris and was surprised to find himself talking to a Maigret devotee.

Harris was introduced to the Police Judiciare detective by the film director John Huston in 1972 and chain-read his way through eighty-odd novels. 'As I read the stories I became Maigret in my head,' explained Harris. 'The clue to Maigret is that he watches everything, throwing people into psychological confrontations to see how they react. It had been an obsession of mine to play him ever since.'

Weingarten, already worried he could not offer his would-be star a big enough share of the series' $3 million budget, was in for another surprise. 'I don't need a salary,' Harris informed him. 'If you like what I do then fine, you can pay me. If not, I'll still do it because I'll enjoy it.' Barbara Shelley would play Madame Maigret and Andrew McCulloch his sergeant Lucas.

With a star of Harris's calibre 'under contract', it was easy to secure the necessary backing from Harlech Television in Britain – the managing director of which was also a self-confessed Simenon addict – and Coca-Cola in America. Location shooting started in late 1987 in Paris, the West Country and on board a luxury cruise liner, with a screen slot already booked for 21 May the following year.

Harris was determined to create his own *le Commissaire*, 'something totally different from Rupert Davies's Maigret'. To fill out his thin six-foot frame he wore a bulky cardigan beneath and an outsized suit. And to force himself into Maigret's slow, shambling gait Harris swapped his size-nine-and-a-half shoes for fifteens. It did not go down well. Nor did the decision to shift the action from the early 1950s to the mid-1980s.

What started as a barrage of disapproval from the critics rumbled on for weeks in various newspaper and magazine letter pages. Searching the archives today, it is impossible to find a single correspondent, professional or member of the public, who enjoyed the two-hour pilot. Like most, Peter Waymark, of *The Times*, missed the old, gentler Maigret:

For those of us who admired Rupert Davies as Simenon's ruminative, pipe-smoking detective in the BBC *Maigret* series in the Sixties, anyone else attempting the role must seem like an impostor. Even so, Richard Harris seems to have gone out of his way to make his portrayal as least like Davies's as possible. The trouble is that he is not much like Simenon's Maigret either. As played by Harris, he is a big, shambling figure, with a battered hat, glasses, scruffy blonde hair and croaky Irish accent.

A *Daily Mail* reader from Basingstoke wrote to the paper to announce, 'Simenon is dead. Otherwise I am sure the author would protest strongly at this truly appalling characterisation.' Another from Orpington demanded to know why 'Richard Harris found it necessary to portray Maigret as a shambling, scruffy individual with his trousers hanging down, his shirt hanging out, wearing his hat back to front and needing a good haircut'.

A more reasoned criticism appeared in the *TV Times* post page. 'Simenon's books show the detective and his wife as totally rooted in the French way of life,' complained Joe Wright from Sussex. 'This is the extra dimension – the mysteries are solved because Maigret knows his way round the French character. To project him as a comic Irishman is an absolute betrayal of the life's work of a fine writer.'

Unusually Harris agreed to defend his performance. The following week the *TV Times* published his reply:

I have played Maigret in my head for twenty years. Inevitably, my characterisation was different from that played by Rupert Davies in the old TV series which I never saw. But I don't see why an Englishman should be considered more suitable than an Irishman to play a Frenchman.

When the series was screened in America, Harris arrived for an interview with the *Daily Telegraph* writer Glenys Roberts, looking as far from his Maigret image as it was possible to get. In fact, he was in danger of becoming a serious international eccentric with 'hair to his collar and what can only be described as a turquoise baby grow with no underwear' and accompanied by his two rat-sized Maltese teacup dogs, Demi and Daisy. The pets were a new passion in Harris's life and, as with a new woman, he insisted they go everywhere with him. In restaurants he would order a bowl of lettuce and a glass of water for himself and roast chicken for the dogs. One New York hotel manager complained it cost $5 a day to feed Harris and $25 each for his dogs.

Back in London Harris was occupying his permanently reserved suite at the Savoy Hotel. To everyone who saw him – but knew nothing of his cancer operation – he was a changed man. The alcohol-free regime and vitamins and Caribbean sunshine were producing positive benefits. To manage his insulin levels the Savoy chefs were issued with a strict set of dietary guidelines. His small regular meals, still gourmet by any Savoy standards, contained few if any sugars or starches.

One evening Harris sat through a matinée of *A Whistle in the Dark* at the Royal Court Theatre. After the performance, the tanned Harris went backstage to congratulate the play's star, his friend Godfrey Quigley. The change, recalls Quigley, was astonishing. 'I could scarcely believe I was talking to the same Dickie Harris. He had mellowed from the man I knew in the 1960s. Now there was a wonderful warm truth about the man.'

CHAPTER THIRTEEN

When the British Academy of Film and Television Arts left his performance in *The Field* – for which he would later be Oscar-nominated – off its nomination list, Harris was more than a little unhappy. His revenge came three months later when the academy asked him to deliver the opening address during a royal visit to America. He wrote back, claiming he had a 'previous engagement with his television set', and suggesting five other actors – all of whom BAFTA had nominated instead of him that year.

But *The Field* and its Oscar nomination are far more than a simple milestone in Richard Harris's long career. His portrayal as the doomed farmer Bull McCabe is more a signpost, turning the actor onto a new path and marking a new journey. 'Gone are the days when I'd make life miserable for myself and everyone else because I hated working,' he admitted. 'I still don't like the movies, but I love acting. I feel most alive when I'm working on a film.'

CHAPTER THIRTEEN

The thing about performance, even if it's only an illusion, is that it is a celebration of the fact that we do contain within ourselves infinite possibilities.

— Daniel Day-Lewis

It was ten years since Richard Harris had completed a film of note. And almost thirty since he'd read a script as promising as this. After months of waiting, his patience finally ran out. 'Why don't you fly over and discuss the priest?' he asked Jim Sheridan.

The director had posted a copy of the script of *The Field* to the actor's Paradise Island home three months previously. It told the story of an Irish farmer willing to go to any lengths to keep a field his family has cultivated for generations, and Sheridan thought Harris might be interested in a cameo role of a priest who delivers a long speech in one of the final scenes. Harris disagreed. There was only one part he was willing to consider.

When Sheridan finally arrived in the Bahamas, he was surprised to find that the actor was sporting a beard and porcupine haircut. The pair opened the discussion on how Harris intended to play the priest. Harris became increasingly animated. To Sheridan's amazement the actor began putting on a pair of trousers and then a huge Irish sweater and coat. As he dressed his voice changed. 'My God,' Sheridan exclaimed, jumping to his feet. 'You're him! Your him, you're Bull McCabe!'

It was a superb example of Harris salesmanship. The deal was done and, a few days later, the actor informed the press, 'I want to make worthwhile movies again ... William Shakespeare wrote two plays to really test actors – *Hamlet*, to stretch the young actor to the limits, and *King Lear* for the older actor who could make that leap. For me, *This Sporting Life* was my *Hamlet* and *The Field* will be my *Lear*.'

Sheridan, who received an Academy Award nomination for the direction of his previous film, *My Left Foot*, starring Daniel Day Lewis, adapted *The Field* from a play by John Keene. In the mid-1950s, after a profitable period making ball bearings in England and a less profitable career as a writer, Keane and his wife returned to Ireland to take over a bar in the small north Kerry town of Listowel. 'There were some of the most marvellous and inventive liars on the face of creation in my pub,' recalls Keane, 'with the most wonderful speech and the most vile curses ever heard. I began to discover a new facet to my writing and an interest in drama.' By the late 1980s he had written fifteen plays and sold the film rights on four, including *The Field*.

With *The Field* and Harris's return to acting came the inevitable analysis of his career by the critics. Harris, as ever, was insouciant. 'I don't want to spend the rest of my life thinking, "I was good once," or " That was a great movie back in a 1966." Why bother? I do my job and I do it well. Sometimes I succeed, sometimes I fail. Sometimes I'm a brilliant, sometimes I'm not. It really doesn't matter.'

Acting, he explained, was a matter of concentration and commitment and obsession. 'Any kind of perfection needs a ruthlessness; you just won't take second best. So, if that means I'm a pain in the arse, then I'm a great pain in the arse, and I can be a big problem if other people don't do their homework.'

Failure to recognise all this hard work can lead to a deep but seldom-festering wound in Harris's psyche. When the British Academy of Film and Television Arts left his performance in *The Field* – for which he would later be Oscar-nominated – off its nomination list, Harris was more than a little unhappy. His revenge came three months later when the academy asked him to deliver the opening address during a royal visit to America. He wrote back, claiming he had a 'previous engagement with his television set', and suggesting five other actors – all of whom BAFTA had nominated instead of him that year.

But *The Field* and its Oscar nomination are far more than a simple milestone in Richard Harris's long career. His portrayal as the doomed farmer Bull McCabe is more a signpost, turning the actor onto a new path and marking a new journey. 'Gone are the days when I'd make life miserable for myself and everyone else because I hated working,' he admitted. 'I still don't like the movies, but I love acting. I feel most alive when I'm working on a film.'

Harris was, by this point, one of the most famous people in the world. He was literary material and gossip to people who had seen him once in a restaurant or watched him drinking in a bar. It was a sensation that continued to leave him self-conscious and, remarkably, more than a little humbled. One trick he learned in order to control his vulnerability was never to read anything written about him. Another was the habit of attacking before he was attacked. In later years these pre-emptive strikes on the egos of his fellow performers became almost a sport and fair game for the world's press. Harris has always detested the aura of celebrity and elitism surrounding the majority of superstars: 'There are far too many prima donnas in this business and not enough action.'

After his divorce from Ann Turkel, Harris was dragged to the launch of Planet Hollywood in Los Angeles – 'she loved that sort of thing, one of the reasons we divorced' – where he felt he had been ignored by Bruce Willis, one of the restaurant's co-owners.

The Irishman tapped the *Die Hard* star on the shoulder and said, 'Excuse me, your face seems so familiar, but I can't put a name to it. I was actually talking to my ex-wife when you moved into my space. So would you please fuck off.'

It seemed, at least to his interviewers, that Harris could play his own version of the psychologist's word-association test: you name a personality or industry event and he could trot out a story or offer an opinion.

On the Oscar ceremony:

I mean, why the fuck would I want to participate in any of this Hollywood bollocks? It's fourteen fucking hours there, fourteen fucking hours back, two hours of fucking stupidity and kissing people's fucking cheeks. Fuck that!

On Tom Cruise:

Someone asked me once, 'What is the difference between Tom Cruise now and when you were a major star?' I said there is a great difference. Look at a photograph of me from the old days and I'm going to one of my film premieres with a bottle of vodka in my hand. Tom Cruise has a bottle of Evian water. That's the difference – a bottle of Evian water.

And on Alec Guinness:

I remember Alec say to me once, 'Isn't it funny, how, the older we get, the better we get, and the less we know?'

Socialising with his equals and betters, once a naïve and frustrating ambition, was now an excruciating torture. Steve McQueen, with whom he once spent an afternoon, was, claimed Harris, 'one of the most miserable men' he ever met. Harris ranked among that rare breed of actor who openly confesses his dislike of the film industry. 'Actors are not important,' he says, 'not like Beethoven or van Gogh or Francis Bacon.'

After he had rested and revitalised from his self-exile from acting, his twilight acting style was far less showy and much more controlled. It was, he tried to explain, closer to the way his old friend Sean Connery had taught himself to perform. 'Connery is totally at one with the camera,' said Harris. 'He knows what it can do and can't do. He's got the confidence to reduce and subtract from everything until it's almost nothing. And yet what he does is very powerful.'

There was no loss of undercurrent. Harris remained a shameless off-stage performer, mischievously launching into an impromptu Irish jig in the middle of a crowded restaurant or touring the tables and kissing the hand of every woman present. But by the early 1990s the hellraising had become staged, almost gentlemanly. There were raised voices, but no raised fists. Harris pleaded for attention, instead of demanding it with outrageous and violent behaviour. He picked his arguments the way a farmer picks his fruit: only when the conversation is ripe and almost over.

'Are you going to say I'm vain in your article?' Harris asked the *Independent on Sunday* journalist Lynn Barber during a 1990 interview. They were sitting in the lobby of the Savoy Hotel.

'Yes,' she replied. Her articled continued:

This is clearly the moment he has been waiting for; it is as if someone has shot him full of adrenalin; it is the moment in the Dublin pub when someone swings the first punch and all hell breaks loose.

He gleefully starts thumping the table and shouting: 'That's what you're saying because that's what you want to write about! This is where you journalists are all so cock-eyed! Why have an interview at all? You've written it all beforehand. You can't understand me – obviously you can't because you've got a female mind. I'm too bright for you altogether.'

The best voice in London, at full belt, has immense carrying power, and virtually the entire Savoy grinds to a halt while everyone listens. Harris enlists all the businessmen at nearby tables as witnesses: 'Did you hear what she said? She says I'm vain. Look at me!'

Alarmed by the noise, the shouting and thumping, I try to change the subject, but he is like a boxer who props up his opponent so he can hit him again: 'Go on, go on,' he urges, 'I want to hear how you rationalise things, how you justify yourself.'

As an attention-getting exercise it is peerless, but these bouts of verbal fisticuffs with willing writers are little more than publicity stunts: Harris is the self-publicist supreme.

Luigi Pirandello, the Italian playwright, novelist and Nobel laureate, was born in a small Sicilian village whose name loosely translates as 'chaos'. Almost four decades after Richard Harris had foregone the pleasures of a Dublin dance to watch *Henry IV*, the curse of its author's life – a 'sad piece of buffoonery' – appeared to have settled resolutely on Harris's shoulders.

By mid-April 1990, a pre-West End run of Pirandello's *Henry IV* had lost both its female lead, Sarah Miles, who pleaded exhaustion, and its director, David Thacker, who claimed pressure of other work. The production's first director, Philip Prowse, had also left after a disagreement over interpretation. One reason for this apparent 'chaos' was Harris's obsession with the play. Using translations of Pirandello's original notes and journals, he felt his colleagues were letting the play down by not doing an equal amount of homework.

Henry IV is a play about madness and a man's preferred descent into insanity. For Harris and his beleaguered production it seemed every line was booby-trapped. Two minutes after the curtain rises comes the line, 'This is a disaster.' One character complains, 'We're just sitting here with nothing to do and no one to direct us.' Another challenges, 'Who will stage this scene?' Not even Harris escapes: he screams in exasperation, 'I've got a bit bloody bored with all this!'

Seriously in danger of what producers fear most, a hot flop, *Henry IV* transferred to London's Wyndham's Theatre. They need not have worried. Harris's portrayal of Pirandello's mock-lunatic charmed the public and critics and won him the London *Evening Standard* Best Actor award. The run, originally scheduled to end in July, was hastily extended to October.

Among the audience for one early performance was the actor, writer and former Monty Python star John Cleese. For him the play's one endearing memory is not Harris's performance, excellent as it was, but the moment the star slipped out of character. 'Richard confronted this actor on the side of the stage,' recalls Cleese. 'And this young man gave such a brilliant reaction to Richard's question that Richard burst out laughing. I don't mean he cackled, he just laughed out loud.' Slipping out of his lines Harris quietly but audibly informed his fellow actor, 'You're not supposed to make me laugh,' before returning to the script. It was a 'wonderful moment' insists Cleese. 'Richard has always had this tremendously relaxed quality about him. He is almost as relaxed on stage as he is off, exactly like some of those old music hall comedians you read about. They simply considered the stage to be an extension of their private lives and sometimes you could never tell the difference between the two.'

Once it had settled into its West End run and with the critical acclaim he felt the production deserved, Harris announced himself 'gloriously happy'. Although his advice had been never to look back, and certainly not with any regret, he also considered he had salvaged some of the lost years. 'You do a piece of work like that and think, perhaps arrogantly, that after everything you have been through you can still do your job,' he triumphantly declared. 'You can still deliver the goods and you are actually pretty fucking good at what you do. I like that feeling. I never used to take my work seriously, certainly not while I was boozing, because I was more concerned about having a good life. But now I'm deadly serious. I turn down all the crap, whatever the money they are throwing around, and I am enjoying myself more than I ever did.'

The years touring America were paying off. His voice was holding up and so was his concentration. Harris refused to allow himself to be distracted: his day started at noon with a little light lunch; the afternoon was spent relaxing; a little after six he would leave his Savoy suite for Wyndham's Theatre to prepare for the eight o'clock curtain; by midnight he would be back in bed and reading for the next two or three hours. Harris, at sixty, was treading, perhaps for the first time in his life, that fine line between the madness of youth and the fulfilment of old age.

The success of *Henry IV* set him bubbling with more classic projects: a season of *Macbeth*, *The Merchant of Venice*, a two-hour *Hamlet* he would direct himself, followed by the ultimate goal of playing King Lear. 'People forget Richard is such a powerful figure that he is virtually a producing management in his own right,' explained the theatrical producer Thelma Holt. 'He can do almost anything he wants and if he needs any help from me then I am his humble handmaiden. It may not be a comfortable experience, but it will be bloody well worth it.'

Someone else who found his initial encounter with Harris uncomfortable was Robert Stephens. Harris had sat through the

Shakespearean actor's portrayal of Lear with a fidgeting excitement. At the end of the evening he barged his way backstage to compliment Stephens 'and compare notes'. When the actor's dressing room door failed to open on command Harris resorted to hammering it with his fist. 'I didn't even know the guy, but I had to get in there to tell him what his performance had meant to me.'

Something inside Clint Eastwood told him the time was right. Arriving at his Malpaso office – the company he set up in 1966 to hire himself out to film studios – Eastwood opened a filing cabinet and pulled out a tattered script. The title page read: *The William Munny Killings*.

David Webb Peoples had written this 'revisionist western' in the mid-1970s, just as money in Hollywood was hard to find and cowboy films were out of fashion. It wasn't until Peoples's screenplay for the futuristic *Blade Runner* made him saleable that Malpaso stepped in and scooped up his earlier script. 'I bought it in 1983 and I kind of nurtured it like a little jewel you put on a shelf and polish now and then,' said Eastwood, justifying his investment. 'I figured I'd age into it a little bit. It's a fictional story about a renegade, very stylised, a little different. What appealed to me was the idea that the good guys weren't all that good and the bad guys weren't all that bad.' Only one thing was needed to improve this screenplay. Eastwood crossed out the original title and above it wrote: *Unforgiven*.

Through Malpaso, Eastwood began his search for three bankable actors to play opposite his William Munny. His instinct told him there was only one man capable of developing the part of Munny's old enemy, Sheriff 'Little Bill' Daggett, and that was Gene Hackman. Without seeing the script, Hackman refused, claiming he was 'overdosed on violence'. Eastwood sent the screenplay anyway and followed it with a telephone call, in which he explained the film's antiviolence message. 'He was very explicit about his desire to demythologise violence,' recalls Hackman. 'I'm really glad Clint convinced me it was not a Clint Eastwood film!'

Choosing the black actor Morgan Freeman to play Munny's old friend Ned Logan once again put Eastwood ahead of the game. It would another two years before Mario Van Peebles's black western *Posse* attempted to stake a claim for thousands of Afro–Americans who helped shape and settle the United States.

Despite his powerful performance in *The Field*, many Hollywood producers still viewed Richard Harris's apparent comeback as a stroke of luck. Others were more charitable. *The Field*, they claimed, proved

Harris had lost none of the exciting talent he displayed in the early 1960s. Whatever the state of the Irish actor's career, Eastwood wanted Harris for the part of his third veteran assassin, English Bob, a self-styled aristocrat who earns a living killing errant Chinese railroad workers. 'I loved it,' admitted Harris. 'Clint's idea was that there were no heroes and no villains. It was to be a slice of American life that debunked the myth of the West: cowboys who were always filthy and who can't shoot each other from a hundred paces and scenery that is an infinity of rock and burned-out bush.'

The plot of *Unforgiven* is a simple one. A prostitute's face is slashed by a cowboy, who takes offence at the woman's having laughed at his 'small pecker'. When the sheriff (Hackman) refuses to punish the crime in a manner that the prostitutes consider appropriate – he merely demands that the cowboy repay the saloon owner for the loss of income that will result from the slashed hooker's diminished appeal – they band together to offer a reward to anyone who will administer a more violent and permanent punishment.

In contrast to Martin Ritt's dour pithead vision for *The Molly Maguires*, Malpaso soon found there was nowhere left in America that overlaid Eastwood's ungodly vision of the nineteenth-century West. *Unforgiven* would be shot near Calgary in Canada, where, in the empty wilderness below the Rockies, the crew would build the Daggett homestead, the Munny and Logan farms and the town of Big Whiskey on sites personally selected by Malpaso's chief executive.

Harris was informed that shooting would not start until September 1991 – not through any financial or technical hiccup, but simply because Eastwood, who shoots all his Westerns in the autumn, was waiting for the bright summer colours to fade. In the meantime, Harris had one suggestion to make.

As ever Harris was determined to get as much out of his character as possible. Somehow he felt English Bob's arrival in Big Whisky didn't quite work: 'It didn't flow the way it should have.' After talking through the scene, Eastwood accepted the need for a minor rewrite.

Once the cameras started to roll, Harris found himself pleasantly confused by his director's approach to filmmaking. 'Clint is very, very, very laid back and terribly polite,' admitted Harris. 'But he knows precisely what he wants on the set.' Eastwood, renowned for his tight shooting schedules, was repaid by working with three 'great start-up actors – Harris and Hackman and Freeman are great examples. They're the kind of guys where you start rehearsal and it looks so good you say,

"Wait a second, stop, roll this thing!", because there's no reason to waste it. They're ready to pull the trigger straight away.'

Eastwood's control did not extend to the weather. With seven weeks' work in the can and just two and a half days' shooting left, he was informed the autumn's first snowfall was expected on Monday morning. It was Saturday midday. The cast and crew worked nonstop through Saturday and Sunday nights to beat the forecast by fifteen minutes.

Unforgiven took 52 days to shoot and cost $14.4 million, excluding Eastwood's own fee. Not only was it one of the fastest films Harris had ever made, but it would also prove to be one his most successful.

Deliberately held back until the end of the lucrative summer season, *Unforgiven* was not released until August 1992. In the United States alone it grossed more than $100 million. The following year it earned an equal amount in publicity by scooping no fewer than nine Academy Award nominations. Sadly, Harris was not among the nominees.

At 59, Michael Caine had established himself as a British institution. He was about to be elevated to the knighthood 'for services to the entertainment industry'. But on one particular day in 1992 the millionaire star and restaurateur allowed a half-forgotten anger to bubble through his veins. It was the kind of resentment that, back on the Camberwell streets of his youth, would almost certainly have ended in a fist fight.

A week earlier the *Observer* had attached its own citation to his career: 'His voice sounds as though it comes from a London taxi driver who has seen too many fares. And yet the voice, the spectacles, the laconic manner, and a slightly trimmer version of the physique all helped establish him as the closest England ever gets to a sex symbol.' Now the paper had published a letter attacking Caine and claiming the actor 'was too big for his boots'. Worse, the insult came from someone he had known and respected for more than thirty years – in the early 1960s they had sipped champagne together at the Pickwick Club and had got drunk in the Salisbury pub.

Michael Caine arrived at the Savoy and demanded to see Richard Harris. In the Irish star's suite his irritation broke the surface.

Harris, who was taken aback by the force of his fellow actor's anger, apologised, saying he had had a funny day.

So far life had been good to Harris – good enough to pay for his needs and caprices and women. Now he was turning his back on the film industry, but most of all Hollywood. An actress who shared Harris's sentiments but took another decade to go public was Shirley MacLaine. In her autobiography, *My Lucky Stars*, she admits:

> The lies, the manipulations, the seductions, the tears, the subjugation of one's very soul are usually done in the name of being true and authentic to one's purpose and art. It is a colossal paradox: to be true to one's authentic vision sometimes requires the basest of fakery, disinformation, duplicity, hypocrisy, distortion, spuriousness and unctuous deception! That is why Hollywood is referred to as the 'Big Knife'. That is why civilians are fascinated by how we conduct our 'reality'. We do things in Hollywood in the name of entertainment that most governments do in the name of espionage.

Wrestling Ernest Hemingway would be Shirley MacLaine's 43rd film. At 59 years old, the veteran American actress was only four years younger than her co-star. Exceptionally perceptive, she very quickly buttoned Harris as a 'bombastic Irishman given to high-blown, grand, eloquent stories'. But one scene produced some unexpected doubts.

Late one evening, when the studio was less busy, the crew began preparing the set for a love scene between Harris's Frank and MacLaine's middle-aged and sexually frustrated character of Helen. 'All sorts of jumbled thoughts went through my mind,' admits MacLaine. 'Would the public want to see grey-haired elders enact their conflict? I could not remember having seen a real love scene between people over forty in years. Was this in bad taste?'

Harris was having his own misgivings, particularly the part where his character admits on screen to being impotent. The set was finally ready, but Harris refused to leave his dressing room. Gentle reassurance from the director turned to heated threats. Time was running out. Still, Harris refused to budge. At three in the morning MacLaine's patience ran out. 'Richard,' she yelled, loud enough for the studio's off-duty staff to hear at home, 'get your butt in here so we can get this mutha and go home.'

The door to Harris's dressing room creaked open and the actor slouched on to the set. It took ten takes and another two hours to capture the scene. Both stars felt slightly ashamed by their behaviour. 'Our relationship was not the same after that,' says MacLaine.

On a cold day in 1994, Richard Harris stood alone in Limerick's Mount St Lawrence Cemetery. The interment had ended. The handshakes and hugged condolences were over, the hundreds of mourners had drifted away.

Slowly and deliberately, the 63-year-old actor began reading the names on the family tomb: James Harris (his great-grandfather) had died in 1895; Richard and Harriet Harris (his grandparents) had both died in 1932; Mildred Harris (his mother) had died of cancer in 1960; Ivan Harris (his broken and bankrupt father) had died less than two years later; Dermot Harris (his brother) had died in 1986.

In his own lifetime Richard Harris had lost a father, two sisters and a brother to heart disease. Now he had just buried a second brother, Jimmy. Another victim of hereditary heart disease.

It was death, and the possibility of his own, that had prompted Harris publicly to board the wagon years before. And it was death that was about to nudge him off again. Inside his head, Harris heard himself asking, 'Wouldn't they all like to get up out of there for five minutes and enjoy a pint of Guinness?' Harris turned and slowly walked to the nearest pub. His first pint of stout in thirteen years tasted better than ever.

Harris claimed that story was true. But if the catalyst was really his brother's funeral the pressure had been building for some time. Those thirteen years of abstinence were the most boring years of his life, he claimed, turning him into a social recluse. 'Nothing is worse than a group of people having a drink and you're sipping Perrier water and they're getting funnier and your getting more and more bored.'

After he had survived stomach cancer, it was Harris's physical appearance that was once again causing concern. By the end of 1993 he was looking seriously gaunt. With the Limerick funeral behind him, his doctor agreed that four daily white-wine spritzers could do little harm. When Harris continued to lose weight, he announced he wanted to try Guinness, a four-pint-a-day regime he maintained for the rest of his life.

Predictably Harris plunged into one of his 'ungrateful and ungracious' depressions. He no longer lashed out at those nearest him. Instead, his marriages long dead and three years since his last affair, Harris turned in on himself, salving his sorrow and regret with plans of change. 'When I saw my brother dead I thought, What have I done with my life?' he said. 'Just how important is acting?'

For the first time since acquiring his home on Paradise Island, Harris felt discontented with the Bahamas. Deep inside he sensed it had somehow served its purpose: his own and everyone else's children had grown up there, and so, too, had he, in a way. He no longer needed a bolt hole from his own celebrity. The world's media were no longer hounding him for an explanation or excuse. For the first time he was being questioned – at least by the more serious interviewers – on his performances and plans. And he could do that from anywhere in the world.

Harris talked over his intention to sell the Bahamas house with his ex-wife Elizabeth, 'My gut feeling is that I want to come back to England,' he confessed. Between them they decided it would be best if he rented a house in London for a year before making a final decision.

During August Harris visited Lindsay Anderson. The 71-year-old director of *This Sporting Life* appeared downcast and preoccupied, and Harris hoped a funny story would cheer him up. Harris told him the story about John Huston, about when Anjelica Huston had asked her dying father, 'Dad, is there anything you want?' And how the film director had answered, 'A good script.'

Anderson smiled and said, 'My dear Richard, that has been the story of my life for the last seven years.'

A week or so later Anderson agreed to spend a few days in France with Lois Smith, an old friend who, as Lois Sutcliffe, had started Anderson's career by persuading him to make his first documentary, *Meet the Pioneers*. On 5 September, despite saying he felt 'so very tired', he agreed to go for a swim in the sea. Climbing back out of the water, Lindsay Anderson collapsed and died. The examining surgeon recorded his death as *crise de coeur, massive*.

Lindsay Anderson's last film was a cinematic self-portrait in 1993 called, *Is That All There Is?*. On 20 November, a year after its release, a memorial celebration was held at the Royal Court Theatre in London. The evening was intended not only to mark the life of one of Britain's most notable directors, but also to celebrate forty years of English stage and screen history. Harris took his turn among the line of other stars delivering Anderson remembrances and recalling how *This Sporting Life* had virtually launched his career.

He did not enjoy the experience. Nor did he feel comfortable. After cheating his own self-inflicted destiny on several occasions, Harris was faced the sudden realisation that he was no longer being viewed as a member of an acting generation but increasingly as one of its survivors. He decided to make Christmas 1994 something special, because 'I thought, Wouldn't it be dreadful if I was to fucking drop dead and didn't know all the Harrises in my family?' His holiday guest list sounded more like the agenda for an international conference, with 74 members of Harris's extended family flying in from New York and Los Angeles, Belgium, France, Russia, Australia, New Zealand and South Africa. 'It was the best Christmas of my life,' he admitted.

After the sell-out West End run of *Henry IV*, Harris found himself with an outstanding date with Broadway. Plans to take the play to New York in the spring were abandoned, however, when Warner Bros asked him to clear his diary for an Oscar campaign for *Wrestling Ernest Hemingway*. Then, without explanation, the studio abandoned its promotion and left the actor and the film in limbo. A year late, Harris announced plans to open on Broadway in May 1995, with venues already booked in Boston, Washington and San Francisco.

By the early summer, Harris was back at his Bahamian mansion to recuperate and catch up on his reading. One of the first things he read was a *Sunday Times* magazine profile of Michael Caine. Buried deep in the feature were two barbed comments, which first irritated and then inflamed Harris's aversion to all things pompous. Caine claimed that other top British actors of his generation – including Richard Burton, Peter O'Toole and Richard Harris – 'were all drunks'. The veteran actor went so far as to describe himself as 'a British Gene Hackman, the star character actor with a lot to teach the younger generation'.

Harris had bitten his tongue for three years. Their friendship-turned-standoff was just about to become a very public feud. He replied with a 1,200-word letter, which the *Sunday Times* duly printed the following week. In it the Irish actor called Caine 'an over-fat, flatulent 62-year-old windbag' with 'vast limitations':

I take great exception to anybody who in print attacks his fellow actors. I loved Richard Burton, who is now dead. I am glad that some producer has decided to revive Michael Caine's career by putting him back to work, but spare us the inevitable flood of self-satisfied, self-congratulatory interviews that will follow this incipient actor's resurrection, rendering indigestible our morning coffee.

Caine was foolish to compare himself to Gene Hackman, added Harris, because Hackman 'is an intimidating and dangerous actor. Mr Caine is about as dangerous as Laurel and Hardy, or indeed both, and as intimidating as Shirley Temple.' Nor should Caine fancy himself among the best of British actors. The suggestion that Caine had eclipsed the names of Finney, O'Toole, Burton, Bates, Smith and Courtenay was 'tantamount to prophesying that Rin-Tin-Tin will be solemnised beyond the memory of Marlon Brando.'

But Harris saved his final and hardest hit for Caine's 'drunk' comment, a criticism he perceived as a slur on the memory of Richard Burton. Harris's drinking sessions with Burton and O'Toole were 'a voyage most great actors embarked on where, on occasion, they might touch the Gods to ignite their craft'.

Across the Atlantic, the *People's Daily* delivered the ultimate verdict on the squabble's absurdity when it declared, 'If they were American, they'd be at the "yo' mama" stage already. But they're British and film stars to boot, so Michael Caine and Richard Harris fight as only highbrows can – by exchanging choice insults in the pages of respected London newspapers.'

Whatever Harris's intention, Caine refused to take the bait. This time there would be no face-to-face remonstrations and certainly no public response. His only comment came four years later in Michael Freedland's biography, *Michael Caine*, where Caine admitted:

When he did it again and pretended it was because I'd said he was drunk, I was disgusted with him. I couldn't say anything because I didn't want to take any notice of it … If something is irrelevant, it doesn't mean anything. Someone tells me that somebody got run over in the street. I say, 'that's terrible'. But I don't burst into tears or get upset.

Around the same time Harris was making his own matchless comment on the disagreement. John Naughton was carrying out an interview with him for *Empire* magazine:

Richard Harris has just answered one of my questions with a fart. There's nothing discreet about it, either. He simply anchors his left elbow on the arm of his comfy Savoy Hotel armchair, tilts his body slightly to the left, raises his right knee and lets rip. A long, snorting, very loud, cheese-cutter of a fart. Oh, I say. The question which provoked this violent outburst of flatulence is simply, what does he think of Michael Caine these days.

'Do you hear that?' asks Harris. As I am not wearing industrial ear mufflers, the question scarcely needs a reply. 'That was an automatic fart, after hearing his name.'

Having given his general impression of Michael Caine via one orifice, he confirms it with another . . .

'The point about Michael is that he can say what he likes, I don't mind him opening his mouth and shooting off. I don't care what he says. But don't characterise Richard Burton, Peter O'Toole and me as drunks as if that's all we've achieved in our life, because he could live twenty fucking lives and he couldn't achieve as much as we three have achieved.'

It is productive but hardly fertile ground for most journalists. But, then again, Harris openly admitted his interview-cum-entertainment sessions with the world's press were hardly to be taken seriously. Harris reacted differently to different writers: one, a woman, he attempted to seduce; another, also a woman, he instantly dismissed and ordered out of the room. Another incident around this time earned equal press coverage on both sides of the Atlantic. Once again, someone had said something that offended Harris, but this time it wasn't the actor who lashed out.

Malachy McCourt was a County Antrim farmer and an 'old IRA' fighter who, not long after World War One, fled to America after allegedly offending the organisation's new and more vicious hierarchy. By the early 1930s he felt the threat to his life had receded enough to allow him to return to Ireland with his wife and five children. The family eventually settled in Limerick and it was his 'miserable Irish Catholic childhood' that Malachy McCourt's oldest son – by now returned to New York and a college teacher – used as the raw material for his memoir, *Angela's Ashes*.

The book was an instant success for Frank McCourt, not only winning the 1997 Pulitzer Prize for nonfiction but with its film rights quickly scooped up for an equally successful movie. It was inevitable that Limerick's oldest and newest celebrities, both residents of New York, should meet up for a drink and a chat in one of the city's better-known Irish pubs. What happened next depends on which newspapers you read and who is being interviewed.

According to Harris, he was drinking in a bar called Himself with

Frank McCourt and his younger brother Malachy, when the author made several 'derogative and derisive' remarks about Limerick. 'I was talking to Malachy when Frank raised his fist and hit me a terrible belt on the nose,' claims Harris. 'Like a hare running from a hound he raced towards the exit door and ran out of the pub. I had never been confronted by a Limerickman who ran away from a fight. We don't do that in Limerick, we stand our ground and fight. To run from a fight is not part of the Limerick character at all.'

In his defence, McCourt admitted the punch but claimed he had been 'provoked'. By the time the story broke – first in the American and then Irish press – any hostility, reassured the writer, had been 'quickly reconciled'. Not, it would seem, to Harris's satisfaction.

Questioned on an Irish radio station a year or so later about the assault, the actor criticised the two McCourt brothers, alleging that, when Angela McCourt died, her sons had her body cremated rather than pay out the cost of shipping a coffin back to Ireland.

McCourt denied the allegations and said he and his brother had 'honoured their mother's final wishes'. On the whole, added Frank McCourt, he got on well with everyone from Limerick – 'except for a few cranks'.

The script for Harris's next film arrived with a note from his agent. It suggested he turn the part down because it was too small. Harris read the screenplay anyway and immediately put in a 2 a.m. call to his agent. 'Are you out of your mind?' he demanded. 'Actors dream of roles like this.'

For *Cry, the Beloved Country*, Harris found himself back in South Africa, an experience he always enjoyed. Watching the shoot was Stephen Coan a feature writer with the *Natal Witness*:

It is 1948. In a valley of the Drakensberg foothills a man whose son has been murdered walks into a church to shelter from a storm. Not that there is much shelter. The roof leaks and water bounces out of the metal bowls set on the altar. The man sits on a bench but has to move to avoid another spout coming through the corrugated iron roof. His movements are slow, deliberate, leaden with depression. A movie camera and its attendant crew record every moment.

Outside the church it is 1994, the sun is shining and a dry, hot wind blows across the valley. The rain hitting the church comes via a rubber hose from a water tanker manipulated by a crew stripped to the waist. Make-up artists, props assistants, electricians, are standing around waiting for another take. Huge lights, cables, scrims – the usual detritus of a film location – lie around the rural church on the hillside. Empty chairs under an awning boast the names Darrell Roodt, James Earl Jones and Richard Harris. Director and stars of a new film version of Alan Paton's *Cry, the Beloved Country*.

Harris is playing the farmer Ralph Jarvis whose politically liberal son has been shot in Johannesburg by the son of the pastor of the church where he has taken shelter. While shooting the scenes in the church his absorption in the role, his concentration, is dauntingly tangible. No wonder the assistant director calls him 'sir'.

'It's a wonderful part,' says Harris. 'In the world of movie-making today scripts like this don't come very often. And it's a change for me – I'm always being offered these histrionic parts and then the critics accuse me of over-balancing films! But the great chance with this is that it's the very opposite – Jarvis is this very quiet, very internal guy.'

Now, relaxing under the awning, fumbling to light a cigarette in the wind, the diminished man of the film suddenly bursts into life. Harris's broad Irish accent replacing the flatter, clipped South African vowels. A fellow actor's description of him as 'fabulously Irish' is an apt one. Harris is grand in gesture and mercurial in mood; moving quickly from wistfulness to anger and back again. All offset by a wry self-awareness . . .

For Jarvis, apartheid and, more importantly, the effects of apartheid, do not exist. He is a man who refuses to see beyond the borders of his own property. The film was adapted from Alan Paton's 1940s classic novel, and its real star was to be James Earl Jones as the Zulu pastor Stephen Kumalo, who sets off for Johannesburg in search of his bruised and scattered family.

The film was a remake – with the addition of a comma in the title – of the 1951 version of *Cry the Beloved Country*. The original, directed by Zoltan Korda, starred Sidney Poitier as the preacher and Canada Lee as James Jarvis. Between the two films the black population of South Africa had endured and survived more than thirty years of state-sanctioned apartheid, something the first film dealt with only on a personal level.

As ever, Harris's luggage on his journey to South Africa included the

1912 Mass card that once belonged to his Rosie Harty, whose guiding spirit remained at his shoulder. At times, this presence provided a little more psychic contact than Harris bargained for.

'I can walk into a house and know instantly that its haunted,' he admitted. While filming *Beloved Country*, Harris and his fellow actors were booked into the Old Halliwell's Country Inn at Curry's Post in northern Natal. One evening he decided to go for a walk in the nearby Karkoof Valley: 'The whole air was filled with spirits . . . There was crying and death – some kind of massacre there. When I went to sleep that night the spirits were all over my room. I had shocking nightmares.'

Cry, the Beloved Country premiered at New York's Zeigfeld Theatre on 23 October 1995. In the audience were the South African president Nelson Mandela and the wife of the American president, Hillary Rodham Clinton. A day or so earlier, Mandela had sat through the film – the first film he had watched in more than thirty years – to allow him to make a prescreening introduction:

Cry, the Beloved Country is a film that for my generation will evoke bittersweet memories of our youth.

One of South Africa's leading humanists, Alan Paton, vividly captured his eloquent faith in the essential goodness of people in his epic work – a goodness that helped manage this small miracle of our transition, and arrested attempts by the disciples of apartheid to turn our country into a wasteland. An attribute that is at the foundation of our people's nation-building effort. And Paton was right, in his time and circumstances, to despair at seeing no peaceful way beyond the oppressors' denial of the humanity of armed resistance. He recognised its inevitability.

Much of what is portrayed in *Cry, the Beloved Country* evokes such strong emotions about the terrible past from which South Africa has just emerged. *Cry, the Beloved Country*, however, is also a monument to the future.

Today's premiere of *Cry, the beloved Country* confirms once more our confidence in the future. It is causes such as this which bring to the fore men and women of good will and talent – Anant Singh, Darrell Roodt, Vusi Kunene, Leleti Khumalo. The talent and creativity that was virtually unrecognised under apartheid is able today to shine, combined with the skill and experience of compassionate friends of South Africa, such as James Earl Jones and Richard Harris. This film and its messages reinforce our friendship across oceans and adds value to the treasure house of culture in general.

Harris was also at the premiere and found *Cry, the Beloved Country* one of the few films he appeared in *and* enjoyed watching. At the post-screening reception, Harris asked Nelson Mandela what would have happened to him if he had not spent 27 years in jail. The South African statesman thought for a few seconds and then replied, 'I'd be dead.'

CHAPTER FOURTEEN

Harris's dedication to *My Kingdom* produced some strong disagreements with the co-writer and director Don Boyd, one bringing the entire set to a two-hour standstill. After two 'spectacular' confrontations, Boyd attempted to short-circuit any future problems by calling at his star's trailer first thing in the morning while the rest of the cast were in make-up. Laid out on the table would be the heavily amended script and copious handwritten notes on the day's scenes. 'He was a brilliant professional,' says Boyd.

When the eight-week shoot was over, Boyd asked Harris why he thought they had remained friends. 'He looked into my eyes with his unforgettable stare and said that, despite our differences, he felt that he'd been able to see into my soul.'

CHAPTER FOURTEEN

I don't think there's a punchline scheduled, is there?

— Monty Python

With a reputation like Richard Harris's, it was common for a script to have been read and rejected by Sean Connery, Roger Moore, Anthony Hopkins and even Gene Hackman before it landed on his desk. This time, the director Carl Schultz was adamant. He wanted the 68-year-old Harris.

To Walk With Lions was to be a sequel to *Born Free*, the 1966 Academy Award-winning story of the conservationists George and Joy Adamson. It had all the elements of a good film, including the promise of Sean Bean as co-star. But Harris, who bore a striking resemblance to the ageing Adamson, was not overly impressed by the Keith Ross Leckie script – for one thing there were an awful lot of lions in it.

Harris read one of Adamson's own books about life on his Kora compound – 'He was an amazing man, wasn't he?' – and his constant struggle with big-game poachers and the Kenyan authorities. After six weeks, Harris telephoned Schultz and agreed to take the part.

By the time the cast and crew arrived in Kenya, with Harris insisting – and getting – a 'no-acting-with-lions' clause in his contract, Bean had been replaced by the Scottish actor John Michie, better known to millions of television viewers as the bad-boy detective Robbie Ross in the cult crime drama *Taggart*. The pair finally met for a first-night drink in a Nairobi bar. 'I can't wait to see some lions again,' Michie admitted. 'The last time was when I was on safari out here.'

'Lions?' exploded Harris. 'I don't want to see a lion in the whole of this film, not one.' Having survived to see his seventieth birthday on the horizon, he felt it would be ironic to be mauled to death by a lion.

'In that case,' smiled his co-star, 'I think you're in the wrong film.'

Financed by a Canadian–British–Kenyan consortium, *To Walk With Lions* was to be far grittier story than the original account of the Adamsons' fight to tame and protect a lion called Elsa. Honor Blackman, a friend of Harris's since the 1960s, would play Joy Adamson, now estranged from her husband. But it was the relationship between the male leads, George Adamson (Harris) and the womanising alcoholic conservationist Tony Fitzjohn (Michie), that provided the film's real focus. It is a fraught and intense friendship, which ultimately ends with George Adamson's death at the hands of Kenyan poachers.

During the first few days of shooting, Michie did his best to calm his co-star's fears. 'I spent a lot of time with one of the animal rangers and discovered I had a bit of an affinity with the lions,' he says. 'So I asked Richard if he'd like to come up to the lion camp with me.' First, Harris asked the tamers how to beat his fear. They showed him how to walk and move near the lions – and what *not* to do. Then came the process of building the animals' trust. Each morning, Harris would visit the cages and talk to the lions, careful not to challenge them with his eyes. One lion, called Taboo, instantly took to the actor. Each time Harris appeared, it would trot across the cage to meet him.

When the location shoot finished Harris visited his favourite lion to say goodbye. As with his human relationships, he had invested a good deal of love in a short space of time. 'God, I loved that lion by the end,' he admitted. Taboo said goodbye by licking Harris's face.

Whatever personal pride Harris had in the film was diluted by some unconventional and careless public relations. When *To Walk With Lions* opened in Canada in the spring of 2000, Harris discovered that his name had somehow been omitted from the posters and publicity. It left him so embittered that the round of prerelease press interviews had to be postponed and there was even talk of his boycotting the 26 May British premiere.

Those permitted to see the film, if not its star, came away impressed both by Harris's performance and his ability to last. Adam Mars-Jones commented in *The Times*:

> Physicality has never been the hallmark of British acting, except perhaps among those for whom drinking was almost the first love and real career. Of his rivals and rough contemporaries, Peter O'Toole was always as much fey as manly (his Lawrence of Arabia a case in point), while Oliver Reed let his beefiness slide into self-parody. As he has aged, Richard Harris has become neither ethereal nor course, and at seventy is still pretty much believable as a man of action, a stubborn survivor living on a diet of corned beef and whisky, King Lear with a pipe and a gun.

Less than a month before the film's release, Ian Bannen, who played Terence Adamson, the conservationist's brother, was killed in a car crash.

During the 1960s, Bannen, another reformed alcoholic, was a drinking companion not only of Harris but also Peter O'Toole and Richard Burton. During filming Harris considered the Scotsman's performance so good that his part should be expanded to replace some of the 'Hollywood sixties romantic crap'.

Harris would lose a second, if more distant, friend while making his second film of 1999. On 2 May, Oliver Reed collapsed and died from a massive heart attack during a Sunday lunchtime drinking season in a Valetta pub. He was in Malta to film the $120 million epic *Gladiator*.

For Harris his *Gladiator* role possessed that pinch of irony he so enjoyed in real life. Thirty-five years earlier, he had turned his back on the role of Commodus, the son of Marcus Aurelius, in Anthony Mann's *Fall of the Roman Empire*. He was now being asked to play Marcus ruefully looking back over the last three and half decades of his life and fearing for his son's future – the son Harris almost played. Philosophically, he declared that it was the character (Marcus), not the film (*Gladiator*), that had tempted him out of his self-imposed retirement. 'Marcus is a man in crisis, wrestling with demons,' he explained. 'Marcus was a scholar and a philosopher, but he spent sixteen of his twenty years as emperor fighting battles and spilling blood to expand the empire. Now, nearing the end, he comes to realise that his life has been a fraud and that he has actually ruined his children – especially Commodus.'

For the first time in his career, Harris could not bully his director. Ridley Scott had both the strength and tact to rein in his star's Celtic bluster, so that he demanded, and got, a powerful, almost muted, performance from his star. Two fellow practitioners of Celtic bluster – a style of controlled theatrical bellowing aimed at the back row of the stalls – were Richard Burton and Anthony Hopkins; one was no longer performing, and the other had long ago learned to adjust the volume of his delivery.

While Ridley Scott was directing Harris and the first *Gladiator* scenes in England, his casting director was facing an equally mammoth task: auditioning 22,000 Maltese extras. By the time Scott and the rest of the cast arrived in Malta – via Morocco and North Africa – thousands of part-time actors and actresses had been trained and costumes fitted. They were ready to start filming.

On the British set, Harris found the mechanics of making a hi-tech epic as fascinating as his part in it. Between scenes or over lunch, he would bombard Ridley Scott with questions, listening in awe as the director explained how the stupendous sets and hundreds of extras would later be augmented by multimillion-dollar computer wizardry.

'Computers are the new, modern world which I don't feel part of at all,' Harris commented. 'One day they're going to simulate actors with computers in movies and they will not need us any more.' It was a startlingly accurate piece of prediction that would come true even before *Gladiator's* release. Oliver Reed's character was to have ridden into the sunset at the end of the film. After the actor's death and with just five days shooting left, Scott ordered a script rewrite to give Proximo a redeeming, $2 million death.

Two earlier scenes were adapted to allow Reed's head to be computer-grafted on to the body of an acting double and hi-tech imaging was used to change his expression and add shadows and wrinkles to his face. Additional appearances, filmed weeks earlier, were clawed back from outtakes and already discarded sequences (one entire scene is a repeat of a previous one, but with Reed in different clothes, against a different background and uttering different words). Proximo's death was shot tactfully from behind.

Reunions with fellow actors were rare and invariably well away from theatres and film sets. The exception was rugby. On 27 May 2000, Munster were scheduled to play Northampton in the Heineken Cup final at Twickenham. The night before, Harris would be in London for the premiere of *To Walk With Lions* and telephoned his old friend Peter O'Toole to arrange a pre-match drink – 'To take wine and talk sport.'

Harris, fighting a savage champagne hangover, was the first to arrive at the Roebuck on Richmond Hill. Beneath a tatty Arran sweater he was wearing an immaculately preserved 1948 Munster Schools rugby shirt. Two pints later, O'Toole walked in puffing on his long trademark cigarette holder. 'Mickser,' he bellowed, using Harris's nickname since his Joan Littlewood days.

Suddenly, O'Toole dropped to his knees and clasps his hands in prayer. The bar fell silent. 'Dickie Harris, you're a great man of Limerick,' intoned O'Toole in a mock Gregorian chant. 'Sure you've brought untold honour on the city. Munster rugby is your passion and we respect you for that. One day, God willing, you'll get the Oscar you richly deserve, but in the meantime will you ever fuck off out of Twickenham and leave us in peace. Every time you come to watch Munster we lose.' The bar erupted in laughter, flying ash and spilled beer, and Harris looked happy but desperate to shed his fabled jinx.

Legend has it that, whenever Munster made it to a final and word got round that Harris was thinking of attending, they said novenas all Friday night in churches across the county. 'I'm the kiss of death to Munster,' admitted Harris. And not just the senior team. A few years previously Young Munster had lost seven finals with the actor watching. When Harris arrived for the eighth, the gateman was under strict orders not to let him in. Harris retreated to his car and listened to the game on the radio. At half-time, Young Munster were 9–0 up and the gateman relented. From the stands, Harris watched his former team lose 10–9. As ever, his jinx held good, and later, in the Twickenham changing rooms, Harris was dishing out comfort, not congratulations.

There were fewer and fewer things that interested Harris enough to make him break cover, and his outings to pubs and clubs tended to be low-profile, but never low-key. That winter he joined his one-time Theatre Workshop colleague and friend, Brian Murphy, in a public campaign to save one of his 'secret' drinking haunts.

Though founded in 1877, the Green Room club moved to its present subterranean premises close to the Strand in 1955. Since then the 200-year-old Adam Street cellar, which looked more like Fagin's kitchen set from *Oliver!* than an exclusive drinking establishment, has attracted members from across the entertainment industry. 'You can go there anonymously, have a pint, have a chat, and remain unmolested,' explained Harris. 'It is full of technicians and actors struggling to get a job – people who are far more interesting than so-called stars.' Four years after its lease expired, the club was still clinging to its crumbling premises despite legal threats and eviction notices. 'I love it because it is totally devoid of luvvies and darlings.'

By his 69th year, the fire in Harris's unorthodox persona had mellowed to an eccentric and endearing glow. It was not uncommon for the rheumy-eyed and scatty-haired actor to answer the door of his New York hotel suite at one in the afternoon – having failed to wake up and missed an appearance on America's top-rated morning talk show – still dressed in a stripy nightshirt. 'I hate mornings, anyway,' he confessed.

Despite his protests, the Renaissance Harris was frequently tempted from his island retreat and back into the studio. Of his seventy-odd film roles, two dozen came to him after his 1990 Oscar-nominated performance in *The Field*. 'Every time I get a script, I hope I hate it,' he admitted. 'I don't want to do it. They have to drag me screaming into committing to do a picture, and I'm screaming all the way to the airport, and I'm screaming resentment on the plane and when I land on location. And, the moment I start, I love it.'

Like that of Oliver Reed, the Irish actor's star was once again in the ascendant. He was in demand. He could be trusted. Producers and directors who once added an extra five days to a shooting schedule to cover his hangovers and off-duty shenanigans could once again sleep at night. With *Gladiator* and *To Walk With Lions* both complete, Harris was preparing himself for a movie he had long wanted to make, a modern-day *King Lear*.

Since receiving his 1994 Best Foreign Film Oscar for *Burnt by the Sun*, Nikita Mikhalkov had virtually dominated Mosfilm, the massive, Soviet-built 'Hollywood on the Moskva'. Plagued by underfunding and disorganisation – despite attracting investment cash from France, Italy and the Czech Republic – Mosfilm contributed just two or three of the forty or so films made in Russia each year. By 1998, Mikhalkov was becoming desperate. His latest venture, *The Barber of Siberia*, would cost in excess of £30 million, with £6 million supplied by the Russian government and taking up the state's entire annual film-sponsorship budget. In the hope of securing overseas artistic approval, and a second Academy Award, Mikhalkov recruited Julia Ormond and Richard Harris.

In April it was announced that *Barber* had been chosen as the opening film at the following month's Cannes Film Festival. Harris made plans to attend. The day after he had flown into London from Nassau, he learned that drastic cuts had been made to the movie. The editing reduced the film's screen time from six to three hours – still a marathon by anyone's endurance – with much of Harris's performance ending up on the editing room floor. In protest, he announced he would not be going to Cannes. 'Hollywood is now run by people from Harvard Business School,' he declared. 'Who said they won't sit through it? Just because those fartarses in California are too busy coking and going to restaurants and screwing everybody else's wife. The Russian *War and Peace* was eight hours, for God's sake.'

That night, Alan Parker, the director of the British Film Institute and a man whose directorial credits included *Midnight Express* and *Evita*, was interviewed by the BBC direct from the South of France. Asked about the ethics of editing a film to fit a festival time slot and Harris's subsequent boycott, Parker said that, if something had to be cut, 'a Richard Harris performance is the place that should be going'.

Within hours – the early hours of the morning – the actor delivered an open letter to the *Daily Telegraph*. It was a few lines before the vitriol started flowing. 'What Parker said on television was exceedingly rude,' replied Harris. 'I am sixty-nine years of age in October. I've put the shield down, but not the sword.'

Unlike Michael Caine and Frank McCourt before him, Parker refused to take the bait. But, when Harris's *Barber* co-star, Julia Ormond, was caught off guard a few days later and complained about working with the Irish actor, she, too, was destined for the mincer. She was, Harris claimed, 'wet behind the ears' and 'yet to prove herself'.

The Barber of Siberia came nowhere near recouping its £30-million-plus budget and landed just one award: a Best Supporting Actor prize (for Vladimir Ilyin) from the Russian Guild of Film Critics. Its unedited six-hour version is still popular on Russian television.

As they passed in opposite directions through Heathrow Airport, John Cleese remembers catching a brief sight of Richard Harris and thinking 'what an absolutely wonderful head' he had. 'It was a marvellous face and head,' recalls the actor–producer, 'and I immediately thought that every sculptor in the world would want to sit down and model it.'

By the spring of 2000, the *Daily Telegraph* writer Elizabeth Grice saw Harris more as someone with the 'forehead of an Old Testament prophet and the body of a middle-aged rambler' dressed in a cable-knit jumper, combat trousers and boots. Not that Harris had not tried his utmost to rearrange his physical appearance.

One lifelong habit he could not control, either on set or in private, was rubbing the side of his nose. It was a nervous reaction to the nine times he claimed to have broken his nose – the first on a Thomond Park rugby pitch and in subsequent collisions with walls, doors and fists. The last time was when he plunged headfirst through the windscreen of a car. His already fragile nose disintegrated as his face hit the road.

To rebuild the actor's face his plastic surgeon ordered a five-by-six-foot enlargement of a photograph of Harris in his late twenties. The picture was pinned to the operating theatre wall. First, a piece of bone was removed from Harris's hip. The surgeon then ground and grafted the small section of bone on to his patient's face, using the enlarged portrait as a 'model'.

Satisfying the demands of his ageing body, though still-rampant intellect, Harris would spend most of his time alone, watching classic films, reading poetry and writing. In the 52 weeks up to April 2000, he spent just seven days on a film set. He drifted pleasantly between his native Ireland, New York, the Bahamas – which he still considered his real home – and his permanent suite on the seventh floor of the Savoy.

Elizabeth Grice attempted to describe his 'etiolated existence' at the prestige hotel:

> Harris seldom rises before the afternoon and values his privacy so much that it is sometimes days before he allows the domestic staff into his room. Most modern films make him angry so he rents old movies, reads books, writes poetry and hopes he isn't going to be sent a script he likes in case he's tempted to interrupt his easeful life.
>
> He ventures out only after dark, usually to a pub where there's no danger of being bored by fellow actors. He has a code of understanding with the barman: when he must be left alone and when it is safe to engage him in conversation. These days he drinks only Guinness.
>
> The Savoy's all-knowing switchboard operators reveal nothing of his whereabouts, not even whether he is in the country. 'They know I am a total eccentric,' he says throatily. 'My nickname is Hughes, Howard Hughes. I press a bell that says Waiter and my dinner comes. I press another bell that says Valet and they take my clothes away. I press another bell that says Maid and they come to clean. I ring to say I'm coming and they put flowers in the room. It's better than marriage.'
>
> All he lacks, then, is a button marked Lover. 'Oh, you bring those in yourself.'

For the months he spent on Paradise Island, Harris lived a curious alternation between intense solitude and intense socialising. 'By myself, I'm the best,' he freely admitted. 'I find myself the best company in the world.' His only human contact was with his servants and the products of other 'far more intelligent' minds. He read prodigiously and found his own varied taste in music confusing. Some days he would listen to nothing else but Frank Sinatra and Sammy Davis Jr. At other times he would feel the need for Gregorian chant or opera. Harris had his own theory for this eclecticism: 'I think there's probably three or four of me inside and whoever wakes up first that morning functions.'

There was another person who inhabited Harris's body: a twitchy, restless being who opened his eyes and said to himself, 'The trouble with the Bahamas is that, although it's beautiful and the people are gorgeous, there are no intellectual or artistic challenges here.' This particular Harris would be on a plane by midday, bound for London or Dublin or California or New York to catch a play.

On 1 October 2000, Richard Harris became a septuagenarian. 'I'm surprised to have reached seventy,' he confessed. 'I wasn't supposed to reach thirty.' The inevitable celebrations, organised by his friend, the Irish film producer Noel Pearson, were lavish and profitable. All two hundred guests attending the State Apartments party in Dublin Castle agreed to pay an 'entrance fee' of £300 a head. The £50,000 raised went to the St Jude's Trust for homeless children. Set up in 1991 by a former homeless Dubliner, Michael Joyce, the charity runs a home in Drumcondra and an advice centre in Beaumont.

Harris, who protected his own children from the destructive bloodletting of marriage break-ups, arrived arm in arm with his granddaughter Ella. Inside, he was greeted by his two former wives and his three sons, Damian, Jared and Jamie.

Two months later, Harris used another celebration to deliver a typically barnstorming confession. He was in Paris to receive a Lifetime Achievement Award from the European Film Academy. 'I won't make a long acceptance speech,' Harris told the audience, which included the French prime minister. 'The first reason is that I speak very bad French. The second is I'm dying for a pee. I've been backstage for twenty minutes and I'm so bloody nervous.'

After admitting he was surprised to receive the award – 'I want to congratulate you on choosing me, which is something the British Academy have ignored annually' – he conceded he was not ready to retire. 'I consider myself in God's departure lounge, waiting for that final plane, but luckily some of my scheduled flights have been cancelled – mostly because I've said I'm not going to die yet. And there's still some parts out there, some unwritten scripts I could probably have a bash at – and I'm not very expensive.'

However mutual the disrespect between Harris and the British Academy, the cinemagoers showed their appreciation early in 2001 by voting him worthy of a Lifetime Achievement Award in *Empire* magazine. At the presentation ceremony, the celebrity audience gave him a standing ovation, and Harris, who arrived only just in time for his own award, excused his rapid departure by claiming to have some friends waiting in a nearby pub.

For the second year running, a Harris was making headlines at the Cannes Film Festival, this time for a performance in *Fast Food Fast Women*. Jamie was the youngest of Harris's three sons and the most reluctant to join what was fast becoming a family business. 'A fourth member of the family trying to make a success in film or theatre seemed silly,' he protested. His eldest brother, Damien, is a film director and Jared a successful actor.

It was not just the acting gene Jamie inherited from his father. While in his final year at Downside – the West Country Benedictine boarding school where his grandfather was educated and where, like his two older brothers, Jamie was sent at the age of six to escape his parents' tempestuous marriage – he was fined £1,000 for stealing and driving a cement mixer two miles back to school after a drunken night out. A regular and hard drinker since the age of fourteen, he left Downside to spend the next four years as lead singer with a not-very-good Irish rock band. A frustrating and brief spell at a London drama school ended when his father found him a job as personal assistant to Jim Sheridan. The theatre and film writer eventually persuaded Jamie to take a small part in his 1993 Oscar-nominated film *The Name of the Father*. Since then, Jamie had appeared in ten more pictures, mainly American-financed, low-budget dramas.

Richard Harris allowed the telephone to ring a few times before reluctantly picking it up. It was a long-distance call from eleven-year-old Ella Harris. Grandfather and granddaughter chatted politely for a few minutes. 'Is it right you've been asked to do *Harry Potter*?' she asked.

'Yes.'

'And you know they're my favourite books?'

'Yes.'

'And that you're thinking of turning it down?'

'Yes.'

'If you don't do it, I'll never speak to you again.'

'OK,' said Harris. 'I'll do it.'

Ella Harris was the daughter Harris longed for but never had. Each time his first wife, Elizabeth, became pregnant he would start calling the unborn child Charlotte Emily, just in case. Any chance of a daughter with his second wife ended when Ann miscarried. 'I waited from 1957 to 28 September 1989 for a girl to arrive,' he admitted. 'On that day Ella was born and for the first time in my life I was truly and deeply happy.'

Warner Bros originally approached Sean Connery to play Albus

Dumbeldore, the wizened and kindly Hogwarts headmaster in *Harry Potter and the Philosopher's Stone*, who dedicates himself to protecting and preparing new generations of wizards and witches. When he refused, the studio approached Harris, who also declined the offer. A second invitation, this time with the incentive of more money, was also rejected. Under orders from his granddaughter, Harris accepted at the third asking, but not before upping his fee still further and demanding a percentage of the film and merchandising profits.

Harris, in Dublin to film *The Count of Monte Cristo,* still had his doubts. With casting for the first film not yet complete a script was about to be commissioned for the sequel, *Harry Potter and the Chamber of Secrets.* And, if the series of all seven films about JK Rowling's boy wizard were actually made, that would mean Harris playing Dumbledore until beyond his eightieth birthday. 'But that will be long after I'm dead and gone,' the actor joked with a friend.

At the Edinburgh Book Fair in August 2000, JK Rowling, whose series of children's books catapulted her to international stardom and ranked her among the world's bestselling authors, confessed she was 'very happy' with the first film's line up of stars. Among them were two of her personal favourites: Dame Maggie Smith would play Professor Minerva McGonagall, second in command of Hogwarts School of Witchcraft and Wizardy; and the portly Robbie Coltrane had accepted the role of the friendly giant Hagrid, the school groundkeeper. After a nationwide and well-publicised search the title role of Harry Potter eventually went to twelve-year-old Daniel Radcliffe, who bore an amazing resemblance to the book images of the schoolboy wizard.

Part of Rowling's film rights contract included a condition that the production remained an all British affair. What concerned her most was the risk her stories might be 'devalued and Americanised' or, worse still, they might be turned into a cartoon. Warner Brothers agreed to an all-British cast, but insisted they needed American money to finance the $90-million spectacular. Coca-Cola eventually stepped in with $100-million.

Principal filming would take place in autumn 2000 at Leavesden Studios in Hertfordshire. As a surprise Harris arranged a small *Harry Potter* appearance for his granddaughter. Ella spent two days on the set and was used as an extra in a Hogwarts dining hall scene. Her grandfather was there only slightly more often. His contract demanded just twenty studio days during the six months of shooting.

Whatever Harris's reservations – real or media-invented – about

Harry Potter, he readily agreed to take part in what turned out to be the biggest press launch in cinema history. More than four hundred journalists from around the world descended on Knebworth House, a fifteenth-century home south of Stevenage in Hertfordshire, for the second weekend of November 2001.

One by one the *Potter* stars were introduced to the press before allowing themselves to be subjected to two days of questions and photographs. When it was Harris's turn, he strode into the drawing room, dressed in a long, baggy cream-and-black linen suit jacket, a navy watchman's cap, too-long trousers and trainers, and looking as though he had arrived for the estate's famous summer rock-'n'-roll festival and stayed on for the press conference. 'I'm grand,' he declared before waiting to be asked.

To get himself through the weekend, Harris had issued strict instructions to the film company's publicity staff. He was to be kept well supplied with Coca-Cola and cigarettes and a bowl of boiled sweets must always be within reach. To ensure his answers should remain as well balanced as his insulin level, an assistant sat nearby to jog his memory whenever he forgot a name or detail.

As predicted *Harry Potter and the Philosopher's Stone* was an immediate and record-breaking success. Multiplex cinemas around Britain dedicated half their screens to showing the film; at some cinemas performances were starting every thirty minutes. Box office receipts in the UK soared to £16 million, outstripping the recently released *Star Wars: Episode I – The Phantom Menace* by a clear £6 million.

In America, retitled as *Harry Potter and the Sorcerer's Stone*, box office receipts reached $31 million on the movie's first day. By the end of its third day the figure had topped $93 million, shattering the previous box office record of $72 million set by *The Lost World: Jurassic Park* in 1997. The US critics were not impressed, however. The *New York Times* warned its readers: 'The most highly awaited movie of the year has a dreary, literal-minded competence; of the Quidditch scene, the *Washington Post* wrote, 'Unfortunately, the video game-like sports event stops the movie in its tracks, and it never quite recovers its momentum'; nor did the *Los Angeles Times* appreciate Harris's performance, which it described as '... [more like] someone waving from a float in a Rose Bowl parade than ... a flesh-and-blood individual'.

Harris was far from disappointed. His performance as the kindly wizard probably won him more worldwide fans, as part of the Harry Potter phenomenon, than any of his previous films. As Dumbledore,

Harris was discovered by a new generation – the second since he started acting in the 1950s. Eight- and nine-year-old children knew his name. Some could even recognise him without his flowing white hair and long beard. He had, as Jon Savage the social chronicler, once explained, 'captured the global imagination through a cultural product'.

By the spring of 2002, Harris found himself spending more time in London than he did at his Paradise Island hideaway. Quizzically, he could find more peace in central London, where, at least, he could shut out the encroaching civilisation. 'When I bought a quarter of an island the Bahamas were like a shanty town,' he explained. 'It was super. Now it's like a mini Las Vegas. Huge buildings going up everywhere, skyscrapers and casinos.' Although he still commuted regularly, he was finding the long flight increasingly tiresome. In April he finally decided to sell. The home he had bought for just a few thousand – his final retreat – went on the market for £15 million.

Filming for *Harry Potter and the Chamber of Secrets* began in the early summer of 2002. For many of the cast, who, like Harris, had agreed to at least three *Potter* films, it was a happy reunion.

Maggie Smith was struck by how 'frail and fragile' her co-star had become since the first film. Even into his seventies, though, Harris still showed flashes of his hellraising past. Alan Rickman invariably sat in the next make-up chair to the veteran actor. 'Each morning he would share his marvellous insights into Shakespeare and Beckett,' recalls Rickman. 'He arrived on time and eager to do his bit – even though he may have been out late the previous night.' One evening Harris teamed up with Rickman and Kenneth Branagh. The trio were still drinking and swapping stories at four the next morning.

Harris was now living permanently in his £6,000-a-week suite in the Savoy. 'Sometimes he would come into the American Bar and start to sing,' recalls a member of staff. 'He had a great voice, especially when he went down on one knee and recited Shakespeare. The entire bar would stop to watch his performance.' Approached for an autograph one day, he winked and mischievously signed it 'Peter O'Toole'.

The American's head barman was Salim Khoury. 'Salim,' Harris once asked him, 'why do I have to work?'

'Because you are a star, Richard,' answered the barman. 'And people want to see you.' To honour his celebrated guest, Khoury created the 'Camelot Fizz', a special cocktail of red wine and soda water, which Harris insisted each new friend he took to the American should try.

Filming for *The Chamber of Secrets* was almost over. Making one of his daily telephone calls to Ann Turkel the actor's voice was unusually gruff. He admitted he was running a temperature and it felt like influenza. 'But that must be the tenth bout of flu you've had this year,' scolded his ex-wife. This time, though, Harris sensed something more serious was wrong. He was losing weight and, for the first time in his life, admitted to himself how frail his body was. Without his make-up he began to look sickly pale; his skin itched. Friends began to comment on his skeletal appearance and suggested he see a doctor. He was barely eating and, when even his nightly Guinness proved too painful to digest, Harris finally agreed.

His doctor suggested a round of hospital tests. Harris refused; he still had a few odd days of filming to go before his Dumbledore scenes were complete. He would, he conceded, check himself into hospital the day after shooting was over.

The diagnosis was immediate and shattering. Harris was suffering from Hodgkin's disease, a cancer of the lymph glands. Although increasingly survivable – the ten-year survival rate is now well over 80 per cent – Harris's history of cancer and his age were against him. So, too, was his stubbornness. He refused to be admitted to hospital for treatment until his last day on the *Harry Potter* set.

Characteristically, Harris refused to give in. At 71, and with his 68th film just completed, he insisted on subjecting himself to an aggressive and debilitating regime of chemotherapy and anticancer drugs. Progress was slow and fitful. By September, it was obvious Harris was losing ground, if not his breezy optimism. One friend who visited him in hospital was greeted by 'a broad grin and typical volley of abuse'. But Harris's eye, by now a paler and weaker blue, could not hide the truth.

When he developed pneumonia, he was transferred to London's University College Hospital, across the road from the Royal Academy of Dramatic Art. Two early callers were *Harry Potter* producer, David Heyman, and director, Chris Columbus. They discussed the third picture in the series – *The Prisoner of Azkaban* – and Harris insisted he would be well enough when shooting started in the spring of 2003. 'He threatened to kill me if I recast him,' recalls Columbus, 'only not as politely as that.'

On 11 September *My Kingdom*, the film Harris had wanted to make for more than a decade, received its world premiere at the Toronto Film Festival. He had, by that point, been in hospital for almost a month. His latest illness had been kept a secret from the media and the few journalists in the know had agreed to hold off on the story. Earlier in the summer Harris had agreed to attend the Canadian event and felt guilty at having to cancel for the second time; hospital treatment for 'dehydration and exhaustion' had forced him to pull out in the early 1990s. When My Kingdom was released in Britain a month later Harris was delighted by the reviews.

He had spent eight weeks making the Don Boyd and Nick Davies-scripted film and considered it one of his best. It had been ten years since Harris had begun imagining and planning a modern-day adaptation of Shakespeare's King Lear, five years since it looked as though it might finally happen. When the long-forgotten meetings and half-promises and shared ambitions began to solidify, it was not surprising Harris viewed the project – and his role – with more than an actor's usual sense of possession.

It was Lear's circumstances that fascinated Harris. In the original tragedy, which he read and rehearsed as a teenager in his Limerick sickroom, Lear is a petulant and unwise king who intends to divide his kingdom among his three daughters. The share of his estate depends on the affection each daughter displays for her father. In My Kingdom, Harris plays Sandeman, the ageing patriarch of a Merseyside crime family, who, like Lear, is the father of three very different daughters. In a Liverpool ravaged by poverty and crime, Sandeman is the undisputed ruler. When his wife Mandy – played by Lynn Redgrave – is killed in an apparently motiveless mugging, Sandeman decides it is time to hand over his criminal kingdom to his daughters, but not before he has taken revenge on his wife's killers. His favourite daughter, Jo, rejects the offer, leaving control in the hands of her power-hungry sisters. Sandeman watches helplessly as his empire spirals down and out of control.

Alongside Redgrave, the producers managed to sign some of Britain's best acting talent to play opposite Harris's Learesque gangster. The studious Jo was played by Emma Catherwood, Tracy by Lorraine Pilkington, and the brothel-keeping Kath by Louise Lombard.

Harris's dedication to the project produced some strong disagreements with the co-writer and director Don Boyd, one bringing the entire set to a two-hour standstill. After two 'spectacular' confrontations, Boyd attempted to short-circuit any future problems by calling at his star's trailer first thing in the morning while the rest of the cast were in make-up. Laid out on the table would be the heavily amended script and copious handwritten notes on the day's scenes. 'He was a brilliant professional,' says Boyd.

When the eight-week shoot was over, Boyd asked Harris why he thought they had remained friends. 'He looked into my eyes with his unforgettable stare and said that, despite our differences, he felt that he'd been able to see into my soul.'

On Tuesday 15 October there was an improvement in Harris's condition. His London agent, Sharon Thomas, at last confirmed rumours of her client's cancer and the apparent success of its treatment. 'Richard should be released from the clinic in the very near future,' she said. 'He will definitely be fit enough to start work on the new *Harry Potter* movie next March.' That weekend several of the actor's family flew over from Ireland to visit him in hospital.

It did not last. Eight days later, on Wednesday 23 October, Ann Turkel joined Harris's family at his bedside. Outside his private room she was told there was little hope. The improvement in his condition had soon faded. Now it was just a matter of time.

When Harris had collapsed while touring with *Camelot* Ann had eased his pain by floating her hands over his injured back. It was a healing power she believed in and it seemed to work. Just as she had done then, she placed her hands over his emaciated body, willing the healing energy within her own body to attack his diseased organs. 'I'm going to heal him,' Turkel kept telling herself. 'I'm going to heal him.'

The next day she returned to his private hospital room. She wanted him to see a sixteen-page Italian *Vogue* fashion spread she had worked on in July. Harris was too exhausted to talk. After a long silence he whispered, 'I love you, Ann.'

Friday was a clear bright day. The freak storms and high winds predicted for southern England that weekend were still two days away as hundreds of international journalists – including two dozen Japanese reporters, each partnered by an interpreter – crammed into London's Guildhall. The City venue's Great Hall had been deliberately chosen for the press launch of *The Chamber of Secrets* because of its resemblance to the interior of Hogwarts School. In a corner of the vast room Hedwig and Errol, the two owl stars of the *Chamber of Secrets*, flapped their wings to order.

The unveiling of the second *Harry Potter* movie looked to be as spectacular and promising as the first. In just one year the film franchise on *Philosopher's Stone* had netted more than £600 million. The publicity for the second film in the series was being tipped as one of the most sophisticated marketing operations in British cinema history. The *Chamber of Secrets* release on 15 November would see more than half of the UK's 3,000 cinemas showing the blockbuster; its only pre-Christmas rival was expected to be the twentieth James Bond epic *Die Another Day*.

Only one journalist at the morning launch asked why Richard Harris had not attended. She was told 'ill health' had kept him away.

Across London Richard Harris's condition progressively worsened and he was noticeably weaker. For most of Friday 25 October Elizabeth and Ann took turns to sit by his bedside, holding his hand, waiting for him to speak. Damian, Jared and Jamie Harris were not far away.

A few minutes before seven o'clock in the evening Richard Harris opened his eyes. They were bluer than they had been for a long time. As he focused on each face his smile changed, like a man reminded of different and happy things.

'Don't go yet,' Ann pleaded. 'Don't go. Stay. It's not your time yet to go to the other side. Please stay.'

Harris slowly closed his eyes. His breathing was long and slow.

'I need to sleep now,' he said.

EPILOGUE

Richard Harris always had the desire to unsettle his audience just enough to make them sit up and notice a different way of saying things.

Even so, he managed to produce three memorable characters in three outstanding films and an imposing opus of other movies that will last long after his death. For all his bluster, his high-profile roistering in far-off lands, his stubborn involvement in bad movies, he remained an obsessive craftsman who created through sheer concentration and hard work one of the truly distinctive acting styles of the second half of the twentieth century.

The scale of Harris's omnipresent personality has meant that his performances – which work best by force of personality rather than delicate shading – did not go unchallenged. As someone who operated outside the industry's accepted boundary, Harris, not surprisingly, suffered a certain amount of sniping from within.

Almost from the evening of his death there were plans to reverse that trend and allow Harris the honours and respect that, in his life, had remained just out of reach.

During Harris's final weeks his last truly great performance in *My Kingdom* received a Best Actor nomination in the 2002 British Independent Film Awards. In its stead the organisers honoured the actor with a posthumous and hurriedly created Lifetime Achievement Award. The campaign continued. First Look Pictures, *My Kingdom*'s distributor, rushed through its American release to enable Harris's performance to qualify for a 2003 Academy Award Best Actor nomination.

Richard Harris talked of a lot of things but he never talked of retirement. He always thought he would go on acting and acting and acting because he was part of that special group of people who belong to the theatre and the movies and who will live for ever in the make-believe world they create.

APPENDIX A
FILMOGRAPHY

Alive and Kicking (1958)
Director: Cyril Frankel
Role: Lover
Cast: Sybil Thorndike, Kathleen Harrison, Estelle Winwood, Stanley Holloway, Joyce Carey, Eric Pohlmann, Colin Gordon, John Salew, Liam Redmond

Shake Hands with the Devil (1959)
Director: Michael Anderson
Role: Terence O'Brien
Cast: James Cagney, Don Murray, Dana Wynter, Cyril Cusack, Michael Redgrave, Glynis Johns, Sybil Thorndike, Niall MacGinnis, Ray McAnally, Noel Purcell

The Wreck of the Mary Deare (1959)
Director: Michael Anderson
Role: Second Mate Higgins
Cast: Gary Cooper, Charlton Heston, Michael Redgrave, Emlyn Williams, Cecil Parker, Alexander Knox, Virginia McKenna

A Terrible Beauty (1960)
Also known as: *Night Fighters* (US)
Director: Tay Garnett
Role: Sean Reilly
Cast: Robert Mitchum, Anna Heywood, Dan O'Herlihy, Cyril Cusack, Marianne Benet

The Long and the Short and the Tall (1960)
Also known as: *Jungle Fighters* (US)
Director: Leslie Norman
Role: Corporal Johnstone
Cast: Laurence Harvey, Richard Todd, David McCallum, Ronald Fraser, John Meillon, John Rees, Kenji Takaki

The Guns of Navarone (1961)
Director: J Lee-Thompson
Role: Squadron Leader Howard Barnsby RAAF
Cast: Gregory Peck, David Nivan, Anthony Quinn, Stanley Baker, Anthony Quayle, James Darren, Gia Scala, James Robertson Justice, Irene Papas, Bryan Forbes, Alan Cuthertson, Michael Trubshawe

Mutiny on the Bounty (1962)
Director: Lewis Milestone
Role: Seaman John Mills
Cast: Marlon Brando, Trevor Howard, Hugh Griffith, Tarita, Richard Haydn, Percy Herbert, Duncan Lamont, Gordon Jackson, Chips Rafferty, Noel Purcell

This Sporting Life (1963)
Director: Lindsay Anderson
Role: Frank Machin
Cast: Rachel Roberts, Colin Blakely, Alan Badel, William Hartnell, Vanda Godsell, Arthur Lowe, Leonard Rossiter

Il Deserto Rosso (1964)
Also known as: *Le Desert rouge* (France)
Red Desert
Director: Michelangelo Antonioni
Role: Corrado Zeller
Cast: Monica Vitti, Carlos Chionetti, Xenia Valderi, Rita Renoir, Lili Rheims

Major Dundee (1965)
Director: Sam Peckinpah
Role: Captain Benjamin Tyreen
Cast: Charlton Heston, Jim Hutton, James Coburn, Michael Anderson Jnr, Warren Oates, Senta Berger, Slim Pickens

I Tre Volti (1965)
Also known as: *Three Faces of a Woman*
The Three Faces
Directors: Michelangelo Antonioni, Mauro
Bolognini and Franco Indovine
Role: Robert
Cast: Princess Soraya, Alberto Sordi,
Goffredo Alessandrini, Ivano Davoli,
Albert Giubilo

The Heroes of Telemark (1965)
Director: Anthony Mann
Role: Knut Straud
Cast: Kirk Douglas, Ulla Jacobsson,
Michael Redgrave, Roy Dotrice, Anton
Diffring, David Weston, Sebastian Breaks,
Eric Porter, Barry Jones, Ralph Michael,
Geoffrey Keen, Maurice Denham

Hawaii (1966)
Director: George Roy Hill
Role: Rafer Hoxworth
Cast: Julie Andrews, Max von Sydow,
Jocelyn La Garde, Gene Hackman, Torin
Thatcher, Carroll O'Connor, Robert
Oakley, John Harding, Robert Crawford

La Bibbia (1966)
Also known as: *The Bible* (US)
*The Bible . . . In The
Beginning* (US)
Director: John Huston
Role: Cain
Cast: Michael Parks, Ulla Bergryd, Ava
Gardner, John Huston, Peter O'Toole,
George C Scott, Stephen Boyd

Caprice (1967)
Also known as: *Operation Caprice*
Director: Frank Tashlin
Role: Christopher White
Cast: Doris Day, Ray Walston, Jack
Kruschen, Michael J Pollard, Edward
Mulhare, Lilia Skala, Irene Tsu, Michael
Romanoff, Maurice Marsac, Lisa Seagram

Camelot (1967)
Director: Joshua Logan
Role: King Arthur
Cast: Vanessa Redgrave, Franco Nero,
David Hemmings, Lionel Jeffries, Laurence
Naismith, Estelle Winwood, Gary Marshal,
Anthony Rogers, Peter Bromilow

The Circle (1967)
Director: Mort Ransen
Role: No information available
Cast: Don Francks

Bloomfield (1969)
Also known as: *The Hero* (US)
Director: Richard Harris
Role: Eitan
Cast: Romy Schneider, Kim Burfield,
Maurice Kaufmann, Yossi Yadin, Shraga
Friedman, Aviva Marks, David Hayman,
Sarah Moor, Amnon Bernson, Jacques
Cohen, Nathen Cogen

The Molly Maguires (1970)
Director: Martin Ritt
Role: James McParlan/McKenna
Cast: Sean Connery, Samantha Eggar,
Frank Finlay, Anthony Zerbe, Bethel
Leslie, Art Lund, Anthony Costello, Philip
Bourneuf, Brendon Dillon, Frances
Heflin, John Alderson

Cromwell (1970)
Director: Ken Hughes
Role: Oliver Cromwell
Cast: Alec Guinness, Robert Morley,
Dorothy Tutin, Frank Finlay, Timothy
Dalton, Patrick Wymark, Patrick Magee,
Nigel Stock, Charles Gray, Michael
Jayston, Anna Cropper, Michael Goodliffe

A Man Called Horse (1970)
Director: Elliot Silverstein
Role: John Morgan
Cast: Corinna Topsei, Manu Tupou, Dame
Judith Anderson, Jean Gascon, Dub
Taylor, William Jordan, James Gammon,
Lina Martin

Man in the Wilderness (1971)
Director: Richard C Sarafian
Role: Zachery Bass
Cast: Prunella Ransome, John Huston,
Ben Carruthers, Henry Wilcoxon, Dennis
Waterman, Percy Herbert, John Bindon,
James Doohan, Bryan Marshall, Bruce M
Fisher

The Deadly Trackers (1973)
Also known as: *Riata* (US)
Director: Barry Shear
Role: Sheriff Sean Kilpatrick
Cast: Rod Taylor, Neville Brand, Al
Lettieri, William Smith, Paul Benjamin,
Kelly Jean Peters, Pedro Armendariz Jnr,
Read Morgan, Joan Swift, Isela Vega

99 and 44/100 Per Cent Dead (1974)
Also known as: *Call Harry Crown* (UK)
Director: John Frankenheimer
Role: Harry Crown
Cast: Edmond O'Brien, Ann Turkel,
Bradford Dillman, Constance Ford, David
Hall, Chuck Connors, Janice Heiden,
Max Kleven, Karl Lukas, Anthony
Brubaker, Jerry Summers, Roy Jenson

Juggernaut (1974)
Also known as: *Terror on the Britannic* (US)
Director: Richard Lester
Role: Fallon
Cast: Omar Sharif, David Hemmings, Roy
Kinnear, Freddie Jones, Anthony
Hopkins, Shirley Knight, Ian Knight,
Cyril Cusack, Kristine Howarth, Clifton
James, Mark Burns, Gareth Thomas,
Andrew Bradford

Ransom (1975)
Also known as: *The Terrorists* (US)
Director: Caspar Wrede
Role: Gerald Palmer
Cast: Sean Connery, Ian McShane,
Norman Bristow, Isabel Dean, William
Fox, Richard Hampton, John Cording

Echoes of a Summer (1975)*
Also known as: *The Last Castle*
Director: Don Taylor
Role: Eugene Striden
Cast: Geraldine Fitzgerald, Lois Nettleton,
Jodie Foster, William Windom, Brad Savage
*A Sandy Howard–Richard Harris
production

Robin and Marian (1976)
Also known as: *The Death of Robin* (US)
The Return of Robin Hood
(US: working title)
Director: Richard Lester
Role: King Richard
Cast: Sean Connery, Audrey Hepburn,
Robert Shaw, Nicol Williamson, Denholm
Elliott, Kenneth Haigh, Ronnie Barker,
Bill Maynard, Ian Holm, Esmond Knight,
Peter Butterworth

**The Return of a Man Called Horse
(1976)***
Director: Irvin Kershner
Role: John Morgan
Cast: Gale Sondergaard, Geoffrey Lewis,
Claudio Brook, Enrique Lucero, Bill
Lucking, Jorge Luke, Jorge Russek, Ana
De Sade
* Executive producer: Richard Harris

The Cassandra Crossing (1976)
Also known as: *Cassandra Crossing* (Italy)
Treffpunkt Todesbrucke
(West Germany)
Director: George Pan Cosmatos
Role: Dr Jonathon Chamberlain
Cast: Sophia Loren, Martin Sheen, Ava
Gardner, Burt Lancaster, Martin Sheen,
Ingrid Thulin, Lee Strasberg, John Phillip
Law, Lionel Stander, OJ Simpson, Ann
Turkel, Alida Valli

Gulliver's Travels (1976)
Director: Peter Hunt
Role: Gulliver
Cast: Michael Bates, Julian Glover,

Meredith Edwards, Catherine Schell,
Norman Shelley, Denise Bryer, Julian
Glover, Stephen Jack, Bessie Love

Orca (1977)
Also known as: *The Killer Whale*
           Orca: Killer Whale
Director: Michael Anderson
Role: Captain Nolan
Cast: Charlotte Rampling, Will Sampson,
Keenan Wynn, Bo Derek, Robert
Carradine, Scott Walker, Peter Hooten,
Arnold Wayne Heffley

Golden Rendezvous (1977)
Also known as: *Nuclear Terror* (US: TV
           title)
Director: Ashley Lazarus
Role: John Carter
Cast: Ann Turkel, David Janssen, Burgess
Meredith, John Vernon, Gordon Jackson,
Leigh Lawson, Robert Beatty, Keith Baxter,
Dorothy Malone, John Carradine, Robert
Flemyng

The Wild Geese (1978)
Director: Andrew V McLaglen
Role: Captain Rafer Janders
Cast: Richard Burton, Roger Moore,
Hardy Kruger, Stewart Granger, Frank
Finlay, Kenneth Griffith, Jack Watson,
Barry Foster, Jeff Corey, Roland Fraser,
Percy Herbert, Patrick Allen, Jane Hylton

Ravagers (1979)
Director: Richard Compton
Role: Falk
Cast: Ernest Borgnine, Ann Turkel,
Anthony James, Art Carney, Woody
Strode, Alana Stewart

The Last Word (1979)
Also known as: *Danny Travis*
           The Number
Director: Roy Boulting
Role: Danny Travis

Cast: Karen Black, Martin Landau, Dennis
Christopher, Biff McGuire, Christopher
Guest, Penelope Milford

A Game for Vultures (1979)
Director: James Fargo
Role: David Swansey
Cast: Richard Roundtree, Joan Collins,
Ray Milland, Denholm Elliott, Mark
Singleton, Sven Bertil Taube, Reginald
Sisilana, Sydney Chama, David Phetoe

Your Ticket is No Longer Valid (1981)
Also known as: *Finishing Touch*
           A Slow Decent Into Hell
           L'Ultime passion
           (Canadian: French title)
Director: George Kaczender
Role: Jason
Cast: Jennifer Dale, George Peppard,
Jeanne Moreau, Alexander Stewart,
Michael Kane, Peter Hutt

Tarzan, the Ape Man (1981)
Director: John Derek
Role: Parker
Cast: Bo Derek, John Phillip Law, Miles
O'Keefe, Akushula Selayah, Steven Strong,
Maxime Philoe, Leonard Bailey, Wilfrid
Hyde-White, Laurie Mains, Harold Ayer

Triumphs of a Man Called Horse (1982)
Also known as: *El Triunfo de un hombre
           llamado Caballo* (Spain)
Director: John Hough
Role: John Morgan
Cast: Michael Beck, Ana De Sade, Anne
Seymour, Buck Taylor, Jerry Gatlin,
Vaughn, Lautaro Murua

Highpoint (1984)
Director: Peter Cater
Role: Lewis Kinney
Cast: Christopher Plummer, Beverly
D'Angelo, Kate Reid, Peter Donat, Robin
Gammell, Saul Rublinek

Martin's Day (1985)
Director: Alan Gibson
Role: Martin Steckert
Cast: Justin Henry, Lindsay Wagner, James Coburn, Karen Black, John Ireland, Jeff Braunstein

Wetherby (1985)
Director: David Hare
Role: Sir Thomas
Cast: Vanessa Redgrave, Ian Holm, Judi Dench, Stuart Wilson, Tim McInnerny, Suzanna Hamilton, Tom Wilkinson, Marjorie Yates, Katy Behean, Ted Beyer

Strike Commando 2 (1989)
Director: Bruno Mattei
Role: No information available
Cast: Brent Huff, Mary Stavin, Mel Davidson, Jim Gaines, Luciano Pigozzi, Massimo Vanni, Vic Diaz, Ottaviano Dell'Acqua

Mack the Knife (1989)
Also known as: *The Threepenny Opera*
Director: Menahem Golan
Role: Peachum
Cast: Roger Daltry, Erin Donovan, Miranda Garrison, Russell Gold, Roy Holder, Dong Ji Hong, Raul Julia, Julie Walters

King of the Wind (1989)
Director: Peter Duffell
Role: King George II
Cast: Frank Finlay, Jenny Agutter, Nigel Hawthorne, Navin Chowdhry, Anthony Quayle, Peter Vaughan, Ralph Bates, Neil Dickson, Barry Foster, Jill Gascoine, Joan Hickson, Ian Richardson, Norman Rodway, Peter Vaughan, Glenda Jackson

The Field (1990)
Director: Jim Sheridan
Role: Bull McCabe
Cast: Tom Berenger, John Hurt, Frances Tomelty, Brenda Fricker, Sean Bean, Frank McDonald, Joan Sheehy, Brenda Fricker

Patriot Games (1992)
Director: Phillip Noyce
Role: Paddy O'Neil
Cast: Harrison Ford, Anne Archer, Sean Bean, Thora Birch, Patrick Bergin, Samuel L Jackson, Polly Walker, James Fox, JE Freeman, Hugh Fraser, David Threlfall, Alun Armstrong

Unforgiven (1992)
Also known as: *The Cut Whore Killings*
(US: original script title)
The William Munny Killings (US: working title)
Director: Clint Eastwood
Role: English Bob
Cast: Clint Eastwood, Gene Hackman, Morgan Freeman, Jaimz Woolvett, Saul Rubinek, Frances Fisher, Anna Thomson, David Mucci, Rod Campbell, Anthony James

Wrestling Ernest Hemingway (1993)
Director: Randa Haines
Role: Frank
Cast: Robert Duvall, Shirley MacLaine, Sandra Bullock, Micole Mercurio, Marty Belafsky, Harold Bergman, Piper Laurie, Ron Russell, Aquilla Owens, Greg Paul Meyers

Silent Tongue (1993)
Also known as: *Le Gardien des esprits*
(France)
Director: Sam Shepard
Role: Prescott Roe
Cast: Shiela Tousey, Alan Bates, River Phoenix, Dermot Mulroney, Jeri Arredonno, Tantoo Cardinal, Bill Irwin, David Shiner, Tommy Thompson, Jack Herrick

Savage Hearts (1995)
Director: Mark Ezra
Role: Sir Roger Foxley
Cast: Jamie Harris, Maryam d'Abo,
Myriam Cyr, Steve Marcus, Angus
Deayton, Jerry Hall, Julian Fellowes, Mark
Burns, Oliver Tobias, Andy Mount,
Andrew Rajan, Clive Panto, Jim
McKechnie

Cry, the Beloved Country (1995)
Director: Darrell James Roodt
Role: James Jarvis
Cast: James Earl Jones, Dolly Rathebe,
Jack Robinson, Jennifer Steyn, Darlington
Michaels, King Twala, John Whiteley, Vusi
Kunene, Leleti Khumalo, Charles S
Dutton

Trojan Eddie (1997)
Director: Gillies MacKinnon
Role: John Power
Cast: Stephen Rea, Brendan Gleeson, Sean
McGinley, Angeline Ball, Brid Brennan,
Stuart Townsend, Linda Quinn, Aisling
O'Flanagan, Eugene O'Brien, Maria
McDermottroe, Aoife MacEoin, Delores
Keane, Brid Brennan

Smilla's Sense of Snow (1997)
Also known as: *Fraulein Smillas Gespur fur
    Schnee* (Germany)
    *Froken Smillas kansla for
    sno* (Sweden)
    *Froken Smillas fornemmelse
    for sne* (Denmark)
    Smilla's Feeling for Snow
Director: Bille August
Role: Andreas Tork
Cast: Ona Fletcher, Julia Ormond, Agga
Olsen, Patrick Field, Matthew Marsh, Jim
Broadbent, Charles Lewson,
Maliinannguoq Markussen-Molgard,
Clipper Miano, Bob Peck, Jurgen Vogel

Sibirskij tsiryulnik (1998)
Also known as: *The Barber of Siberia
    Le Barbier de Siberie*
    (France)
    Il Barbiere di Siberia (Italy)
    Сибирский цирюльник
    (Russia)
Director: Nikita Mikhalkov
Role: Douglas McCraken
Cast: Julia Ormond, Oleg Menshikov,
Aleksei Petrenko, Marina Neyolova,
Vladimir Ilyin, Daniel Olbrychski,
Vladimir Zaitsev, Alexander Yakovley,
Evgeny Tsimbal, Mambo Syril, Alexey
Shutov, Roman Radov, Andrew
O'Donnels, MacMacDonald, John
Higgins, Robert Hardy, Elizabeth Spriggs

This is the Sea (1998)
Director: Mary McGuckian
Role: Old Man Jacobs
Cast: Samantha Morton, Ross McDade,
Gabriel Byrne, John Lynch, Dearbhla
Molloy, Ian McElhinney

Grizzly Falls (1999)
Director: Stewart Raffill
Role: Old Harry
Cast: Bryan Brown, Tom Jackson, Oliver
Tobias, Daniel Clark, Chantel Dick,
Trevor Lowden, Marnie McPhail

To Walk with Lions (2000)
Director: Carl Schultz
Role: George Adamson
Cast: John Michie, Kerry Fox, Ian
Bannen, Hugh Quarshie, Honor
Blackman, Geraldine Chaplin, Guy
Williams, Kamau Wa Mbugwa, Raymond
Ofula, Caroline Kere, Sasha Hurt, Omar
Godana, Edward Kwach

Gladiator (2000)
Also known as: *The Gladiators* (US)
Director: Ridley Scott
Role: Emperor Marcus Aurelius

Cast: Russell Crowe, Joanquin Phoenix, Connie Nielson, Oliver Reed, Derek Jacobi, Jimon Housou, David Schofield, John Shrapnel, Tomas Arana, Ralph Moeller

The Royal Way (2000)
Director: Andrei Konchalovsky
Role: No information available
Cast: Kiefer Sutherland

The Pearl (2001)
Director: Alfredo Zacharias
Role: No information available
Cast: Lukas Haas, Litefoor, Tere Lopez-Tarin, Jorge Rivero, Ryan James

Harry Potter and the Philosopher's Stone (2001)
Also known as: Harry Potter and the
Sorcerer's Stone (US)
Director: Chris Columbus
Role: Professor Albus Dumbledore
Cast: Daniel Radcliffe, Rupert Grint, Emma Watson, Robbie Coltrane, Maggie Smith, Alan Rickman, Tom Felton, Zoe Wanamaker, Terence Baylor, Sean Biggerstaff, Emily Dale, Warwick Davis, Tom Felton, Simon Fisher-Becker, Richard Griffiths, Ian Hart, Joshua Herdman, Harry Melling

San Giovanni – L'Apocalisse (2002)
Also known as: The Apocalypse
Role: St John/Teophilus
Cast: Vittoria Belvedere, Benjamin Sadler, Christian Kohlund, Erol Sander, Ian

Duncan, Bruce Payne, Alessandro Bertolucci, Walter Nudo, Constantine Gregory, Luca Ward

My Kingdom (2002)
Director: Don Boyd
Role: Sandeman
Cast: Lynn Redgrave, Tom Bell, Emma Catherwood, Aidan Gillen, Louise Lombard, Paul McGann, Jimi Mistry

The Count of Monte Cristo (2002)
Also known as: Alexandre Dumas' The
Count of Monte Cristo
Director: Kevin Reynolds
Role: Abbe Faria
Cast: James Caviezel, Guy Pearce, James Frain, Dagmara Dominczyk, Luis Guzman, Michael Wincott, Albie Woodington

Harry Potter and the Chamber of Secrets (2002)
Director: Chris Columbus
Role: Professor Albus Dumbledore
Cast: Daniel Radcliffe, Rupert Grint, Emma Watson, Kenneth Branagh, Robbie Coltrane, Alan Rickman, Maggie Smith, John Cleese

Keana: The Prophecy (2002)
Directors: Chris Delaporte, Pascal Pinon
Role: Opaz
Cast: Kirsten Dunst, Anjelica Huston, Keith David, Michael McShane, Greg Proops

APPENDIX B
AWARDS, NOMINATIONS AND DECORATIONS

Year: **1963**
Award: Cannes Film Festival
Category: Best Actor
Film: *This Sporting Life*
Result: Won

Year: **1964**
Award: Oscar
Category: Best Actor in a Leading Role
Film: *This Sporting Life*
Result: Nominated

Year: **1964**
Award: BAFTA Film Award
Category: Best British Actor
Film: *This Sporting Life*
Result: Nominated

Year: **1968**
Award: Golden Globe
Category: Best Motion Picture Actor –
Musical/Comedy
Film: *Camelot*
Result: Won

Year: **1971**
Award: Golden Berlin Bear
Category: Best Film
Film: *Bloomfield*
Result: Nominated

Year: **1971**
Award: Moscow International Film
Festival
Category: Best Actor
Film: *Cromwell*
Result: Won

Year: **1982**
Award: Razzie Award
Category: Worst Actor
Film: *Tarzan, the Ape Man*
Result: Nominated

Year: **1985**
Decoration: Danish Knighthood

Year: **1987**
Decoration: Honorary Doctorate from
University of Scranton

Year: **1990**
Award: *Evening Standard*
Category: Best Actor
Film: *Henry IV*
Result: Won

Year: **1991**
Award: Oscar
Category: Best Actor in a Leading Role
Film: *The Field*
Result: Nominated

Year: **1991**
Award: Golden Globe
Category: Best Performance by an Actor
in a Motion Picture – Drama
Film: *The Field*
Result: Nominated

Year: **2000**
Award: European Film Awards
Category: Lifetime Achievement Award

Year: **2000**
Award: Wine Country Film Festival
Category: Lifetime Achievement Award

Year: **2001**
Award: London Film Critics' Circle
Awards
Category: Special Achievement Award

Year: **2001**
Award: Screen Actors' Guild Awards
Category: Outstanding Performance by
the Cast of a Theatrical Motion Picture
Film: *Gladiator*
Result: Nominated

Year: **2001**
Award: *Empire*
Category: Lifetime Achievement Award

Year: **2002**
Award: British Independent Film Award
Category: Outstanding Contribution by
an Actor
Result: Won

Year: **2002**
Award: British Independent Film Award
Category: Best Actor
Film: *My Kingdom*
Result: Nominated

SOURCES AND ACKNOWLEDGMENTS

There are so many people I need to thank and who made this book possible. Some have preferred to stay anonymous. My gratitude is nonetheless sincere.

A special thank-you must go to my full-time partner and part-time secretary, Sarah Berry, and her family – Philip, Elsie and Claire – all of whom gave their support. Thanks also to my agent, Jane Judd, who continues to amaze with her loyalty and endless advice. Also Stuart Slater at Virgin Books, who provided reassurance when I needed it most, and my editor Kirstie Addis, for all her hard work and long hours.

My gratitude and thanks must also go to Simon Harries at Carlton Television and Brendan Halligan of the *Limerick Leader*, and Stephen Coan, of the *Natal Witness*, all of whom took a great interest in this project and never failed to find the answers to my questions.

For help with photographs and illustrations I am indebted to Tony Hillman, whose film archive and collection of movie memorabilia continues to provide an everlasting source of material and pictures. Permission to use copyrighted photographs was also granted by the *Irish Times*. I must also thank Trevor Ermel of Monochrome, Newcastle, who exercised great care and enthusiasm when copying some very valuable material.

Finally, I must show my indebtedness to the following authors, publishers, institutions, individuals and societies on whose sources I have drawn and who gave their time and goodwill and helped in the creation of this book.

Principal printed material cited and quoted

Books

Bragg, Melvyn, *Rich: The Life of Richard Burton*, Hodder & Stoughton, 1987.
Brando, Marlon, *Songs My Mother Taught Me*, Century, 1994.
Braun, Eric, *Doris Day*, Weidenfeld & Nicolson, 1991.
Clinch, Minty, *Clint Eastwood: A Biography*, Hodder & Stoughton, 1994.
Dunaway, Faye, *Looking for Gatsby: My Life*, HarperCollins, 1995.

Falk, Quentin, *Anthony Hopkins*, Virgin Publishing, 1989.

Freedland, Michael, *Michael Caine*, Orion, 1999.

Haining, Peter, *The Complete Maigret*, Boxtree, 1994.

Hall, William, *Raising Caine: The Authorised Biography*, Sidgwick & Jackson, 1981.

Harrison, Elizabeth, *Love, Honour and Dismay*, Weidenfeld and Nicolson, 1976.

Harrison, Rex, *Rex: An Autobiography*, Conundrum Ltd, 1992.

Heston, Charlton, *In the Arena*, HarperCollins, 1995.

Kingsley, Hilary and Tibballs, Geoff, *Box of Delights*, Macmillan, 1989.

Lambert, Gavin, *Mainly About Lindsay Anderson*, Faber & Faber, 2000.

McCourt, Frank, *Angela's Ashes*, Flamingo, 1997.

McGilligan, Patrick, *Clint: The Life & Legend*, HarperCollins, 1999.

MacLaine, Shirley, *My Lucky Stars*, Transworld, 1995.

Morley, Sheridan, *Robert: My Father*, Weidenfeld & Nicolson, 1993.

Moseley, Roy, with Masheter, Philip and Martin, *Roger Moore: A Biography*, New English Library, 1985.

Munn, Michael, *Burt Lancaster: The Terrible-Tempered Charmer*, Robson Books, 1995.

Munn, Michael, *Hollywood Rogues*, Robson Books, 1991.

O'Brien, Daniel, *Clint Eastwood: Film-maker*, BT Batsford, 1996.

O'Connor, Garry, *Alec Guinness: Master of Disguise*, Hodder & Stoughton, 1994.

Parker, John, *Sean Connery*, Victor Gollancz, 1993.

Pendreigh, Brian, *The Film Fan's Guide to Britain and Ireland*, Mainstream, 1995.

Richardson, Tony, *Long Distance Runner*, Faber & Faber, 1993.

Roberts, Rachel, *No Bells on Sunday: The Journals of Rachel Roberts*, Pavilion Books, 1984.

Sellers, Robert, *Sean Connery: A Celebration*, Robert Hale, 1999.

Smith, Gus, *Richard Harris: Actor by Accident*, Robert Hale, 1990.

Spada, James, *Streisand: The Intimate Biography*, Little, Brown, 1995.

Todd, Richard, *In Camera*, Hutchinson, 1989.

Walker, Alexander, *Audrey: Her Real Story*, Weidenfeld & Nicholson, 1994.

Walker, Alexander, *Fatal Charm: The Life of Rex Harrison*, Weidenfeld & Nicholson, 1992.

Walker, Alexander, *Hollywood England: The British Film Industry of the Sixties*, Michael Joseph, 1974.

Wapshott, Nicholas, *The Man Between: A Biography of Carol Reed*, Chatto & Windus, 1990.

Wapshott, Nicholas, *Rex Harrison: A Biography*, Chatto & Windus, 1991.
Williams, Kenneth, (ed. Russell Davies), *The Kenneth Williams Diaries*, HarperCollins, 1993.
Windeler, Robert, *Julie Andrews*, Aurum Press Ltd, 1997.
Wogan, Terry, *Is It Me?*, BBC Worldwide, 2000.

Periodicals and newspapers

Anon

'Actor battles for club', *Empire*, January 2000.
'Actor fights to save green room', *Coventry Evening Telegraph*, January 2000.
'Bush telegraph on stage upset', *Daily Telegraph*, March 1997.
'Cut the sob story, Richard', *Daily Telegraph*, December 2000.
'Fellow actor dismisses Caine as "a Whinger" ', *Guardian*, April 2000.
'Harris gets a gong', *Empire*, December 2000.
'Harris in drinking club fight', BBC News, January 2000.
'Harris revisits his sporting life for documentary', *Irish Times*, May 2001.
'Hello, cruel world', *Daily Telegraph*, April 1999.
'History of heartache, mushrooms and ghosts', *Sunday Times*, South Africa.
'Lifetime Achievement Award: Richard Harris', *Empire*, 2001.
'Merry ex-wives of Harris', *Sunday Times*, October 2000.
'Obituary: Donald Cotton', *Daily Telegraph*, January, 2000.
'Obituary: Ian Bannen', *Daily Telegraph*, November 1999.
'Obituary: Ken Hughes', *The Times*, May 2001.
'Reviews', *Scotsman*, September 1994.
'Richard Harris LP', *Limerick Leader*, July 2000.
'Shakespeare's lost movies', *Daily Telegraph*, November 2000.
' "Stab city" tag at odds with reality', *Irish Times*, January 2000.
'The Jimmy Woulfe interview', *Limerick Leader*, July 1999.
'The row over Angela McCourt's ashes rumbles on', *Munster Express*, January 2000.
'The vulture's top 100 actors: 100–81', *The Times*, December 2000.
'The vulture's top 100 actresses: 80–61', *The Times*, December 2000.
'Today's other news: Casting couch', *Guardian*, February 2000.

Andrews, Nigel, 'Olivier rides again', *Financial Times*, May 1982.
Barber, Lynn, 'The hellraiser in a tracksuit', *Independent*, July 1990.

Bickley, Claire, 'The reluctant Harris falls under the spell of Harry', *Toronto Sun*, November 2001.

Branigan, Tania, 'Honoured by Europe, actor berates British', *Guardian*, December 2000.

Brett, Anwar, 'There's nobody in this business who's done as much c. as me: says Richard Harris after a pint or five', *Daily Record*, March 1997.

Brook, Danae, ' "Don't die" I pleaded with Richard ... but he slowly slipped away', *Mail on Sunday*, October 2002.

Brooks, Angela, 'I told Dad I thought Lovejoy was rubbish', *Daily Mail*, March 1995.

Brown, Geoff, 'Ivory towers over cardboard Russian houses', *The Times*, February 1991.

Chapman, Sandra, 'Health: illness rings curtain on Brian's stage act', *Belfast News Letter*, November 1997.

Chittenden, Maurice, 'Harris leaves behind a wizard role to fill', *Sunday Times*, October 2002.

Cleary, Mick, 'Galway lays down Munster marker', *Daily Telegraph*, May 2000.

Collins, Laura, 'I loved working with lions in the *Born Free* sequel, but Richard Harris was scared to go near them; From *Taggart* to working with a screen legend', *Daily Mail*, June 2000.

Connolly, Ray, 'Richard Harris', *The Times*, May 1990.

Corr, Aidan, 'Feat of a Riverdancer', *Limerick Leader,* November 2000.

Dempsey, Iain, 'Harris blasts rugby's Euro cup officials', *Limerick Leader*, May 2001.

Dempsey, Iain, 'New gallery opens with a real splash', *Limerick Leader*, December 2001.

Dempsey, Iain, 'Sell-out bash for Richard's party', *Limerick Leader,* September 2000.

Dening, Penelope, 'Selling Harry Potter', *Irish Times*, November 2001.

Dinning, Mark, 'Richard Harris: rink! feck! arse! girls! dr', *Empire*, July 2000.

Doran, Mike, 'Harris upset as "Saint" goes marching out', *Limerick Leader*, September 1999.

Dougary, Ginny, 'The arts: A foul-mouthed genius', *Daily Telegraph*, April 1994.

D'Silva, Beverley, 'Why I play the wild rover', *Daily Telegraph*, March 1997.

Duff, Gavin, 'Hellraiser Harris got star drunk', *Daily Mirror*, May 2000.

Elliott, John, 'Moving on', *Sunday Times*, April 2002.

Feinstein, Sharon, ' "When I die there'll be six people at my funeral ... and five will be debt collectors" ' *People*, February 1994.

Francke, Lizzie, 'Screen: Ode to sadness', *Guardian*, September 1994.

French, Philip, 'Irish wild man who brought passion to the big screen', *Observer*, October 2002.

Gallagher, Brendan, 'Frustrated Harris follows Munster's fortune from afar', *Daily Telegraph*, May 2000.

Gallagher, Brendan, 'Sport: Old devils reunite for day of celebration: Acting greats meet at Twickenham and drink to Munster and rugby', *Daily Telegraph*, May 2000.

Garland, Patrick, 'Rex – the very model of a rakish English gentleman', *Sunday Telegraph*, June 1990.

Garvey, Anthony, 'Munster call up the big guns for Euro clash', *Mid Week Pink*, January 2000.

Grant, Brigit, 'Cool it, Liam!: Hellraiser Harris warns Oasis star', *Daily Mirror*, March 1997.

Grice, Elizabeth, 'I was badly miscast as a husband', *Daily Telegraph*, April 2000.

Halligan, Brendan, 'How Dickie Harris got a nose job to match his character', *Limerick Leader*, December 2001.

Hastings, Chris, 'Sad farewell to Harris, wizard to the stars', *Sunday Telegraph*, October 2002.

Hobson, Louis B, 'Richard Harris hangs out with feline friends', *Calgary Sun*, March 2000.

Hobson, Louis B, 'No longer down for the count', *Calgary Sun*, January 2002.

Hoyle, Martin, 'Star turns and preposterous poses – Television', *Financial Times*, April 1994.

Ingle, Roisin, 'Irish fans pay tribute', *Irish Times*, May 1998.

Johnson, Boris, 'Reduced, alas, to the cutting room floor', *Daily Telegraph*, May 1999.

Johnstone, Iain, 'Brando: from rebel to recluse', *The Times*, January 1990.

Kelly, Keith, 'Harris bemoans Limerick's Lions snub', *Limerick Post*, January 2002.

Khan, Frank, 'Charity banquet honours actor on his 70th birthday', *Irish Independent*, October 2000.

Kirkland, Bruce, 'Richard the Lionheart', *Toronto Sun*, March 2000.

Kirkland, Bruce, 'Harris not keen on "Potter" shoot', *Toronto Sun*, February 2001.

Kirkland, Bruce, 'Film art "a mirror" of free world', *Toronto Sun*, September 2001.

Lagnado, Alice, 'Putin to privatise Russia's "Hollywood" film studios', *The Times*, April 2001.

Lawson, Mark, 'The comedy of exits or Pirandello's revenge', *Independent*, April 1990.

Lister, Sam, 'Rise and rise of Potter star may break spell', *The Times*, October 2002.

Lockyer, Daphne, 'A lion among men', *The Times*, May 2000.

Low, Valentine, 'Now actors have a place to behave badly again', *Evening Standard*, March 2001.

McLaughlin, Brian, 'Call for addiction centre after death of brothers', *Irish Times*, January 2002.

Macaulay, Sean, 'Dried out but not so dusty', *The Times*, May 2000.

Mansfield, Paul, 'The born-again Irishman – Richard Harris is tired of Hollywood portraying "gombeen leprechaun assholes"', *Guardian*, February 1991.

Martin, Nicole, ' "I have been forgotten in Britain," says Harris', *Daily Telegraph*, December 2000.

Mars-Jones, Adam, 'Heaven on earth – and paradise', *The Times*, May 2000.

Millar, John, 'Rise and fall of a roman emperor', *Mail on Sunday*, May 2000.

Naughton, John, 'Richard', *Empire*, May 1997.

O'Riordan, Ian, 'Sidelines: This week in quotes', *Irish Times*, May 2000.

O'Sullivan, John, 'Powerful images from Munich Games', *Irish Times*, September 2000

Parsons, Jill, 'Taming the wild son of a hellraiser', *Mail on Sunday*, October 1994.

Parsons, Sandra and Porter, Monica, 'The woman who won Bond's love', *Daily Mail*, June 1994.

Phelan, Eugene, 'Harris and McCourt in pub fight', *Limerick Leader*, January 2000.

Pulver, Andrew, 'Profile: Michael Caine: Now don't mess abaht', *Guardian*, February 1998.

Quigley, Maeve, 'Confessions of a hellraiser: "They said I'd have to give up drinking so I gave cocaine a try instead" ', *Sunday Mirror*, August 2000.

Quinn, Jessica, 'Richard Harris: Thank you for one shining moment', *Limerick Leader*, November 2002.

Ranson, Geraldine, 'The true voice of the Kerry publican', *The Times*, December 1990.

Reynolds, Nigel, 'Harris raises hell over film director's cutting remark', *Daily Telegraph*, May 1999.

Reynolds, Nigel, 'Harris finds himself cast as chip off old block at Cannes Film Festival', *Daily Telegraph*, May 2000.

Roberts, Glenys, 'A round with Richard: Rumbustious actor Richard Harris is back on the booze, even if it is only shandy', *Daily Telegraph*, December 1995.

Ross, Deborah, 'The woman who saved my career', *Daily Mail*, September 1992.

Ryon, Ruth, 'Supreme puts home on sale', *Los Angeles Times*, January 1998.

Taki, 'The truth hurts', *Sunday Times*, August 1995.

Thompson, Bob, 'Richard Harris a no-show at this year's fest', *Toronto Sun*, September 1999.

Woods, Richard, 'Reed buried with one last mighty binge', *The Times*, May 1999.

Young, Robin, 'Bad reviews can't stop Potter in US', *The Times*, November 2001.

Advertising

Associated British Picture Corporation, *Alive and Kicking*, 1958.

Columbia, *Major Dundee*, 1965.

Columbia, *Cromwell*, 1970.

EMI, *Gulliver's Travels*, 1976.

Metro-Goldwyn-Mayer, *The Wreck of the Mary Deare*, 1959.

Metro-Goldwyn-Mayer, *Mutiny on the Bounty*, 1962.

Paramount Pictures Corporation, *The Molly Maguires*, 1970.

Paramount Pictures Corporation, *Patriot Games*, 1992.

Rank Films, *The Heroes of Telemark*, 1965.

Rank Films, *Golden Rendezvous*, 1977.

20th Century Fox, *Cleopatra*, 1963.

20th Century Fox, *A Man Called Horse*, 1970.

20th Century Fox, *99 and 44/100 Per Cent Dead*, 1974.

United Artists, *Shake Hands with the Devil*, 1959.

United Artists, *Echoes of a Summer*, 1975.

United Artists, *The Return of a Man Called Horse*, 1976.

Warner Bros, *Man in the Wilderness*, 1971.

Warner Bros–Seven Arts, *Camelot*, 1967.

Warner-Pathé, *The Long and the Short and the Tall*, 1960.

PERSONAL INTERVIEWS

I wish to thank the following people, whom I had the pleasure of interviewing or corresponding with during my research for this book:

Honor Blackman
Michael Brown
Bill Burrows
John Cleese
James Coburn
Mary Dennehy
Simon Harries (Carlton Television)
Theresa Hughes
Sheila Grey
Gareth James (theatre manager, Young Vic Theatre Company)
Sean Leonard

Finally to Mike Maguire, reference librarian at Limerick City Library, and Larry Walsh, curator at Limerick City Museum, whose endless research and enthusiasm for this book deserve special thanks.

Every effort was made to trace and seek permission from those holding the copyright to material used in this book. My deepest apologies to anyone I may have inadvertently omitted. Any omissions or errors in the form of credit will be corrected in future printings.

– Cliff Goodwin, 2003

INDEX

Mack the Knife 247
MacLaine, Shirley 210
MacLiammóir, Michael 26
MacOwen, Michael 30–31
Maigret 195–8
Major Dundee 95–8, 243
Man, Beast and Virtue 53
Man Called Horse, A 159, 174–6, 244
Man in the Wilderness 158, 159–60, 245
Man of Destiny 50
Mandela, Nelson 218–19
Mankowitz, Wolf 132
Mann, Anthony 102–4
Marceau, Marcel 34
Maritana 15
Mars-Jones, Adam 224
Martin, Bill 169
Martin's Day 247
Marvin, Lee 168
McCallum, David 67
McCourt, Frank 15–16, 215–17
McCourt, Malachy (actor)153, 158
McCourt, Malachy 215–17
McCulloch, Andrew 196
McDowell, Malcolm 84
McQueen, Steve 203–4
Mercer, Johnny 146
Merchant of Venice, The 206
Meredith, Burgess 178
Michener, James A 99
Michie, John 223
Mikhalkov, Nikita 228
Miles, Sarah 205
Milestone, Lewis 80
Miller, Arthur 46
Minnelli, Vincente 130
Mitchum, Robert 62–3, 117–18, 139, 188
Molly Maguires, The 151–5, 208, 244
Montand, Yves 130
Moore, Roger 156, 176, 178
Morley, Robert 141

Morrison, Van 169
Munster News 11
Murphy, Brian 48, 52, 227
Murphy, Gerry 18
music 15, 130–32, 133–4, 169–70, 230 *see also Camelot*
Mutiny on the Bounty 76–80, 156, 243
My Boy 170
My Kingdom 236–8, 243, 249

Name of the Father, The 232
Natal Witness 216–17
Naughton, John 214–15
New York Morning Telegraph 115
New York Post 171
New York Times 234
New Yorker 129, 154, 162, 172
Newman, Alfred 125
Newman, David 106
Nimoy, Leonard 188
99 and 44/100 Per Cent Dead 162, 245
Niven, David 68, 178
nominations 253–4
Norman, Leslie 68
Nova 104
Nureyev, Rudolf 113

Oberon, Merle 187–8
O'Brien, Edna 181
Observer 49, 209
O'Connor, Joseph 534
O'Donovan, Jack 25
Ogmore, Lord 35, 38, 61
O'Grady, Desmond 16–17, 25, 38–9
Olin, Lena 123
Olivier, Lawrence 19
O'Mahoney, Michael 133–4
O'Meara, Mary 20
On a Clear Day 130
O'Neal, Ryan 188
Orca: Killer Whale 176, 246
Ormond, Julia 228, 229